FLUID AND ELECTROLYTE MANAGEMENT IN SURGICAL PATIENTS

DR. OWAIS ZARGAR

Made with ♥ on the Notion Press Platform
www.notionpress.com

Dedicated to my parents

Sh. A.W. Zargar

Smt. Parveen Kousar

Contents

Preface *vii*

Acknowledgements *ix*

1. Introduction 1
2. Body Fluids 4
3. Physiologic Stress Response To Surgery 12
4. Monitoring Body Fluid Status 22
5. Intravenous Fluids 31
6. Fluid Resuscitation Strategies 41
7. Perioperative Fluid Management 48
8. Calculation Of Fluid And Electrolytes 69
9. Gibbs – Donnan Equilibrium 80
10. Fluid And Electrolyte Abnormalities 89
11. Acid–base Physiology 130
12. Acid Base Disorders 139
13. Clinical Cases 153
14. Acidosis Due To Toxins 155
15. Case Scenarios 163
16. Conclusion 167
17. References 168

Preface

First of all I would like to thank all my colleagues, friends, teachers and family because this book is the result of encouragement and guidance from all of them. I can proudly say that all my students have contributed a lot by their constant feedback regarding improvement of the book and making the book as the bestseller They have helped me in becoming a better teacher, a better author and, most importantly, a better human being. I take this opportunity to thank all of you. The happiness you all give me keeps me telling always to work harder, to bring a positive change in the life of my students. This will be reflected in the pages of this book. I always strive to provide a winning edge to my students. This book has become the bestseller chiefly because of the suggestions, love and even critics that I come across and am informed of. Higher education has become necessary, as graduation alone is found inadequate in this highly competitive and dynamic world. The information provided is cogent but concise to save the precious time, as we all know the clock is ticking. Time is one thing that can never be recovered once gone. Be careful! I am passionate about excellence. Excellence in the field of education, and in my efforts to groom my students to make them confident enough that they lose the fear of failure. My aim, as an author and as a teacher, is to provide students with a learning experience which when amalgamated with perseverance and commitment helps them in achieving goals. I am still not sure about one thing that who is more happy when a student achieves something, the student or the teacher, but I am very sure that the teacher is more satisfied when he sees his students achieving what they deserve and desire. I always tell my students to dream big but not while sleeping. But, these dreams should always be accompanied with intelligence and hard work. To guide your work intelligently, this book and the author, both are there, with you throughout the year. But, the hard work is totally in your hands. Accept responsibility for your life. Know that it is you who will get you where you want to go, no one else. It is a pleasure now to give outlet to the overflowing appreciation and thanks to all my colleagues, friends, teachers and family because this book is the result of encouragement and guidance from all of them. I am pleased to acknowledge the overwhelming love I have received from my students, who are my ultimate source of inspiration. Wishing you all the best and looking forward for your feedback and suggestions...

Dr. Owais Zargar
MBBS, MS Surgery, FMAS
Cert. in Bariatric & Metabolic Surgery
(AIIMS New Delhi)

Acknowledgements

I would like to express my greatest gratitude to the people who have helped and supported me throughout my project. I wish to thank my parents for their undivided support and interest, who inspired me and encouraged me to go my own way, without whom I would be unable to complete my project. I would like to thank my co-authors Dr Nashrah Ashraf and Dr. Ayat Albina, for their constant support and motivation. They helped me in updating the book from the latest editions of standard textbooks. They helped me throughout this project by giving their valuable advises and feedbacks regarding improvement of the book. I am very thankful to Dr N.C. Dhingra, Prof. and Ex. HOD of Surgery, Govt. Medical College, Jammu, for the valuable help. He was always there to show us the right track when we needed his help. It is with the help of his valuable suggestions, guidance and encouragement, that I was able to complete this project. I am grateful to Dr K.S. Mehta, Head of Department, Surgery ASCOMS and Dr. H.S. Bali (Assoc. Proffessor), Dr. Akshat Sharma (Asstt. Professor), Dr. Ravinder Singh Ghai (Asstt. Professor), Dr. Manish Sharma (Asstt. Professor), Dr. Samia Mohan (Asstt. Professor) for their continuous support, valuable advice and encouragement for completion of this project. I sincerely thank Dr. R.K. Chrungoo (Prof. Emeritus Surgery), for his valuable advice and knowledge regarding the subject, which helped me a lot in preparation of certain topics of this book. I wish to express my sincere thanks to Dr. Gurpreet Singh, Professor of Surgery, ASCOMS, for his valuable suggestions, guidance and encouragement for helping me throughout this project. I am very thankful to Dr. Rattnakar Sharma, Head of Department Surgery, GMC Jammu, Dr Javed Iqbal, Dr. Talib Hussain, Dr. Zahoor Hussain, Dr. Sanjay Bhasin, Dr. Sanjay Sharma, Dr. Hamid Wani, Dr Satish Parihar, Professor of Surgery, GMC Jammu, for their valuable and indispensable help. Last but not the least i would like to thank my friends Dr. Sanjeev, Dr Azhar, Dr. Dawood, Dr. Ishtiyaq, Dr. Adnan, Dr. Zahid, Dr. Deepak, Dr. Shahnawaz, Dr. Subash, Dr. Nitesh, Dr. Aman, Dr. Yarik, Dr. Maqsood for their constant help and support throughout this journey.

CHAPTER ONE

INTRODUCTION

Fluid management is an important part of overall surgical therapy. Proper administration of fluids is critical, especially in patients who undergo major surgeries such as emergency laparotomies, bowel resections and hepatectomy procedures. Body fluid composition may change in minutes or hours, resulting in impaired wound healing and homeostasis. Briefly, choice of strategy in intraoperative and postoperative fluid management may be significant.

Postoperative management of patients, who undergo surgery, is carried out by intensive care specialists, anesthesiologists and surgeons in postoperative care units, in all over the world. On the other hand, intraoperative management is a quite different expertise, which is totally put into practice by anesthesiologists only. Although postoperative care units are mostly managed by a team of both anesthesiologists and surgeons or only by anesthesiologists in Europe and Japan, surgeons' presence and co-leadership is of great importance in postoperative care.

Types of the fluids, amount of the fluid given and timing of the administration are the main topics that determine the fluid management strategy. Several debates have been continued about each of these topics. In early times of modern medicine, administering large amounts of fluids was favored, instead of facing the risk of hypovolemia. In 1961, Shires et al defined the "third space" fluid deficit as non-functional fluid which can be accounted as fluid loss and they suggested use of large quantities of fluids to substitute this functional loss. After this strategy becomes popular, reports of adverse effects of high volume states induced by excessive saline use began to arise. Today, exact amount of fluid to maintain ideal homeostasis is still controversial. Similarly, there are varying types of intravenous fluids and all vary in their biological and chemical properties which results in varying distribution forms and varying effects on homeostasis, vascular integrity, and other hemodynamic variables. Apparently, fluid management is admitted to be an art of medicine and based on personal judgments. Although this approach may not be totally wrong, plenty of evidence acquired by large volume studies should be considered wisely.

Postoperative fluid management plays a key role in providing adequate tissue perfusion, stable hemodynamics and reducing morbidities related with hemodynamics. Understanding body fluid physiology and possible outcomes of different fluid management strategies is crucial.

Terminologies and definition:

Solvent: is the liquid where particles dissolves in (e.g. Water) that can be measured in liters and milliliters.

Solutes: are the dissolving particles

A molecule: is the smallest unit with chemical identity (e.g.Water consist of one oxygen and two hydrogen atoms = water molecule)

Ions: are dissociated molecule into parts that have electrical charges (e.g. NaCl dissociates into Na+ and Cl-) Cations are positively charged ions (e.g. Na+) due to loss of an electron (e-) anions are nega:vely charged ions (e.g. Cl-) due to gain of an electrone (e-)

Electrolytes: are interac:ng ca:ons and anions (e.g. H^+ + Cl^- = HCL [hydrochloric acid])

Univalent ion: has one electrical charge (e.g. Na+)

Divalent ion: has two electrical charges (e.g. Ca++)

Molecular weight: the sum of atomic weights of different parts of a molecule (e.g. H+ [2 atoms] + O2 [16 atoms] = H2O [18 atoms]).

A mole: is a measuring unit of the weight of each substance` in grams (e.g. 1 mole of Na+ = 23 grams, 1 mole of Cl- = 35 grams, 1 mole of NaCl = 58 grams). It can be expressed in moles/L, millimoles x 10-3/L, micromoles x 10-6/L of the solvent.

Equivalence: refers to the ionic weight of an electrolyte to the number of charges it carries (e.g. 1 mole of Na+ = 1 Equivalent, whereas 1 mole of Ca++ = 2 Equivalents). Like moles, equivalence can also be expressed in milliequivalent/L and microequivalent/L of the solvent.

Osmosis: is the movement of a solution (e.g. water) through a semi permeable membrane from the lower concentration to the higher concentration.

Osmole/L or milliosmole/L: is a measuring unit for the dissolu9on of a solute in a solvent.

Osmotic coefficient: means the degree of dissolution of solutes (molecules) in a solvent (solution). For example the osmotic coefficient of NaCl is 0.9 means that if 10 molecules of NaCl are dissolved in water, 9 molecules will dissolve and 1 molecule will not dissolve.

Osmolarity: is the dissolution of a solute in plasma measured in liters.

Osmolality: is the dissolution of a solute in whole blood measured in kilograms. Therefore, Osmolality is more accurate term because dissolution of a solute in plasma is less inclusive when compared to whole blood that contains plasma (90%) and Proteins (10%).

Gibbs – Donnan Equilibrium: refers to movement of chargeable particles through a semi permeable membrane against its natural location to achieve equal concentrations on either side of the semi permeable membrane. For example, movement of Cl- from extra cellular space (natural location) to intracellular space (unusual location) in case of hyperchloremic metabolic acidosis because negatively charged proteins (natural location in intravascular space) are large molecules that cannot cross the semi permeable membrane for this equilibrium.

Tonicity: of a solution means effective osmolality in relation to plasma (=285 milliosmol/L). Therefore, isotonic solutions [e.g. 0.9% saline solution] have almost equal tonicity of the plasma, hypotonic solutions [e.g. 0.45% saline solution] have < tonicity than plasma, and hypertonic [e.g. 3% saline solution] solutions have > tonicity than plasma.

Fluid and electrolyte management is paramount to the care of the surgical patient. Changes in both fluid volume and electrolyte composition occur preoperatively, intraoperatively, and postoperatively, as well as in response to trauma and sepsis. The sections that follow review the normal anatomy of body fluids, electrolyte composition and concentration abnormalities and treatments, common metabolic derangements, and alternative resuscitative fluids. These concepts are then discussed in relationship to management of specific surgical patients and their commonly encountered fluid and electrolyte abnormalities.

BODY FLUID COMPARTMENTS

Total body water is approximately 60% of total body weight. One third of this water is extracellular and it can be divided to as intravascular (20%) and extravascular (80%). The remaining two-third of body water is intracellular, which also exists in intravascular and extravascular compartments. From another perspective, intravascular fluid contains of both intracellular (40%) and extracellular (60%) compounds and plasma is the intravascular-extracellular compound of total body water (approximately 4% of body weight; in example, about 2.8 L in a 70 kg individual).

The endothelium is the separating wall between intravascular and extravascular compartments, thus it is the cell wall that separates the intracellular and extracellular compartments. There are various control mechanisms on these separating walls that regulate volumes of each compartment. Cell membrane is completely permeable to water, whereas it is selectively permeable to ions and organic molecules. It has also the Na^+/K^+-adenosine triphosphatase enzyme that actively expels Na^+ ions and maintains the Na^+ gradient between compartments. There are also endocrine mechanisms that control the cellular intake of certain molecules, such as glucose.

On the other hand, the earliest theory on vascular barrier by Ernest Starling declared that the hydrostatic pressure gradient in blood vessels creates a flow and the oncotic pressure of interstitial tissue allows only reasonable amount of fluid to cross through endothelium. Later studies showed the intravascular osmotic pressure is significantly higher than interstitial osmotic pressure, however this doesn't result in interstitial edema. As a result, this unexplained situation led researchers to look for another actor in this fluid distribution balance. The endothelial glycocalyx is a carbohydrate-rich coating over endothelial surface which is supported by proteoglycans and glycoproteins. It is a dynamic formation, consisting of membrane-bound and soluble molecules. Existence of this glycocalyx layer forms a distinct space in the interior neighborhood of the endothelium, and there develops a notable oncotic pressure in this particular protein-free space. This definition brings out the "double-layer concept" for the vascular barrier. This concept is quite capable of clarifying oncotic pressure balance between two compartments.

CHAPTER TWO

BODY FLUIDS

Total Body Water

Water constitutes approximately 50% to 60% of total body weight. The relationship between total body weight and total body water (TBW) is relatively constant for an individual and is primarily a reflection of body fat. Lean tissues such as muscle and solid organs have higher water content than fat and bone. As a result, young, lean males have a higher proportion of body weight as water than elderly or obese individuals. Deuterium oxide and tritiated water have been used in clinical research to measure TBW by indicator dilution methods. In an average young adult male, TBW accounts for 60% of total body weight, whereas in an average young adult female, it is 50%. The lower percentage of TBW in females correlates with a higher percentage of adipose tissue and lower percentage of muscle mass in most. Estimates of percentage of TBW should be adjusted downward approximately 10% to 20% for obese individuals and upward by 10% for malnourished individuals. The highest percentage of TBW is found in newborns, with approximately 80% of their total body weight comprised of water. This decreases to approximately 65% by 1 year of age and thereafter remains fairly constant.

Fluid Compartments

TBW is divided into three functional fluid compartments: plasma, extravascular interstitial fluid, and intracellular fluid. The extracellular fluids (ECF), plasma and interstitial fluid, together compose about one third of the TBW, and the intracellular compartment composes the remaining two thirds. The extracellular water composes 20% of the total body weight and is divided between plasma (5% of body weight) and interstitial fluid (15% of body weight). Intracellular water makes up approximately 40% of an individual's total body weight, with the largest proportion in the skeletal muscle mass. ECF is measured using indicator dilution methods. The distribution volumes of NaBr and radioactive sulfate have been used to measure ECF in clinical research. Measurement of the intracellular compartment is then determined indirectly by subtracting the measured ECF from the simultaneous TBW measurement.

Figure1. Functional body fluid compartments. TBW = total body water.

Figure1. Functional body fluid compartments. TBW = total body water.

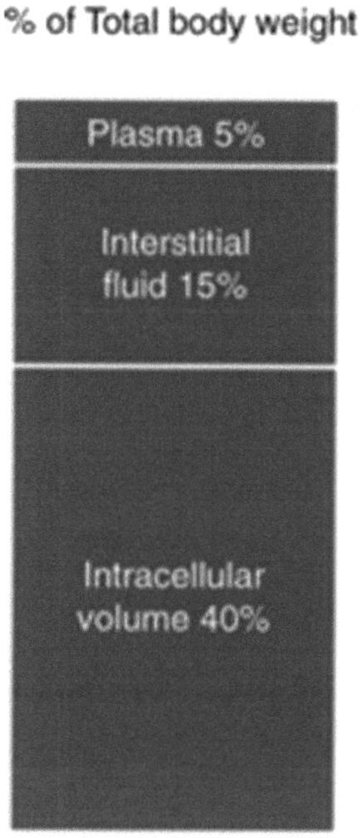

% of Total body weight	Volume of TBW	Male (70 kg)	Female (60 kg)
Plasma 5%	Extracellular volume	14,000 mL	10,000 mL
Interstitial fluid 15%	Plasma	3500 mL	2500 mL
	Interstitial	10,500 mL	7500 mL
Intracellular volume 40%	Intracellular volume	28,000 mL	20,000 mL
		42,000 mL	30,000 mL

Fig.1

➲ Distribution of fluid between the intra- and extravascular compartments is dependent upon:

↳ The oncotic pressure of plasma (which is determined by albumin primarily) and the permeability of the endothelium

↳ Size of compartment available.

↳ Tonicity (mainly): water balance is adjusted to maintain osmolality.

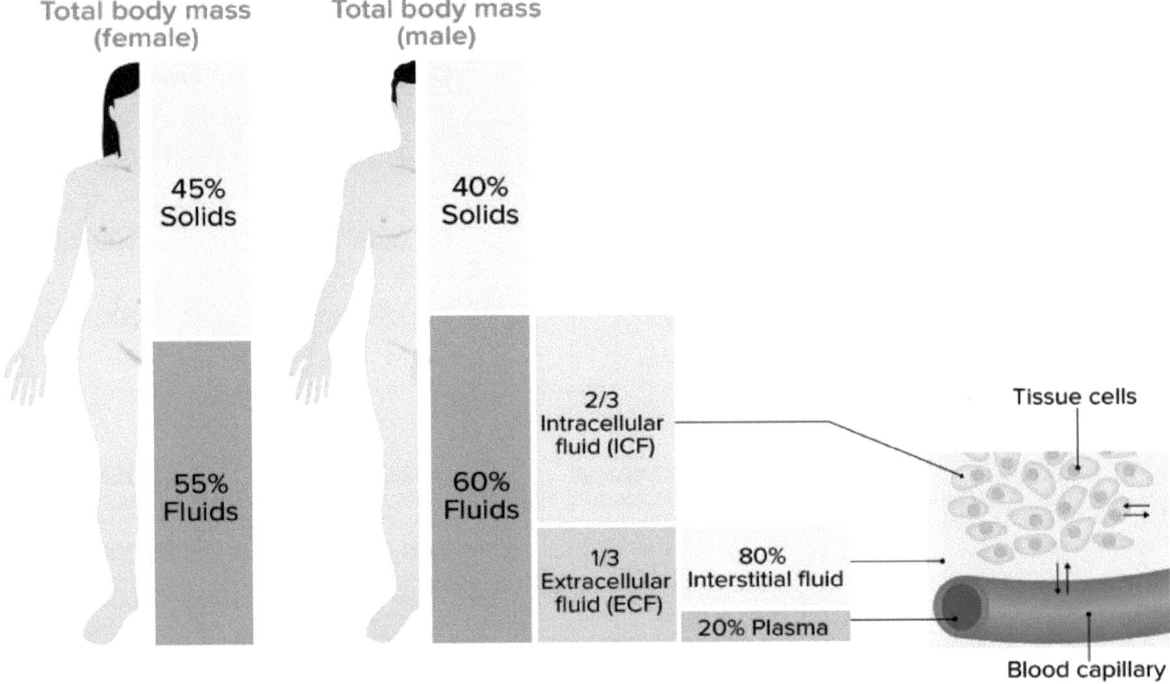

➲ Distribution of fluid and electrolytes between the intracellular and extracellular fluid compartments.

Fig. 2

Distribution of fluid and electrolytes between the intracellular and extracellular fluid compartments.

- In our day-to-day use, fluids can only be given into, or taken from the vascular space (5%) which is the most important compartment for clinicians.
- Fluid losses occur mainly from the vascular compartment as well. We lose water through our renal and gastrointestinal tracts, and this can be seen and measured.
- The water we lose from our skin and respiratory tract cannot be measured with ease, and makes up our insensible losses. These amount to 500 ml a day in health, and increase in sickness, particularly when febrile (200 cc/day for each degree)

Composition of Fluid Compartments

The ECF compartment is balanced between sodium, the principal cation, and chloride and bicarbonate, the principal anions. The intracellular fluid compartment is composed primarily of the cations potassium and magnesium, and the anions phosphate and sulfate, and proteins. The concentration gradient between compartments is maintained by adenosine triphosphate–driven sodium-potassium pumps located within the cell membranes. The composition of the plasma and interstitial fluid differs only slightly in ionic composition. The slightly higher protein content (organic anions) in plasma results in a higher plasma cation composition relative to the interstitial fluid, as explained by the Gibbs-Donnan equilibrium equation. Proteins add to the osmolality of the plasma and contribute to the balance of forces that determine fluid balance across the capillary endothelium. Although the movement of ions and proteins between the various fluid compartments is restricted, water is freely diffusible. Water is distributed evenly throughout all fluid compartments of the body so that a given volume of water increases the volume of any one compartment relatively little. Sodium, however, is confined to the ECF compartment, and because of its osmotic and electrical properties, it remains associated with water. Therefore, sodium-containing fluids are distributed throughout the ECF and add to the volume of both the intravascular and interstitial spaces. Although the administration of sodium-containing fluids expands the intravascular volume, it also expands the interstitial space by approximately three times as much as the plasma.

Osmotic Pressure

The physiologic activity of electrolytes in solution depends on the number of particles per unit volume (millimoles per liter, or mmol/L), the number of electric charges per unit volume (milliequivalents per liter, or mEq/L), and the number of osmotically active ions per unit volume (milliosmoles per liter, or mOsm/L). The concentration of electrolytes usually is expressed in terms of the chemical combining activity, or equivalents. An equivalent of an ion is its atomic weight expressed in grams divided by the valence:

Equivalent = atomic weight (g)/valence

For univalent ions such as sodium, 1 mEq is the same as 1 mmol. For divalent ions such as magnesium, 1 mmol equals 2 mEq. The number of milliequivalents of cations must be balanced by the same number of milliequivalents of anions. However, the expression of molar equivalents alone does not allow a physiologic comparison of solutes in a solution.

The movement of water across a cell membrane depends primarily on osmosis. To achieve osmotic equilibrium, water moves across a semipermeable membrane to equalize the concentration on both sides. This movement is determined by the concentration of the solutes on each side of the membrane. Osmotic pressure is measured in units of osmoles (osm) or milliosmoles (mOsm) that refer to the actual number of osmotically active particles. For example, 1 mmol of sodium chloride contributes to 2 mOsm (one from sodium and one from chloride). The principal determinants of osmolality are the concentrations of sodium, glucose, and urea (blood urea nitrogen, or BUN):

Calculated serum osmolality = 2 sodium + (glucose/18) + (BUN/2.8)

The osmolality of the intracellular and extracellular fluids is maintained between 290 and 310 mOsm in each compartment. Because cell membranes are permeable to water, any change in osmotic pressure in one compartment is accompanied by a redistribution of water until the effective osmotic pressure between compartments is equal. For example, if the ECF concentration of sodium increases, there will be a net movement of water from the intracellular to the extracellular compartment. Conversely, if the ECF concentration of sodium decreases, water will move into the cells. Although the intracellular fluid shares in losses that involve a change in concentration or composition of the ECF, an isotonic change in volume in either one of the compartments is not accompanied by the net movement of water as long as the ionic concentration remains the same. For practical clinical purposes, most significant gains and losses of body fluid are directly from the extracellular compartment.

BODY FLUID CHANGES

Normal Exchange of Fluid and Electrolytes

The healthy person consumes an average of 2000 mL of water per day, approximately 75% from oral intake and the rest extracted from solid foods. Daily water losses include 800 to 1200 mL in urine, 250 mL in stool, and 600 mL in insensible losses. Insensible losses of water occur through both the skin (75%) and lungs (25%) and can be increased by such factors as fever, hypermetabolism, and hyperventilation. Sensible water losses such as sweating or pathologic loss of gastrointestinal (GI) fluids vary widely, but these include the loss of electrolytes as well as water (Table1). To clear the products of metabolism, the kidneys must excrete a minimum of 500 to 800 mL of urine per day, regardless of the amount of oral intake.

Table1: Water exchange (60 to 80 kg man)

Table1: Water exchange (60 to 80 kg man)

ROUTES	AVERAGE DAILY VOLUME (mL)	MINIMAL (mL)	MAXIMAL (mL)
Oral fluids	800–1500	0	1500/h
Solid foods	500–700	0	1500
Insensible:			
Water of oxidation	250	125	800
Water of solution	0	0	500
H_2O loss:			
Sensible:			
Urine	800–1500	300	1400/h
Intestinal	0–250	0	2500/h
Sweat	0	0	4000/h
Insensible:			
Lungs and skin	600	600	1500

Table 1

The typical individual consumes 3 to 5 g of dietary salt per day, with the balance maintained by the kidneys. With hyponatremia or hypovolemia, sodium excretion can be reduced to as little as 1 mEq/d or maximized to as much as 5000 mEq/d to achieve balance except in people with salt-wasting kidneys. Sweat is hypotonic, and sweating usually results in only a small sodium loss. GI losses are isotonic to slightly hypotonic and contribute little to net gain or loss of free water when measured and appropriately replaced by isotonic salt solutions.

Classification of Body Fluid Changes

Disorders in fluid balance may be classified into three general categories: disturbances in (a) volume, (b) concentration, and (c) composition. Although each of these may occur simultaneously, each is a separate entity with unique mechanisms demanding individual correction. Isotonic gain or loss of salt solution results in extracellular volume changes, with little impact on intracellular fluid volume. If free water is added or lost from the ECF, water will pass between the ECF and intracellular fluid until solute concentration or osmolarity is equalized between the compartments. Unlike with sodium, the concentration of most other ions in the ECF can be altered without significant change in the total number of osmotically active particles, producing only a compositional change. For instance, doubling the serum potassium concentration will profoundly alter myocardial function without significantly altering volume or concentration of the fluid spaces.

Disturbances in Fluid Balance

Extracellular volume deficit is the most common fluid disorder in surgical patients and can be either acute or chronic. Acute volume deficit is associated with cardiovascular and central nervous system signs, whereas chronic deficits display tissue signs, such as a decrease in skin turgor and sunken eyes, in addition to cardiovascular and central nervous system signs (Table-2). Laboratory examination may reveal an elevated blood urea nitrogen level if the deficit is severe enough to reduce glomerular filtration and hemoconcentration. Urine osmolality usually will be higher than serum osmolality, and urine sodium will be low, typically <20 mEq/L. Serum sodium concentration does not necessarily reflect volume status and therefore may be high, normal, or low when a volume deficit is present. The most common cause of volume deficit in surgical patients is a loss of GI fluids (Table 3) from nasogastric suction, vomiting, diarrhea, or enterocutaneous fistula. In addition, sequestration secondary to soft tissue injuries, burns, and intra-abdominal processes such as peritonitis, obstruction, or prolonged surgery can also lead to massive volume deficits.

Table2: Signs and symptoms of volume disturbances

Table2: Signs and symptoms of volume disturbances

SYSTEM	VOLUME DEFICIT	VOLUME EXCESS
Generalized	Weight loss	Weight gain
	Decreased skin turgor	Peripheral edema
Cardiac	Tachycardia	Increased cardiac output
	Orthostasis/hypotension	Increased central venous pressure
	Collapsed neck veins	Distended neck veins
		Murmur
Renal	Oliguria	—
	Azotemia	
GI	Ileus	Bowel edema
Pulmonary	—	Pulmonary edema

Table 2

Table-3: Composition of GI secretions

Table-3: Composition of GI secretions

TYPE OF SECRETION	VOLUME (mL/24 h)	Na (mEq/L)	K (mEq/L)	Cl (mEq/L)	HCO_3^- (mEq/L)
Stomach	1000–2000	60–90	10–30	100–130	0
Small intestine	2000–3000	120–140	5–10	90–120	30–40
Colon	—	60	30	40	0
Pancreas	600–800	135–145	5–10	70–90	95–115
Bile	300–800	135–145	5–10	90–110	30–40

Table 3

Extracellular volume excess may be iatrogenic or secondary to renal dysfunction, congestive heart failure, or cirrhosis. Both plasma and interstitial volumes usually are increased. Symptoms are primarily pulmonary and cardiovascular (Table 2). In fit patients, edema and hyperdynamic circulation are common and well tolerated. However, the elderly and patients with cardiac disease may quickly develop congestive heart failure and pulmonary edema in response to only a moderate volume excess.

Volume Control

Volume changes are sensed by both osmoreceptors and baroreceptors. Osmoreceptors are specialized sensors that detect even small changes in fluid osmolality and drive changes in thirst and diuresis through the kidneys. For example, when plasma osmolality is increased, thirst is stimulated and water consumption increases, although the exact cell mechanism is not known. Additionally, the hypothalamus is stimulated to secrete vasopressin, which increases water reabsorption in the kidneys. Together, these two mechanisms return the plasma osmolality to normal. Baroreceptors also modulate volume in response to changes in pressure and circulating volume through specialized pressure sensors located in the aortic arch and carotid sinuses. Baroreceptor responses are both neural, through sympathetic and parasympathetic pathways, and hormonal, through substances including renin-angiotensin, aldosterone, atrial natriuretic peptide, and renal prostaglandins. The net result of alterations in renal sodium excretion and free water reabsorption is restoration of volume to the normal state.

Concentration Changes

The management of fluid in the postoperative surgical patient can vary from simple to complex. Postoperative intravenous maintenance fluid therapy ensures adequate organ perfusion, prevents catabolism, ensures electrolyte- and pH-balance, and may be all that is required for patients who undergo surgical procedures that do not significantly alter the hemodynamic milieu. Typically, such procedures are associated with a small volume of blood loss (<250 mL), a short course of anesthesia and surgery (<3 hours), a small volume of intravenous fluid administration (<30 mL/kg), and little to no extravascular fluid shift in patients without significant organ dysfunction.

However, in many cases, postoperative patients with extensive traumatic or surgical tissue injury, burns, critical illness, or sepsis require more complex resuscitative fluid therapy in addition to maintenance therapy to compensate for preoperative and intraoperative losses, the stress response to surgery, the underlying disease state, ongoing gastrointestinal fluid loss, blood loss, and other bodily fluid loss. Such complex fluid management is often needed for patients who undergo surgical procedures that result in significant blood loss (>500 mL or 7 mL/kg), fluid shifting out of the vascular space ("third-spacing"), large-volume intravenous fluid administration (>30 mL/kg), or hemodynamic instability.

CHAPTER THREE

PHYSIOLOGIC STRESS RESPONSE TO SURGERY

The stress response to traumatic or surgical tissue injury is a primal collection of biochemical pathways designed to facilitate survival following a major insult. The "fight or flight" response promotes expansion of the blood volume, glucose availability, perfusion of vital organs, and inflammation. This stress response is triggered by entry into a major body cavity (eg, chest, abdomen, joint, cranium), significant tissue disruption (eg, severe burn wounds, long bone fracture, penetrating gunshot wound, pancreatitis), significant blood loss (>500 mL or 7 mL/kg), hemodynamic instability, and sepsis.

The stress response to surgery is a pattern of physiological and pathophysiological changes that occur in response to the stimulus of surgery. The response consists of two broad categories:

- (i) neuroendocrine–metabolic response
- (ii) inflammatory–immune response

The magnitude, invasiveness, and duration of surgery are central in determining the degree of the body's integrated stress response. Major open vascular and abdominal surgery, joint replacement surgery, and cardiac surgery using cardiopulmonary bypass (CPB) elicit the greatest stress response. The body's attempt to maintain physiological homeostasis perioperatively induces a non-specific adaptation response that can be detrimental and lead to systemic inflammatory response syndrome (SIRS), hyper-metabolism, and hyper-catabolism. Further injury may cause loss of normally functioning negative-feedback systems leading to muscle wasting, impaired immune function, impaired wound healing, and the potential for organ failure and death.

Physiological responses to surgical stress

Neuroendocrine–metabolic response

Sympathetic nervous system response

The paraventricular nucleus (PVN) is a group of neurones in the hypothalamus that plays a central role during stress. The PVN can detect physiological changes, such as hypotension and inflammation. It acts to relay afferent impulses originating at the site of surgical tissue damage via the limbic system, particularly the amygdala and brainstem nuclei (Fig 3). Paraventricular nucleus fibres project directly to the posterior pituitary and also control various anterior pituitary functions. Adrenaline (epinephrine) is secreted directly from the adrenal medulla in response to hypothalamic activation by the sympathetic nervous system (SNS) (Fig 4). Circulating adrenaline strengthens the sympathetic response and mobilises carbohydrate and fat stores. Rapid sympathetic responses are mediated neurally. However, slower sustained sympathetic responses are also seen, and these result from hormonal responses (i.e. circulating adrenaline and noradrenaline [norepinephrine]).

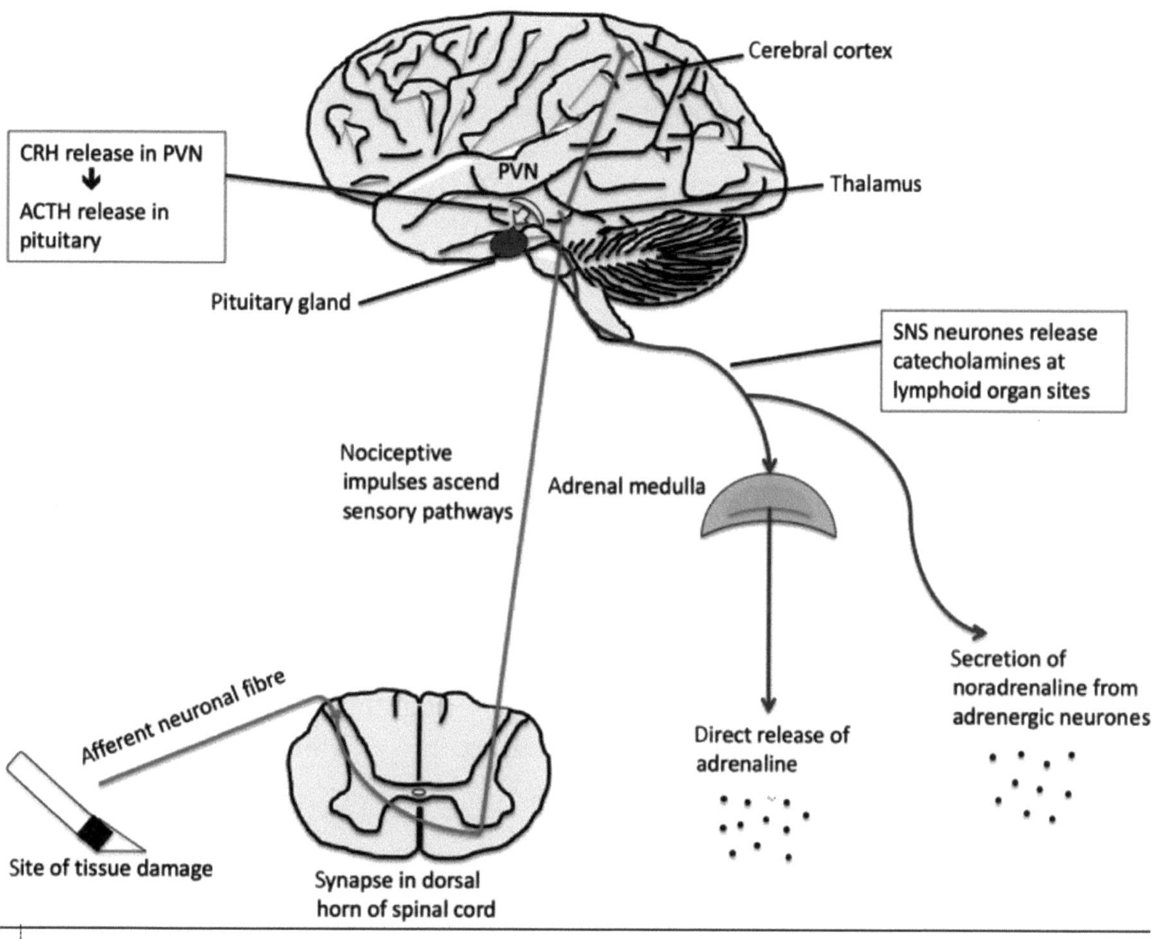

Fig. 3

Fig. 3. Hypothalamic activation of the neuroendocrine response.

Heart rate and vascular smooth muscle tone are controlled by the SNS. Sympathetic nervous system activation increases efferent signals to vascular smooth muscle, thereby increasing systemic vascular resistance and arterial blood pressure. Blood flow to active muscles is increased alongside a concurrent reduction in blood flow to organs not prioritised for rapid motor activity, such as the kidneys and gastrointestinal tract. Hepatic and muscle lipolysis and glycogenolysis increase, leading to hyperglycaemia. In addition, cellular metabolic activity and the coagulability of blood increase.

Endocrine system response

The hypothalamus both directly and indirectly coordinates the complex hormonal stress response. Corticotrophin-releasing hormone (CRH), secreted in response to surgical stress, activates the hypothalamic–pituitary–adrenal (HPA) axis cascade and its metabolic consequences. Corticotrophin-releasing hormone stimulates the anterior pituitary gland to secrete adrenocorticotropic hormone (ACTH). Adrenocorticotropic hormone acts on cells in the *zona fasciculata* of the adrenal cortex to promote glucocorticoid (cortisol) secretion.

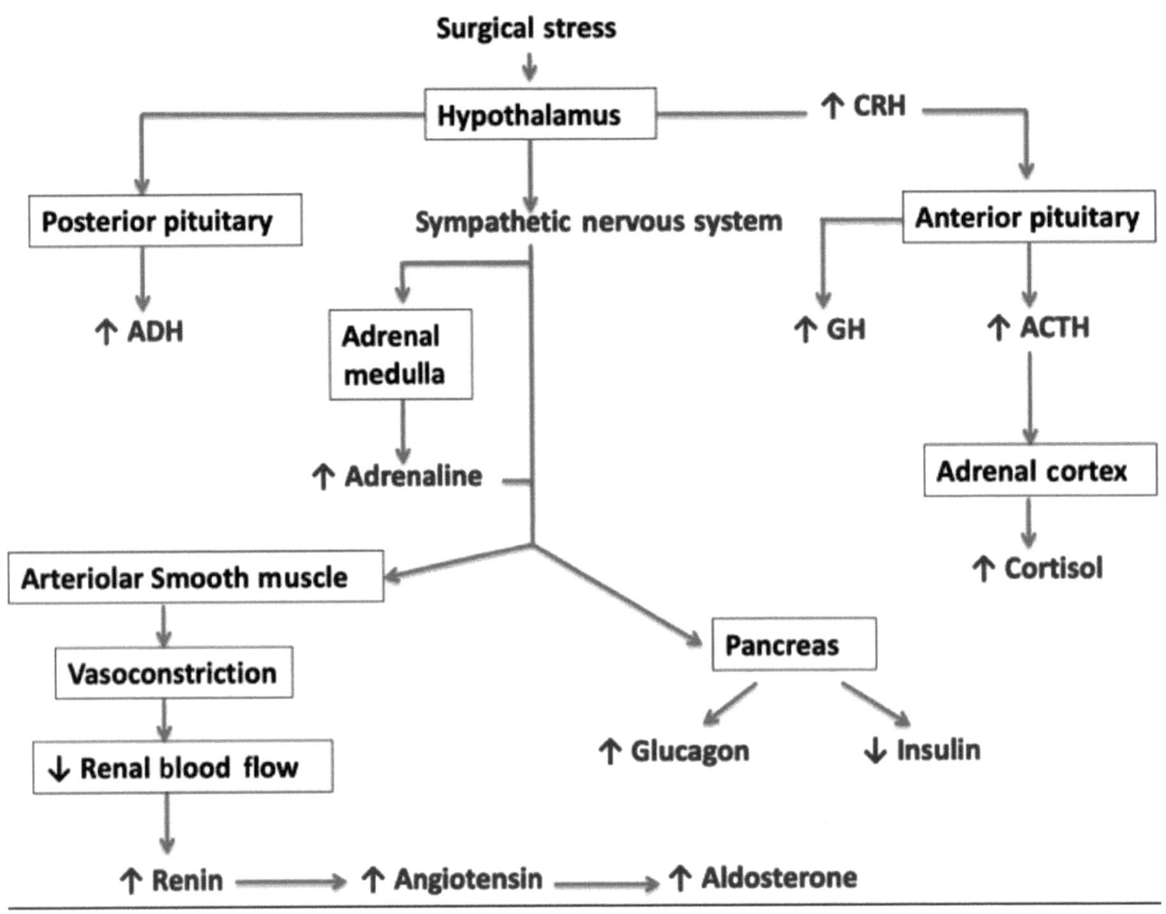

Fig. 4

Fig 4. Integration of the stress response by the hypothalamus, sympathoadrenal, and sympathorenal responses.

In the normal 'unstressed' state, physiological levels of glucocorticoid hormones participate in conventional negative-feedback mechanisms to inhibit ACTH and CRH secretion, predominantly at the level of the anterior pituitary gland, but also at the PVN. Activity of the HPA axis is characterised by a circadian rhythm with superimposed ultradian pulsatile release of glucocorticoids (i.e. there is a recurrent cycle of release repeated throughout a 24 h period). The circadian pattern of cortisol release is controlled by the suprachiasmatic nucleus in the hypothalamus. The HPA axis is a stress-responsive neuroendocrine system that adapts and responds to homeostatic challenges, such as surgery. Immediately after surgery, ultradian pulses in ACTH and cortisol both increase. Adrenocorticotropic hormone concentrations return to baseline within 24 h, but plasma concentrations of cortisol remain increased for at least 7 days after major surgery. In minimally invasive surgical procedures, when compared with open surgical techniques, the cortisol 'peak' is delayed, and in severe critical illness, the circadian variation is flattened in proportion to the degree of circadian disruption.

Chronic activation of the HPA axis before surgery is associated with HPA axis dysfunction. Increasing age and frailty are associated with a progressive loss of hypothalamic sensitivity, with higher cortisol concentrations and a decrease in its diurnal variation. Negative-feedback mechanisms of the HPA axis are blunted: CRH (and also vasopressin, discussed in more detail later) in the PVN of elderly people is increased despite increased circulating plasma cortisol concentrations. Pre-existing cardiovascular deconditioning leading to decreased physical activity, as a result of conditions, such as heart failure, chemotherapy for cancer, or chronic joint pain, can contribute to perioperative disruption of neuroendocrine function. Hypothalamic–pituitary–adrenal axis dysfunction also occurs in a variety of non-cardiac medical conditions, including clinical depression; anxiety and depression are associated with worse perioperative outcomes. Central hypersecretion of CRH, and consequently increased production of glucocorticoids, may contribute to the HPA axis dysregulation that occurs in 80% of patients with depression. This may partly account for the increased incidence of upper respiratory tract infections, disruption in wound healing, and psychosocial stress when these patients undergo surgery.

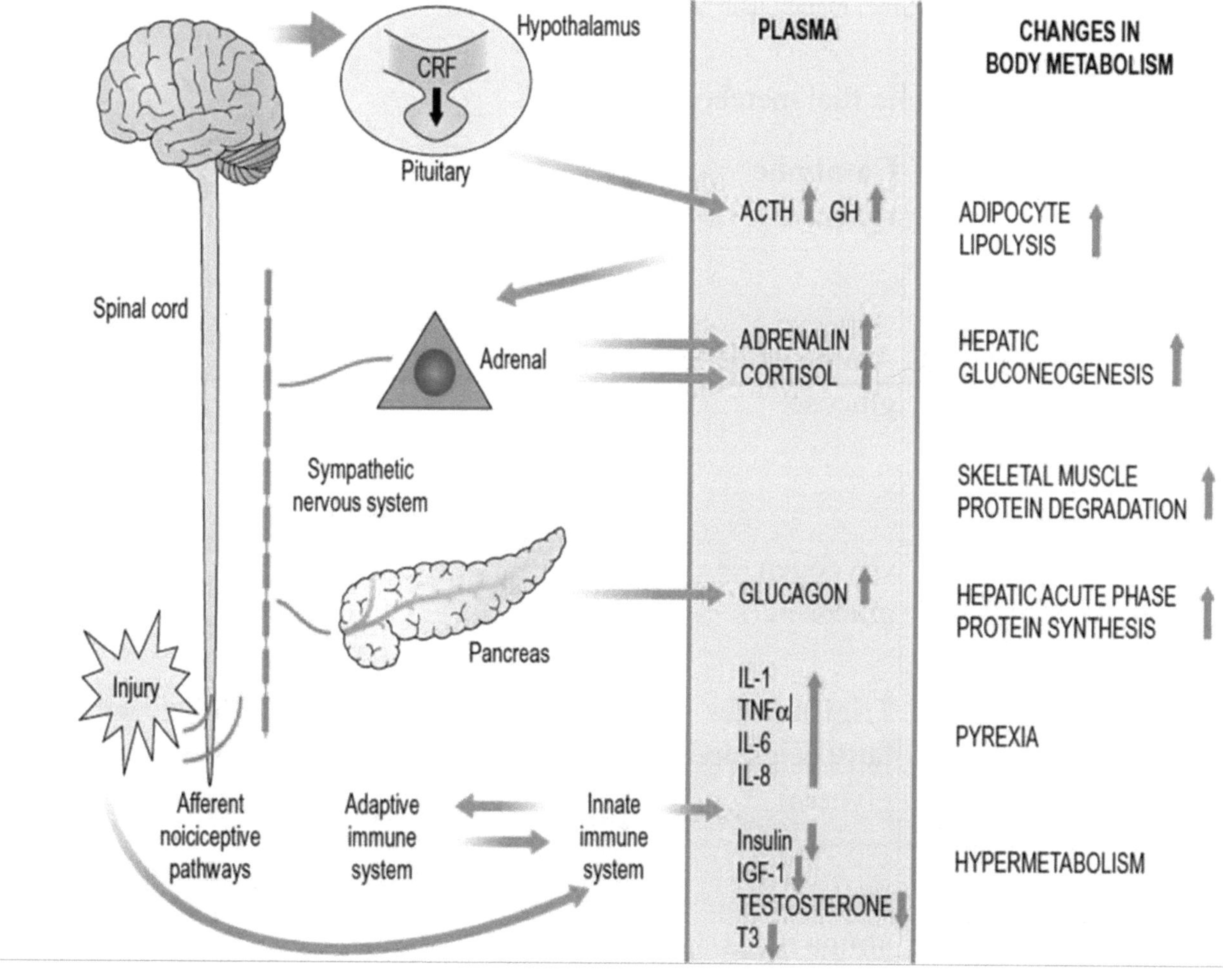

Fig. 5

Growth hormone (GH) secretion by the anterior pituitary gland increases in response to the magnitude of the surgical stress response. Growth hormone increases hepatic glycogenolysis leading to hyperglycaemia. Growth hormone also causes insulin resistance, although the molecular mechanism is uncertain.

Antidiuretic hormone (ADH) is a peptide hormone that is synthesised in the hypothalamus before being transported via axons to the posterior pituitary gland and released into the circulation. This process occurs in response to hypovolaemia, hypotension, hyperosmolarity, and an increase in angiotensin II concentrations. The primary function of ADH, also termed vasopressin or arginine vasopressin, is to regulate extracellular fluid volume. Antidiuretic hormone release leads to a reduction in renal free-water clearance by an action on the renal collecting ducts. Antidiuretic hormone stimulates the insertion of aquaporins into the walls of the renal collecting system. This favours free-water resorption down its concentration gradient back into the renal medulla and causes a reduction in urine volume with an increase in urine concentration.

Other hormonal changes associated with the stress response include increased prolactin concentrations and reduced testosterone, thyroxine (T4), and triiodothyronine (T3) concentrations. These normalise to preoperative baseline within a few days and are not thought to exert a significant effect on patient-centred functional outcomes.

Metabolic response

A state of hypermetabolism and hypercatabolism occurs with the mobilisation of readily useable energy sources. Hepatic glycogen stores are converted to glucose, skeletal muscle undergoes proteolysis, and fat reserves undergo lipolysis. The body uses these substrates in tissue repair and as an energy source.

Table 4. Summary of catabolic fuel metabolism

Summary of catabolic fuel metabolism

Metabolic process	Catabolic reaction	Caused by	Effect
Hepatic gluconeogenesis	Amino acids → glucose	Increased adrenaline, glucagon, and cortisol concentrations stimulate this mobilisation of fuel stores	Increased blood glucose Protein catabolism
Hepatic glycogenolysis	Glycogen → glucose		Increased blood glucose
Lipolysis	Triglycerides → fatty acids and glycerol		Increased plasma fatty acids
Proteolysis	Protein → amino acids		Increased plasma amino acids

Table 4

The release of adrenaline seen alongside SNS activation results in the stimulation of glucagon and inhibition of insulin release. Secretion of the key anabolic hormone insulin is reduced by the SNS effect on pancreatic α_2-adrenergic receptors, and later a decrease in insulin sensitivity occurs in peripheral cells. These hormonal changes lead to hyperglycaemia and the release of fatty acids with relatively unopposed catabolism of muscle tissue.3

Increased sympathetic activity to the kidneys activates the renin–angiotensin–aldosterone system (RAAS). Adrenaline-induced vasoconstriction of the renal afferent arterioles causes reduced renal blood flow, promoting the secretion of renin. Renin initiates conversion of angiotensin I to angiotensin II by angiotensinogen, which in turn stimulates the release of aldosterone from the adrenal cortex. In addition, the posterior pituitary gland secretes ADH in response to both increased sympathetic activity and angiotensin II. Together, the hormones aldosterone and ADH promote the retention of salt and water. These changes play a role in the sustained maintenance of blood volume and increased vascular tone. Fluid retention, oliguria, and accumulation of extracellular fluid are common in the acute postoperative period. This may act as a protective feature to help maintain arterial blood pressure in the setting of acute loss of plasma volume through, for example, haemorrhage. In addition, ADH and angiotensin have a direct vasopressor effect.

Inflammatory–immune response

The stress response to surgery involves both the innate and cell-mediated adaptive (acquired) immune systems. In addition to the magnitude of surgical trauma, factors, such as malnutrition, infection, and cancer status, contribute to the impact of surgery on the inflammatory–immune system. The innate immune response is non-specific, and activation occurs early in the surgical stress response. Monocytes migrate to sites of tissue injury where they differentiate into macrophages. Innate immune cells with phagocytic properties capable of antigen presentation, such as macrophages, and neutrophils and natural killer (NK) cells, move into the wound and produce proinflammatory mediators called cytokines. If there is excessive production of inflammatory mediators, a SIRS response characterised by non-specific whole-body response may occur. Natural killer cells are a type of uncharacterised cytotoxic lymphocyte and an important component of the innate immune system. Natural killer cells are activated in response to cytokines and induce apoptosis in damaged, neoplastic, and virally infected cells. Later after operation, immune cells may have reduced cytotoxicity.

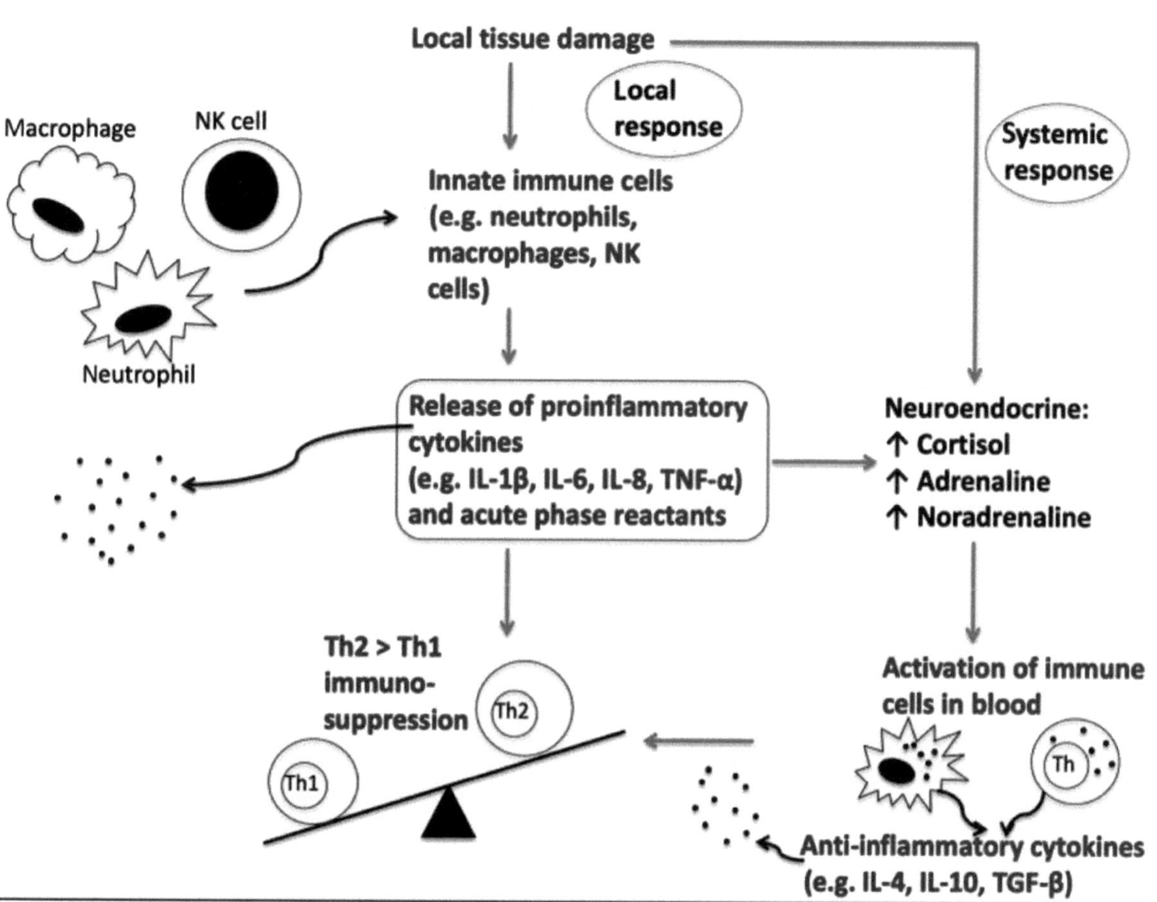

Fig. 6

Fig 6. Surgery-induced immunological response. TGF, transforming growth factor.

Cytokines are a vast family of small proteins with diverse biological activity that include interleukins (ILs), interferons, chemokines, and tumour necrosis factors (TNFs). Cytokines are responsible for mediating and maintaining the local inflammatory response to tissue damage. Early in the inflammatory cascade, pro-inflammatory cytokines IL-6, IL-1β, TNF-α, and IL-8 are produced. Cytokine concentrations are highest on the first postoperative day. Anti-inflammatory cytokines IL-4, IL-10, transforming factor-β, IL-1 receptor antagonist, and soluble TNF receptors (sTNFR1 and sTNFR2) are also produced. They help to reduce the magnitude and duration of the SIRS response. If the overall balance between the pro- and anti-inflammatory mediated responses is unregulated, immunodeficiency and sepsis are more likely.

The acute phase response is an increase in the concentration of serum proteins (acute phase proteins [APPs]) in response to tissue injury and inflammation, and is a component of early innate immunity. Acute phase proteins are a large group of proteins produced by hepatocytes in response to stimulation by cytokines, especially IL-6. The acute phase response is characterised by the production of APPs in the liver, such as C-reactive protein (CRP), fibrinogen, D-dimer, and α_2 macroglobulin, and also fever, granulocytosis, and a reduction in transport proteins, such as albumin and transferrin.

Initiation of the cell-mediated adaptive immune response requires interaction between T-lymphocytes and antigen-presenting cells. Antigen-presenting cells, such as macrophages, take up antigens, such as damaged tissue cells in the surgical wound or tumour cells. The surgical stress response promotes a relative increase in T-helper 2 (Th2) lymphocytes compared with T-helper 1 (Th1) lymphocytes. The shift in Th1:Th2 balance causes impaired cell-mediated immunity, and this is associated with poor outcomes, such as impaired wound healing, an increased incidence of sepsis, and cancer recurrence; it can also contribute to the development of postoperative multi-organ failure. The suppression of Th1 response and an increase in Th2 response leading to impaired cell-mediated immunity may be detrimental after all major surgery. Furthermore, in cancer surgery, this shift may result in deficient NK cell function, and therefore higher risk of perioperative tumour cell immune evasion and possibly increasing the chance of cancer recurrence or metastasis.

Recovery after surgery has been tracked by serial measurement of a number of blood markers, such as cortisol, IL-6, white blood cell count (WCC), and CRP. The postoperative concentrations for these peak at different times: cortisol (0–4 h), IL-6 (12–24 h), WCC (24–48 h), and CRP (24–72 h). Only IL-6 and CRP concentrations are consistently associated with the magnitude of surgical stress. Peak cortisol concentrations and WCC are not considered to reflect the magnitude of systemic inflammatory response in elective surgery. C-reactive protein may be monitored after major surgery as a potential early indicator of infection or excessive inflammation.

Modulation of the perioperative stress response

Anaesthetic drugs

I.V. and volatile anaesthetic agents

A single induction dose of propofol (1–2 mg kg^{-1}) suppresses circulating cortisol concentrations, but does not completely block the secretion of cortisol and aldosterone. A continuous infusion of propofol (TIVA with plasma concentration of 4–8 μg ml^{-1}) may completely block cortisol secretion.

This inhibition of cortisol secretion is postulated to take place at the level of the adrenal glands because the ACTH response to surgery is similar during maintenance of anaesthesia with both propofol and volatile anaesthetics. Propofol results in the lowest proteolytic response to surgery, when compared with other i.v. and inhaled anaesthetic agents. This may be because the propofol emulsion contains triglycerides, which allows the body to preferentially use them as a substrate.

Etomidate suppresses adrenocortical function by the reversible inhibition of 11β-hydroxylase and 17α-hydroxylase enzymes. Etomidate inhibits synthesis of cortisol and aldosterone for up to 8 h after a single induction dose (0.3 mg kg^{-1}). Etomidate is considered obsolete because of its association with increased mortality when used as a sedative infusion in patients with sepsis in intensive care. Thiopental and ketamine have both been shown to suppress NK immune cell activity in *in vitro* animal models, but propofol has not.

Volatile anaesthetic agents inhibit ACTH, cortisol, catecholamine, and GH to a greater extent than i.v. anaesthetic agents, such as propofol combined with remifentanil. In laparoscopic surgery, ACTH, cortisol, and GH concentrations are significantly reduced when sevoflurane is used compared with isoflurane. In cardiac surgery, there was no difference in mortality or other outcomes when volatile anaesthesia and TIVA with propofol were compared.

Volatile agents impair platelet aggregation and clot stability to a greater extent than propofol. Volatile anaesthetic agents have a multitude of both immunosuppressive and immunoactivating effects. These immune-modulatory effects include decreased NK cell cytotoxicity by sevoflurane, isoflurane, and halothane; decreased cytokine release by sevoflurane; decreased neutrophil cell number and adhesion by sevoflurane, isoflurane, and halothanc; and increased neutrophil cell number by desflurane.

Analgesics and other medications

Benzodiazepines

Benzodiazepines (e.g. midazolam 0.2–0.4 mg kg^{-1} or infusion of 0.9–0.125 mg kg^{-1} h^{-1}) inhibit cortisol production at the hypothalamic–pituitary level of the HPA axis. This effect has been reported in both limb and abdominal surgeries. The significance of this suppression is not clear.

α_2-adrenergic agonists

Clonidine and dexmedetomidine are centrally acting α_2-adrenoceptor agonists that inhibit the surgical stress response mediated by the SNS. Central sympathetic outflow is reduced when α_2-receptors in the lateral reticular nucleus are stimulated. In the spinal cord, α_2-receptor stimulation augments endogenous opioid release and modulates the descending pathways involved in spinal nociceptive processing. By these mechanisms, the sympathoadrenal and cardiovascular responses to a surgical stimulus are reduced.

Dexmedetomidine reduces cortisol and renin concentrations, which imparts haemodynamic stability and impaired pancreatic insulin secretion. A single dose of dexmedetomidine 0.5 μg kg^{-1} before induction attenuates the increase in heart rate and MAP during laryngoscopy and tracheal intubation. After major abdominal surgery, a bolus of dexmedetomidine (0.5–1.0 μg kg^{-1}) before induction followed by an infusion (0.2–0.5 μg kg^{-1} h^{-1}) during the operation significantly suppressed postoperative IL-6, IL-8, TNF-α, cortisol, and glucose concentrations.

Opioids

Systemic opioids reduce ACTH and GH secretion by reduced CRH release at the hypothalamic level. High-dose opioids have been shown to completely suppress both ACTH and cortisol secretion if administered before CPB in cardiac surgery (but not after CPB), and before knife to skin incision in open cholecystectomy. At high doses (fentanyl >50 μg kg^{-1}), the hormonal response to pelvic and abdominal surgery is prevented. However, this dose level would significantly prolong re-emergence from anaesthesia and is associated with a requirement for postoperative ventilatory support. Systemic opioids may attenuate the hyperglycaemic response to surgery.

Morphine, fentanyl, remifentanil, methadone, and codeine have an immunomodulatory role, whereas oxycodone, tramadol, hydrocodone, and buprenorphine do not. One hypothesis to explain this is that opioids that can cross the blood–brain barrier (BBB) exert more of an immunomodulatory effect than opioids that cannot cross the BBB. Morphine shows dose-dependent, immunosuppressive effects to impair monocyte and neutrophil function, NK-cell-mediated cytotoxicity, cytokine release, and lymphocyte and macrophage proliferation. There is conflicting and inconsistent evidence in relation to the effect of opioids on tumour growth and cancer metastasis. Emerging preclinical literature in both *in vitro* and *in vivo* studies suggests that opioids may influence tumour cell growth by their action on the mu-opioid receptor (MOR). This receptor is overexpressed on the surface of certain cancers. In non-small cell lung cancer, the MOR antagonist methylnaltrexone may be beneficial in reducing cancer progression and metastasis. Similar to the relationship between opioids and cancer recurrence, the clinical consequences of the immunomodulation caused by high-dose opioids on perioperative infection rates are not yet fully understood.

Regional anaesthesia

Wide-ranging neuraxial analgesia with local anaesthetic agents block the endocrine and metabolic response to surgery in the pelvis and lower limbs. Much of the literature examining this does so as a comparative study with volatile or i.v. general anaesthesia agents. Neuraxial epidural and spinal anaesthesia block the HPA axis response by blocking the afferent activation of the hypothalamus and efferent stimulation of the liver, adrenals, and pancreas. Adrenocorticotropic hormone, cortisol, adrenaline, and GH secretions are impaired. Proposed benefits of regional techniques over general anaesthesia include an earlier return of gut function, reduced incidence of pulmonary dysfunction, reduced inflammatory response to surgery, and beneficial effects on the coagulation system.

In abdominal aortic surgery, epidural anaesthesia when combined with general anaesthesia reduces the increase in cortisol and urinary adrenaline concentrations during surgery, when compared with general anaesthesia alone. Thoracic epidural anaesthesia combined with general anaesthesia can suppress the catecholamine response during CPB and up to 24 h after surgery. In patients undergoing hip surgery, combined spinal and epidural blockade (compared with general anaesthesia) reduced the amount of amino acid oxidation, as a marker of protein catabolism in the acute postoperative period. The hyperglycaemic response during surgery is inhibited by regional anaesthesia. Spinal anaesthesia showed suppression of serum cortisol and blood glucose concentrations compared with general anaesthesia in patients undergoing elective abdominal, urological, and orthopaedic surgery.

Thoracic epidural combined with general anaesthesia can suppress the catecholamine response during CPB and up to 24 h after surgery.

Surgical techniques

Minimally invasive surgical techniques, including laparoscopic and robotic surgeries, have an independent impact on the magnitude of the inflammatory–immune response. When used alongside enhanced recovery after surgery (ERAS) programmes, minimally invasive surgery can reduce hospital length of stay, surgical complication rates, and incidence of readmission to hospital.

The duration of surgery and the extent of intraoperative surgical manipulation and tissue injury are proportional to the associated stress response. The use of less invasive surgical techniques over traditional open techniques where possible reduces the inflammatory response (e.g. concentrations of IL-6 and CRP are reduced in laparoscopic surgery when compared with open techniques). A major advantage of minimally invasive surgery is the reduced incision size and associated tissue injury, resulting in a reduction in requirements for postoperative analgesia.

There is an increase in intra-abdominal pressure during minimally invasive pelvic and abdominal surgery with a pneumoperitoneum. This results in reduced renal blood flow with activation of the RAAS and an increase in ADH secretion. Permissive oliguria of 0.3 ml kg^{-1} h^{-1} and increased ADH secretion may be accepted as an appropriate physiological response that is not associated with an increased incidence of acute kidney injury.

Glucocorticoids

The impact on the surgical stress response by the perioperative supplementation of glucocorticoids is an uncertain area, and there is significant heterogeneity between studies. In patients undergoing elective endovascular abdominal aortic aneurysm repair, for which there is a recognised pronounced pro-inflammatory response, a single preoperative dose of methylprednisolone (30 mg kg^{-1}) reduced serum pro-inflammatory biomarkers (IL-6, IL-8, and CRP) and increased concentrations of the anti-inflammatory cytokine IL-10. The anti-inflammatory benefits of perioperative glucocorticoids have also been reported in colorectal, hepatobiliary, and orthopaedic lower-limb joint replacement surgeries. There is also evidence showing reduced pulmonary complications without affecting duration of stay or incidence of infection.

The inflammatory–immune response is strongly activated in cardiac surgery with high peak values measured for CRP and IL-6. High-dose glucocorticoid administration (methylprednisolone 30 mg kg^{-1} or dexamethasone 1 mg kg^{-1}) before CPB leads to a significant decrease in pro-inflammatory mediators (IL-6, IL-8, TNF, and CRP). Glucocorticoid use has been associated with a reduction in duration of postoperative mechanical ventilation, postoperative infection, hyperthermia, and length of stay after cardiac surgery.

Concerns remain regarding the possibility of a glucocorticoid-induced hyperglycaemic response, and caution should be taken, especially in diabetic patients, where no conclusive data exist. Perioperative outcomes in patients with a reduced cortisol response to surgery, such as elderly, frail, depressed, or critically ill patients, may be worse if supplemental glucocorticoids are not given.

Nutrition and fluids management

Enhanced recovery after surgery is a combination of measures that, when used together, reduce the component parts of the surgical stress response to improve postoperative outcomes and recovery times. There is an emphasis on a multidisciplinary approach to measures, including multimodal optimal analgesia, early mobilisation, minimally invasive surgical techniques, and early enteral feeding. Hyper-metabolism and hyper-catabolism occur after surgical tissue injury in an attempt to restore homeostasis within the body. This may lead to impaired immune function, impaired wound healing, muscle wasting, and a change in nutrition requirements. Malnutrition and underfeeding are risk factors for postoperative complications.

A reduction in fasting time and preoperative carbohydrate loading have been shown to reduce the amount of fluid administered during surgery and reduce postoperative insulin resistance and associated catabolism. Immunonutrition with glutamine, arginine, and omega-3 fatty acid supplementation may reduce immune-mediated changes seen after surgery. However, no clear recommendation currently exists for enteral supplementation as evidence of the benefit is insufficient.

Conclusions

The stress response to surgery is a complex neuroendocrine–metabolic and inflammatory–immune process. The physiological changes that this stress induces in the body have been discussed; it triggers a catabolic cascade with the release of growth factors and energy substrates. There is a release of inflammatory mediators, suppression of anabolic hormones, and sodium and fluid retention. The increase in sympathetic tone and its physiological sequelae plays a key role. Knowledge in this area is continuing to develop, and it is becoming clear that overexpression of inflammatory mediators and immune suppression puts the patient at increased risk of perioperative complications. A major aim of perioperative care should be to attenuate this response by the judicious selection and conduct of anaesthetic techniques.

Fluid and electrolyte balance may be altered in the surgical patient for several reasons:

- ADH and aldosterone secretion.
- Loss from the gastrointestinal tract (e.g; bowel preparation, ileus, stomas, fistulas)
- Insensible losses (e.g; sweating secondary to fever).
- Third space losses
- Surgical drains
- Medications (e.g.diuretics)
- Underlying chronic illness (e.g; cardiac failure, portal hypertension).
- Note: ↳ 1 mEq/L = 1 mmol/L ↳ 1 cc = 1 ml

CHAPTER FOUR

MONITORING BODY FLUID STATUS

WHAT HAPPENS TO THE FLUID BALANCE IN SURGERY?

Homeostasis defines the tendency of the organism to maintain stability and balance. In this manner, body fluid balance is controlled by previously described compartment mechanisms. On the other hand, any physical intervention may cause imbalance of the body fluids. During relatively long lasting major surgeries, which are performed with general anesthesia, whole intake is controlled by the anesthesiologist and fluid loss happens in numerous different ways such as bleeding, drainage of ascites, urination, insensible water loss and "third space losses". However, long term effects of these intraoperative events, such as possible over-hydrating, dehydration, and bleeding should be considered in the postoperative care unit.

The third space is a term for spaces in which body fluids lose their function to affect fluid balance between intravascular and extravascular compartments. In other words, it can be called as non-functional extracellular volume. Bowel lumen, peritoneal and pleural cavities are thought to be the major examples of the third space. Studies that tried to explain the third space loss measured the extracellular volume (ECV) and functional ECV (FECV). FECV is defined as fluid accumulations within the interstitial space combined with plasma. Shires showed that, there is up to 28% loss in extracellular volume after two hours of operative time, during elective surgeries of thirteen adult patients. Subsequent studies in 1960s support this finding and existence of the third space. However, numerous trials with improved methodology proved that FECV levels do not decrease in or after surgery. This correction of data couldn't be recognized well enough, but still, favored common belief is in the presence and importance of the third space. Current evidence supports that FECV is not negatively affected by surgery, however over-hydration with saline and surgical trauma cause endothelial dysfunction and interstitial edema due to fluid shift to ECV. In conclusion, "the third space" term should only refer to anatomical cavities like bowel lumen, peritoneum and pleura, and should only be considered in certain cases. Moreover, possible endothelial glycocalyx dysfunction and fluid shift to ECV should be our guiding facts for determining the right strategy in postoperative fluid management.

K^+ and Na^+ are the predominant cations in the ICF and ECF, respectively. Distribution and movement of water between the intracellular and interstitial spaces is governed by the osmotic forces created by differences in non-diffusible solute concentrations. The cell membrane separating the fluid compartments is selective and allows the free passage of water, but not solutes. Diffusion occurs by one of several mechanisms; directly through the lipid bilayer of the cell membrane, through protein channels within the membrane or by reversible binding to a carrier protein that can traverse the membrane (facilitated diffusion). Because of the charged lipid nature of the cell membrane, cations (such as Na^+ and K^+) cannot easily cross the membrane. These cations can diffuse only through specific voltage-dependent protein channels; thus, the cell transmembrane voltage potential (which is positive to the outside) created by the Na^+–K^+ pump is maintained. The solutions on each side of the cell membrane are therefore not identical and relative changes in osmolality between the intracellular and interstitial compartments result in a net water movement from the hypo-osmolar to the hyper-osmolar compartment.

In contrast, the capillary endothelium is non-selective and freely permeable to both water and ions; plasma and interstitial fluids have similar solute compositions. Therefore, the major determinant of water flux is plasma protein concentration. Proteins do not normally pass out of the capillaries into the interstitium because of the tight intercellular junctions between adjacent endothelial cells. As a result, plasma proteins are the only osmotically active solutes in fluid exchange between plasma and interstitial fluid with albumin contributing 75% of the total colloid osmotic pressure (oncotic pressure). Compromising the integrity of the capillary membrane allows passage of albumin to the interstitial compartment and subsequent accumulation of tissue fluid.

Regulation of ECF volume and composition

The volume of the ECF is determined mainly by the total amount of osmotically active solutes (i.e.Na^+ and Cl^-). Because changes in Cl^- are mainly secondary to changes in Na^+, the amount of Na^+ in the ECF is the most important determinant of ECF volume; thus, the mechanisms that control Na^+ balance are the major mechanisms defending ECF volume. However, the need to ensure optimal circulating volume is paramount and volume stimuli can override the osmotic regulation of vasopressin secretion. A rise in ECF volume inhibits vasopressin secretion, and a decline in ECF volume increases its secretion. In addition, expansion of ECF volume increases the secretion of natriuretic hormones, the most important being secretion of atrial natriuretic peptide (ANP) by the heart causing natriuresis and diuresis.

Thirst and osmolality

Thirst occurs in response to hypovolaemia (mediated via baroreceptors) and to changes in osmolarity detected by osmoreceptors in the hypothalamus. Drinking in response to thirst restores central circulating volume in hypovolaemia, ensures adequate hydration and allows additional fluid loss during the renal excretion of excess osmotic loads.

Total body osmolality is directly proportional to the total body sodium and potassium divided by TBW, so changes in osmolality occur when there is disproportionate change. When osmolality increases, the thirst mechanism is stimulated and vasopressin secretion (anti-diuretic hormone, ADH) is increased. Water is drunk and retained by the kidney, thus diluting the hypertonic plasma. Opposite effects occur when the plasma becomes hypotonic. Plasma osmolality ranges from 280 to 295 mosmol $litre^{-1}$.

The role of the kidney and renal sodium excretion

While thirst and ADH control the intake and excretion of water, respectively, the electrolyte composition of urine is largely determined by renal mechanisms. Urinary sodium excretion is affected by changes in glomerular filtration rate (GFR) and tubular reabsorption of sodium. Decrease in intravascular volume causes a decrease in GFR and filtration of salt and water. Tubular reabsorption of sodium is affected by renal sympathetic tone, which results in diminished Na^+ excretion and by the renin–angiotensin–aldosterone system, which plays a vital role in increasing sodium reabsorption and renovascular tone. Subsequent release of aldosterone from the adrenal cortex acts on the collecting ducts causing a further increase in sodium reabsorption.

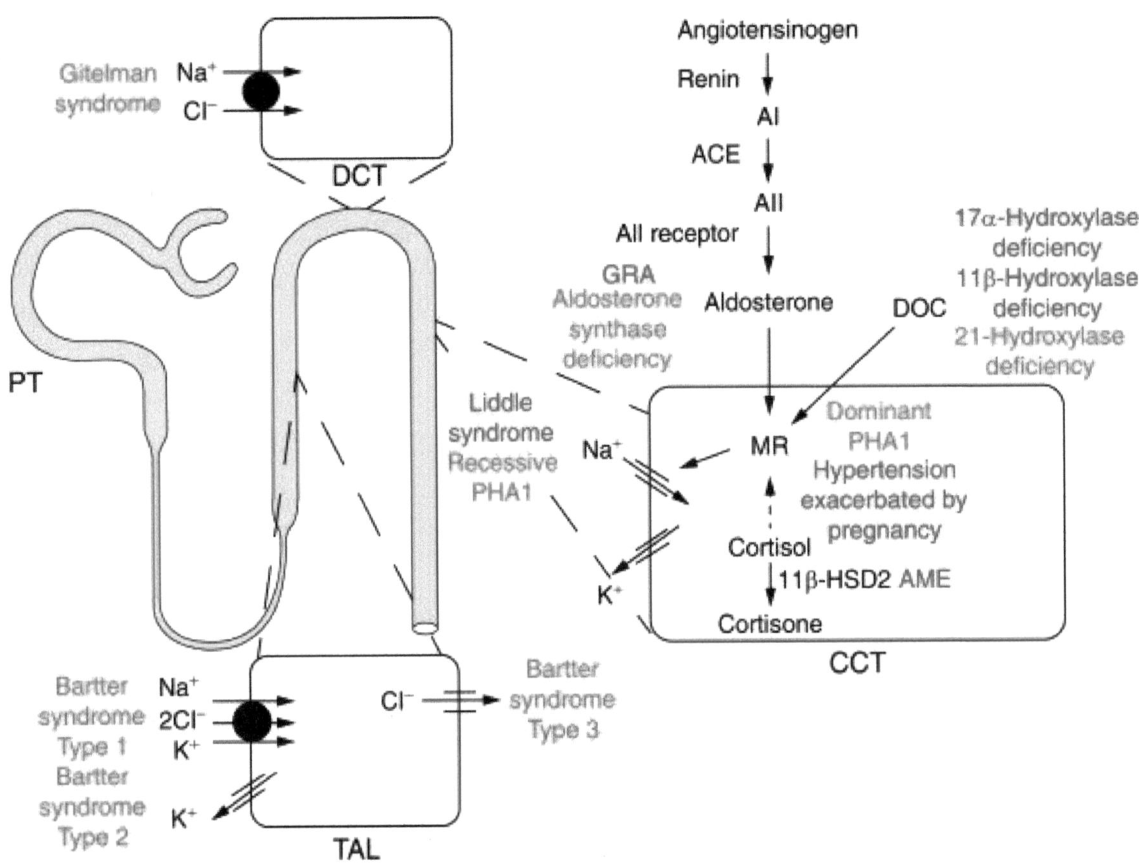

Fig. 8

Water balance

Normal balance is maintained with intake and losses of 2.5–3 litres per day. Intake from ingested fluid (1300 ml), solid food (800 ml) and metabolic waste (400 ml) is balanced by insensible fluid losses of 0.5 ml kg^{-1} h^{-1} (850 ml) from skin and lungs; plus sensible losses from urine (1500 ml) and faeces (100 ml). These values are those in health, at normothermia and at rest.

Electrolyte balance and clinical implications

Sodium

Sodium balance is related to ECF volume and water balance; daily ingestion has a wide range (50–300 mmol). It is regulated by the kidneys in which the volume and constitution of filtrate reaching the collecting ducts is dependent on GFR, sympathetic tone and angiotensin II acting via the effects of ADH and aldosterone to conserve water and sodium (see above). Normothermic extra-renal losses are minimal (~10 mmol day^{-1}).

Hypernatraemia leads to pyrexia, nausea, vomiting, convulsions, coma and focal neurological signs. Correction is advisable over 48–72 h with 5% dextrose. In hyponatraemia, symptoms depend on the cause, magnitude and rapidity. Acute symptomatic hyponatraemia is a medical emergency. The aim of treatment is to raise plasma concentration to 125 mmol $litre^{-1}$ gradually over a period of no less than 12 h while treating the underlying cause.

Potassium

The total amount of potassium in the ECF is less than the average daily intake (50–200 mmol), so a potassium load must be cleared rapidly from this compartment. The physiological mechanisms that contribute to this are the release of both insulin and glucagon to increase intracellular transport and aldosterone release which stimulates the active transport of potassium from peritubular fluid into the cells of the distal convoluted tubule. K^+ regulation is also inversely related to the pH. Potassium regulation is less efficient than sodium regulation and extrarenal losses are minimal.

Hypokalaemia leads to anorexia, nausea, muscle weakness, paralytic ileus and cardiac conduction abnormalities. Treatment is with potassium supplements and treatment of the underlying causes. Hyperkalaemia results in cardiac arrhythmias which may be life threatening. Immediate treatment is necessary if plasma potassium concentration exceeds 7 mmol litre^{-1} or if there are serious ECG abnormalities. Treatment options include calcium gluconate, glucose and insulin, sodium bicarbonate, calcium resonium, and peritoneal or haemodialysis.

Chloride

Chloride is the main anion in the ECF. It is important in maintaining a normal acid–base state, normal renal tubular function and in the formation of gastric acid. Chloride loss is mainly from the stomach, bile, pancreatic and intestinal secretions. Regulation of chloride is passively related to sodium and inversely related to plasma bicarbonate. In the renal proximal tubule, chloride is excreted with ammonium ions to eliminate hydrogen ions in exchange for sodium and can result in the production of acid urine. In the erythrocytes, carbon dioxide is converted by the action of carbonic anhydrase to bicarbonate. About 70% of the bicarbonate produced will diffuse into the plasma and chloride shifts into the cell to maintain electrochemical neutrality. The reverse occurs when the blood reaches the lungs. In respiratory disturbances (acidosis or alkalosis), 30% of an acid load can be buffered by such shifts between the ICF and ECF.

It is important to recognise the clinical implication of excessive use of chloride (normal saline) in fluid resuscitation. According to Stewart, the major determinant to H^+ concentration is the strong ion difference (SID) in the body. A normal SID (42–46 mmol litre^{-1}) is obtained by adding together the concentrations of the main cations in solution (Na^+, K^+, Ca^{2+}, Mg^{2+}) and subtracting the concentrations of the main cations (Cl^-, lactate). A decrease in SID is associated with a metabolic acidosis and this can be precipitated by large volume of saline because renal excretion of Na^+ occurs in preference to Cl^- and H^+. The cause of metabolic acidosis may be erroneously attributed to tissue hypoperfusion and cellular hypoxaemia and treating acidaemia with liberal volume infusions may worsen the acidosis rather than correcting it.

Bicarbonate

Bicarbonate forms the main buffer and facilitates the carriage of carbon dioxide in the blood (80% as bicarbonate). Most of the filtered bicarbonate is reabsorbed in the proximal tubule as a result of H^+ secretion from tubular cells into the lumen, the remainder is reabsorbed in the distal tubule and collecting ducts. Bicarbonate regulation is related to renal acid secretion; this in turn is altered by changes in $PaCO_2$, K^+ concentration, carbonic anhydrase level, and adrenocortical hormone concentration. When $PaCO_2$ is high (respiratory acidosis) more intracellular bicarbonate is available to buffer the hydroxyl ions and acid secretion is enhanced, whereas the reverse is true when $PaCO_2$ falls. Acid secretion is also increased by aldosterone owing to increase reabsorption of Na^+ and when there is K^+ depletion because this causes intracellular acidosis even though the plasma pH may be elevated. Acid secretion is inhibited when carbonic anhydrase is inhibited because the formation of bicarbonate is decreased.

When the plasma bicarbonate concentration is high, it appears in urine, which becomes alkaline. Conversely, when the plasma bicarbonate falls, more H^+ becomes available to combine with other buffer anions and the urine becomes more acidic.

The main implications of bicarbonate in perioperative fluid therapy are in the correction of metabolic acidosis and the emergency treatment of hyperkalaemia. However, over-treatment can lead to deleterious effects including an increase in $PaCO_2$, worsening intracellular acidosis, hypokalaemia, hypernatraemia and fluid overload.

Anaesthesia, surgery and fluid balance

Fluid shifts during the perioperative period and the physiological responses to surgical stress have significant implications for perioperative fluid prescribing. Many patients are dehydrated before theatre owing to prolonged fasting, the use of purgatives or diuretic therapy. Intraoperative losses are frequently underestimated and excess losses, both surgical and third-space losses, persist into the early postoperative period. Therefore, a general tendency towards hypovolaemia is usually present leading to thirst and vasopressin secretion.

There are two main components to the stress response to surgery the neuroendocrine response and the cytokine response. The neuroendocrine response is stimulated initially by painful afferent neural stimuli reaching the CNS.

It may be diminished by dense neural blockade from regional anaesthesia. The cytokine response is stimulated by local tissue damage at the site of surgery itself (the more extensive the surgery the higher the response) and is independent of neural blockade.

The most important response to anaesthesia and surgery in the perioperative period is sodium and water retention. In general, the tendency to retain water is directly related to the magnitude of surgery. A number of factors may contribute to this including: the effects of anaesthetic agents on renal blood flow and GFR; effects of intraoperative hypotension or hypovolaemia on renal function; increased sympathetic tone and circulating catecholamines causing renal vasoconstriction; the salt and water retaining effects of increased plasma cortisol and aldosterone levels in response to the stress of surgery; and increased ADH activity. One of the most important of these is the increase in ADH activity. This is almost invariable; during surgery the ADH concentration may increase 50–100-fold. This concentration falls at the end of surgery but does not return to normal for 3–5 days (similar to the period of postoperative oliguria). This response is partly related to drugs, pain and other factors attributable to the stress of surgery; however, mostly it is a physiological response to the loss of intravascular fluid into cells or by its sequestration and immobilization in damaged tissues (i.e.'third-space'). The difference is important because it determines the choice between fluid loading and fluid restriction as the most physiological approach to fluid therapy in the peroperative period.

Changes in capillary membrane porosity occur during surgery largely as a result of the cytokine-mediated responses to tissue injury and bacteraemia. Despite a considerable increase in lymphatic drainage, fluid accumulates in previously 'dry' tissues. The situation often exists where circulatory hypovolaemia is significant enough to threaten organ perfusion whilst these 'third-space' tissues are waterlogged. More fluid is required in this situation to maintain circulatory volume and adequate organ perfusion.

Table 5 Electrolyte composition of body fluids

Solutes	*Plasma mEq / L*	*Interstitial fluid (mEq/L)*	*Intracellular fluid (mEq/L)*
Cations:			
Sodium	140	146	12
Potassium	4	5	160
Calcium	5	3	–
Magnesium	1.5	1	34
Anions:			
Chloride	105	117	2
Bicarbonate	24	27	10
Sulfate	1	1	–
Phosphate	2	2	140
Protein	15	7	54

Table 5

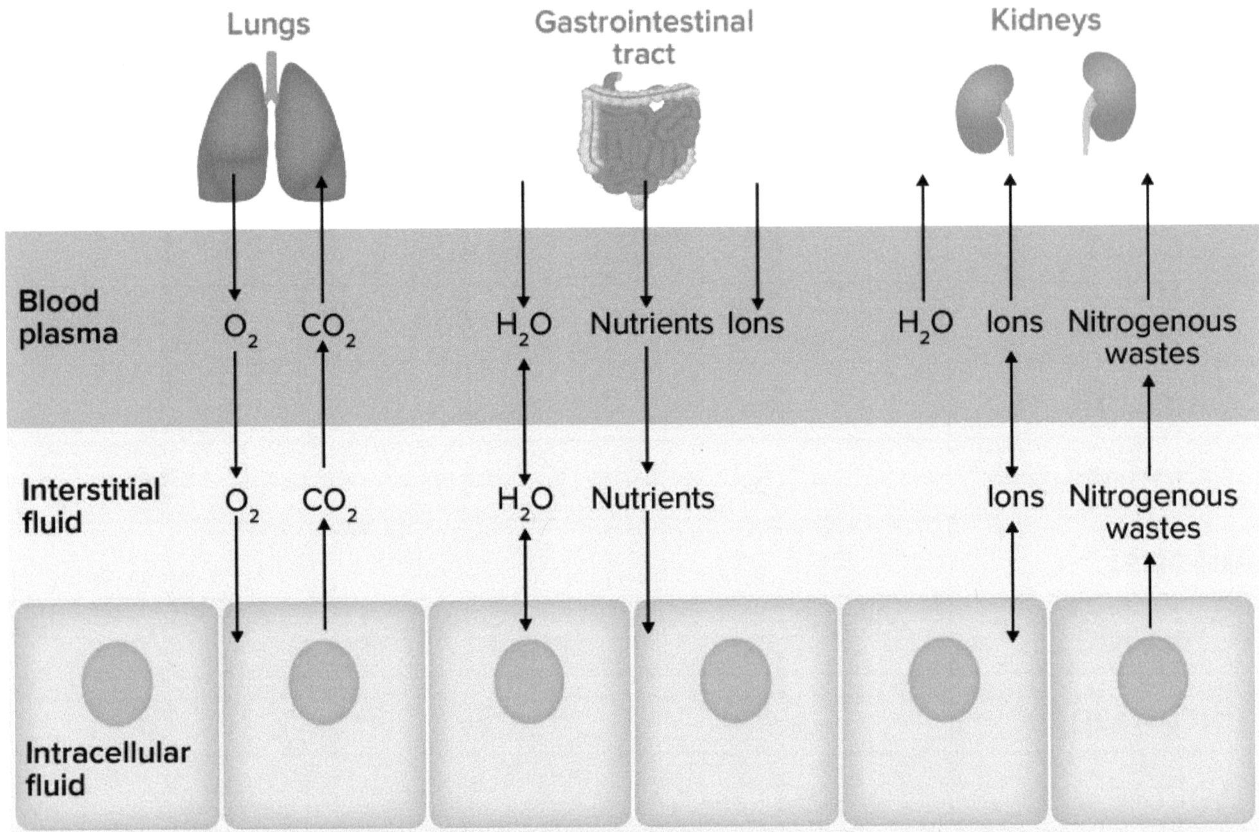

Fig. 7

Common causes of electrolyte disturbance
Table 6:

ELECTROLYTE DISORDER	COMMON CAUSES	SYMPTOMS AND SIGNS	INITIAL TREATMENT RECOMMENDATIONS
Hyponatremia	Vomiting, diarrhea, excess free water intake	Mental status changes, seizures, hyporeflexia	IV normal saline starting with a 20 mL/kg bolus For seizures: 4 mL/kg of 3% saline over 30 minutes
Hypernatremia	Vomiting, diarrhea, insensible losses, diabetes insipidus, renal disease	Diarrhea, mental status changes, ataxia, doughy skin, seizures, hyperreflexia	IV normal saline starting with a 20 mL/kg bolus Further correction to take place slowly over 48 hours
Hypokalemia	Vomiting, DKA	Muscle weakness, ileus	Generally tolerated well, replace orally over several days If severe: IV 0.2-0.3 mEq/kg/h of KCl
Hyperkalemia*	Cortical adrenal hyperplasia (neonates), renal failure. May be due to hemolysis of blood sample	ECG changes: peaked T waves, prolonged PR interval, widening of QRS	Insulin 0.1 unit/kg *plus* 25% glucose, 0.5 gram/kg IV Calcium gluconate 10%, 1 mL/kg IV, no faster than 1 mL/min Albuterol, 0.5% solution, 2.5 milligrams via nebulization
Hypocalcemia	Dietary or, vitamin D deficiency, hypoparathyroid and chronic renal failure	Vomiting, irritability, muscle weakness, tetany, seizures	Calcium gluconate 10%, 1 mL/kg IV, no faster than 1 mL/min
Hypercalcemia	Malignancy, hypervitaminosis D or A	Fatigue, irritability, anorexia, vomiting, constipation	IV normal saline starting at 20 mL/kg Bisphosphonates if admission required
Hypomagnesemia	Diarrhea, short gut, diuretics, chemotherapy	Muscle spasms, weakness, ataxia, nystagmus, seizures ECG changes: prolonged PR and QTc, torsades de pointes	For seizures or arrhythmia: IV magnesium sulfate 1 mEq/kg slowly over 4 hours Asymptomatic patients can be treated with oral supplements
Hypermagnesemia	Ingestion of antacids or renal dysfunction	Hypotension, respiratory failure, loss of deep tendon reflexes ECG changes: widening of QRS, PR, QTc	Remove exogenous source of magnesium If severe: calcium gluconate 10% 1 mL/kg IV, no faster than 1 mL/min

*Mild hyperkalemia usually well tolerated in neonates.

Table 6

Hypernatraemia

If urine output is *low* and urine osmolality *high*, then both ADH secretion and the renal response to it are present. The cause here is most likely extrarenal water loss. If *both* urine output and urine osmolality are *high*, then osmotic diuresis is suspected. If urine osmolality is *less* than plasma osmolality, then the cause is attributable to reduced ADH secretion or abnormal renal response to ADH; in both cases, urine output is high.

Hyponatraemia

If hypovolaemia is present, then the loss is either *renal* (urine sodium >20 mmol litre^{-1}) or *extrarenal* (urine sodium <15 mmol litre^{-1}); in these conditions, saline is required. If hypervolaemia (oedema) is present, the cause could be cardiac, hepatic or renal (nephrotic) and urine sodium is usually <20 mmol litre^{-1}. However, if hyponatraemia is associated with normovolaemia, the most common causes are SIADH (syndrome of inappropriate ADH release), postoperative stress, drugs and renal failure; plasma osmolality is usually decreased and fluid restriction is required.

MONITORING BODY FLUID STATUS

Mostly, the main goal of fluid resuscitation is to provide adequate tissue perfusion without harming the patient. It can be also said that fluid resuscitation is generally the first step in patients with inadequate tissue perfusion. However, it should be kept in mind that infusion of large volumes of fluids to patients who don't have enough preload reserves may result in unbalanced fluid shift to interstitial tissue, having no useful effect on tissue perfusion. Intravenous fluid administration will have no effect on tissue perfusion, unless it increases the stroke volume. Studies show that nearly half of the unstable patients are not hemodynamically responsive to fluid resuscitation. This means that, fluid resuscitation may not always be the right way to provide adequate tissue perfusion, especially in unstable patients. Thereby, assessment of the patient's responsiveness to fluid resuscitation should determine the need of extra volume.

Thus, we need to determine the actual body fluid status of the patient and build a strategy accordingly. For this purpose, static measures of intravascular volume are being used for decades and central venous pressure (CVP) has been the most favorite tool. CVP is widely believed to indicate general intravascular volume status of the patient. Moreover, many intensivists think that, CVP is directly correlated with right ventricle stroke volume and indirectly correlated with left ventricle stroke volume. However, a systematic review of 24 studies showed no relation between CVP and left ventricle stroke volume. Due to lack of evidence that supports CVP as an indicator of body fluid needs, we should not make our fluid resuscitation decisions based on CVP levels. Similarly, pulmonary capillary wedge pressure is another static measure of intravascular volume and is incapable of predicting fluid responsiveness, in contrast to the common assumption. Besides, the two even less favored static measures are left ventricular end-diastolic area and inferior vena caval diameter.

On the other hand, recent studies claim that monitoring of the interactions of heart and lung in mechanically ventilated patients, so called dynamic measures, can be used to determine patient's fluid status. According to Marik et al, non-invasive techniques such as the pulse pressure variation, the stroke volume variation, and systolic pressure variation can significantly predict fluid responsiveness in mechanically ventilated patients. These techniques are based on physiological facts. The patients, whose pulse pressures or stroke volumes are more dependent on intra-thoracic pressure variations provided by the ventilator, tend to be more responsive to fluid resuscitation.

The physiological principles underlying the pulse pressure variation (PPV) and the stroke volume variation (SVV) are based on the effects of increased pleural pressure. As the mechanical ventilator increases the pleural pressure, the increased resistance in the pulmonary system causes a decrease in the right ventricle preload and an increase in the right ventricle afterload. Meanwhile, the left ventricle preload and afterload are affected exactly the opposite way of right ventricle is: Left ventricle preload increases and afterload decreases at the end of inspiration. The pulse pressure and the left ventricle stroke volume are at their highest values at this moment. Afterwards, prolongation of blood transit time through pulmonary system results in a decrease in the left ventricle preload and reduction in the left ventricle stroke volume (and the pulse pressure) during expiratory period. Echocardiographic evaluations of aortic flow velocity and stroke volume and vena caval diameter variation are two other dynamic parameters based on similar physiological reactions.

Another technique for predicting fluid responsiveness is called the passive leg raising (PLR). While previously mentioned techniques are used for mechanically ventilated patients especially who has no spontaneous breathing, PLR can be used on any patient. Raising the legs to provide a better cardiac preload has been used for a long time in emergency patients. Recently PLR gained interest as a predictor for fluid responsiveness. Monnet pointed out that lifting the legs passively in a lying patient induces a significant blood flow towards the heart. Therefore, Marik et al called this physiologic condition as "autotransfusion". In a study on mechanically ventilated patients, PLR-induced changes have been found to be strongly similar with the effects of 300 mL colloid infusion. As a result, PLR simulates the state after fluid administration. In other words, if the patient has enough preload reserve, PLR will increase left ventricle preload and stroke volume correspondingly. It is also been reported that, these effects are reversible, and when legs are returned to their horizontal positions, this preload increasing effect disappears. Another important point is that PLR reaches its maximal effect in 1 min and its effects disappear gradually in time. Accordingly, when PLR is used to predict fluid responsiveness changes in arterial pulse pressure, descending aorta blood flow, pulse contour-derived stroke volume, or pulsed Doppler-derived velocity-time integral should be monitored closely at the first minute.

Briefly, fluid management must be done based on the patient's body fluid status. Patients who are responsive to fluids can benefit from fluid resuscitation, whereas patients who are not fluid responsive are more likely to suffer complications of over-hydration.

Therefore, common use of CVP, which is proved to be inefficient to predict fluid responsiveness, should be avoided and attempts should be made to extend the use of techniques like PLR, pulse pressure variation and the stroke volume variation. Practical tools should be manufactured and made available for common use.

CHAPTER FIVE

INTRAVENOUS FLUIDS

Substances that may be infused intravenously

- Volume expanders (crystalloids and colloids)
- Blood-based products (Whole blood, fresh frozen plasma, cryoprecipitate)
- blood substitutes.
- medications.

Types of intravenous fluid:

A. Colloid solutions:

- Containing water and large proteins and molecules, so tend to stay within the vascular space and increase intravascular pressure.
- Used for volume expanding (in hypotension), or protein replacement (low albumin)
- Very expensive.
- Examples: Dextran, hetastarch, albumin

B. Crystalloid solutions:

- Containing water and electrolytes (sodium, potassium, calcium, chloride).
- Do not contain large proteins and molecules.
- crystalloid's osmolality related to the blood's.
- Classified according to their "tonicity:

1. Isotonic (0.9% NaCl 'normal saline' and Lactated Ringer's)
2. Hypotonic (2.3 % dextrose)
3. Hypertonic (D5 NaCl)

Intravenous therapy (abbreviated as IV therapy) is a medical technique that administers fluids, medications and nutrients directly into a person's vein. The intravenous route of administration is commonly used for rehydration or to provide nutrients for those who cannot, or will not—due to reduced mental states or otherwise—consume food or water by mouth. It may also be used to administer medications or other medical therapy such as blood products or electrolytes to correct electrolyte imbalances. Attempts at providing intravenous therapy have been recorded as early as the 1400s, but the practice did not become widespread until the 1900s after the development of techniques for safe, effective use.

The intravenous route is the fastest way to deliver medications and fluid replacement throughout the body as they are introduced directly into the circulatory system and thus quickly distributed. For this reason, the intravenous route of administration is also used for the consumption of some recreational drugs. Many therapies are administered as a "bolus" or one-time dose, but they may also be administered as an extended infusion or drip. The act of administering a therapy intravenously, or placing an intravenous line ("IV line") for later use, is a procedure which should only be performed by a skilled professional. The most basic intravenous access consists of a needle piercing the skin and entering a vein which is connected to a syringe or to external tubing. This is used to administer the desired therapy. In cases where a patient is likely to receive many such interventions in a short period (with consequent risk of trauma to the vein), normal practice is to insert a cannula which leaves one end in the vein, and subsequent therapies can be administered easily through tubing at the other end. In some cases, multiple medications or therapies are administered through the same IV line.

IV lines are classified as "central lines" if they end in a large vein close to the heart, or as "peripheral lines" if their output is to a small vein in the periphery, such as the arm. An IV line can be threaded through a peripheral vein to end near the heart, which is termed a "peripherally inserted central catheter" or PICC line. If a person is likely to need long-term intravenous therapy, a medical port may be implanted to enable easier repeated access to the vein without having to pierce the vein repeatedly. A catheter can also be inserted into a central vein through the chest, which is known as a tunneled line. The specific type of catheter used and site of insertion are affected by the desired substance to be administered and the health of the veins in the desired site of insertion.

Placement of an IV line may cause pain, as it necessarily involves piercing the skin. Infections and inflammation (termed phlebitis) are also both common side effects of an IV line. Phlebitis may be more likely if the same vein is used repeatedly for intravenous access, and can eventually develop into a hard cord which is unsuitable for IV access. The unintentional administration of a therapy outside a vein, termed extravasation or infiltration, may cause other side effects.

Intravenous (IV) access is used to administer medications and fluid replacement which must be distributed throughout the body, especially when rapid distribution is desired. Another use of IV administration is the avoidance of first-pass metabolism in the liver. Substances that may be infused intravenously include volume expanders, blood-based products, blood substitutes, medications and nutrition.

Volume expander and Buffer solution

Fluids may be administered as part of "volume expansion", or fluid replacement, through the intravenous route. Volume expansion consists of the administration of fluid-based solutions or suspensions designed to target specific areas of the body which need more water. There are two main types of volume expander: crystalloids and colloids. Crystalloids are aqueous solutions of mineral salts or other water-soluble molecules. Colloids contain larger insoluble molecules, such as gelatin. Blood itself is considered a colloid.

The most commonly used crystalloid fluid is normal saline, a solution of sodium chloride at 0.9% concentration, which is isotonic with blood. Lactated Ringer's (also known as Ringer's lactate) and the closely related Ringer's acetate, are mildly hypotonic solutions often used in those who have significant burns. Colloids preserve a high colloid osmotic pressure in the blood, while, on the other hand, this parameter is decreased by crystalloids due to hemodilution. Crystalloids generally are much cheaper than colloids.

Buffer solutions which are used to correct acidosis or alkalosis are also administered through intravenous access. Lactated Ringer's solution used as a fluid expander or base solution to which medications are added also has some buffering effect. Another solution administered intravenously as a buffering solution is sodium bicarbonate.

Medication and treatment

Medications may be mixed into the fluids mentioned above, commonly normal saline, or dextrose solutions. Compared with other routes of administration, such as oral medications, the IV route is the fastest way to deliver fluids and medications throughout the body. For this reason, the IV route is commonly preferred in emergency situations or when a fast onset of action is desirable. In extremely high blood pressure (termed a hypertensive emergency), IV antihypertensives may be given to quickly decrease the blood pressure in a controlled manner to prevent organ damage. In atrial fibrillation, IV amiodarone may be administered to attempt to restore normal heart rhythm. IV medications can also be used for chronic health conditions such as cancer, for which chemotherapy drugs are commonly administered intravenously. In some cases, such as with vancomycin, a loading or bolus dose of medicine is given before beginning a dosing regimen to more quickly increase the concentration of medication in the blood.

The bioavailability of an IV medication is by definition 100%, unlike oral administration where medication may not be fully absorbed, or may be metabolized prior to entering the bloodstream. For some medications, there is virtually zero oral bioavailability. For this reason certain types of medications can only be given intravenously, as there is insufficient uptake by other routes of administration, such is the case of severe dehydration where the patient is required to be treated via IV therapy for a quick recovery. The unpredictability of oral bioavailability in different people is also a reason for a medication to be administered IV, as with furosemide. Oral medications also may be less desirable if a person is nauseous or vomiting, or has severe diarrhea, as these may prevent the medicine from being fully absorbed from the gastrointestinal tract. In these cases, a medication may be given IV only until the patient can tolerate an oral form of the medication. The switch from IV to oral administration is usually performed as soon as viable, as there is generally cost and time savings over IV administration. Whether a medication can be potentially switched to an oral form is sometimes considered when choosing appropriate antibiotic therapy for use in a hospital setting, as a person is unlikely to be discharged if they still require IV therapy.

Some medications, such as aprepitant, are chemically modified to be better suited for IV administration, forming a prodrug such as fosaprepitant. This can be for pharmacokinetic reasons or to delay the effect of the drug until it can be metabolized into the active form.

Blood products

A blood product (or blood-based product) is any component of blood which is collected from a donor for use in a blood transfusion. Blood transfusions can be used in massive blood loss due to trauma, or can be used to replace blood lost during surgery. Blood transfusions may also be used to treat a severe anaemia or thrombocytopenia caused by a blood disease. Early blood transfusions consisted of whole blood, but modern medical practice commonly uses only components of the blood, such as packed red blood cells, fresh frozen plasma or cryoprecipitate.

Nutrition

Parenteral nutrition is the act of providing required nutrients to a person through an intravenous line. This is used in people who are unable to get nutrients normally, by eating and digesting food. A person receiving parenteral nutrition will be given an intravenous solution which may contain salts, dextrose, amino acids, lipids and vitamins. The exact formulation of a parenteral nutrition used will depend on the specific nutritional needs of the person it is being given to. If a person is only receiving nutrition intravenously, it is called total parenteral nutrition (TPN), whereas if a person is only receiving some of their nutrition intravenously it is called partial parenteral nutrition (or supplemental parenteral nutrition).

Contrast agent

Medical imaging relies on being able to clearly distinguish internal parts of the body from each other. One way this is accomplished is through the administration of a contrast agent into a vein.The specific imaging technique being employed will determine the characteristics of an appropriate contrast agent to increase visibility of blood vessels or other features. Common contrast agents are administered into a peripheral vein from which they are distributed throughout the circulation to the imaging site.

Use in sports

IV rehydration was formerly a common technique for athletes. The World Anti-Doping Agency prohibits intravenous injection of more than 100mL per 12 hours, except under a medical exemption.[19] The United States Anti-Doping Agency notes that, as well as the dangers inherent in IV therapy, "IVs can be used to change blood test results (such as hematocrit where EPO or blood doping is being used), mask urine test results (by dilution) or by administering prohibited substances in a way that will more quickly be cleared from the body in order to beat an anti-doping test". Players suspended after attending "boutique IV clinics" which offer this sort of treatment include footballer Samir Nasri in 2017 and swimmer Ryan Lochte in 2018.

Use for hangover treatment

In the 1960s, John Myers developed the "Myers' cocktail", a non-prescription IV solution of vitamins and minerals marketed as a hangover cure and general wellness remedy.The first "boutique IV" clinic, offering similar treatments, opened in Tokyo in 2008. These clinics, whose target market was described by Elle as "health nuts who moonlight as heavy drinkers", have been publicized in the 2010s by glamorous celebrity customers. Intravenous therapy is also used in people with acute ethanol toxicity to correct electrolyte and vitamin deficiencies which arise from alcohol consumption.

Others

In some countries, non-prescription intravenous glucose is used to improve a person's energy, but is not a part of routine medical care in countries such as the United States where glucose solutions are prescription drugs. Improperly administered intravenous glucose (called "ringer"), such as that which is administered clandestinely in store-front clinics, poses increased risks due to improper technique and oversight.[24] Intravenous access is also sometimes used outside of a medical setting for the self-administration of recreational drugs, such as heroin and fentanyl, cocaine, methamphetamine, DMT, and others.

Intravenous therapy is also used for veterinary patient management.

Types

Bolus

Some medications can be administered as a bolus dose, which is called an "IV push". A syringe containing the medication is connected to an access port in the primary tubing and the medication is administered through the port. A bolus may be administered rapidly (with a fast depression of the syringe plunger) or may be administered slowly, over the course of a few minutes. The exact administration technique depends on the medication and other factors. In some cases, a bolus of plain IV solution (i.e. without medication added) is administered immediately after the bolus to further force the medicine into the bloodstream. This procedure is termed an "IV flush". Certain medications, such as potassium, are not able to be administered by IV push due to the extremely rapid onset of action and high level of effects.

Infusion

An infusion of medication may be used when it is desirable to have a constant blood concentration of a medication over time, such as with some antibiotics including beta-lactams. Continuous infusions, where the next infusion is begun immediately following the completion of the prior, may also be used to limit variation in drug concentration in the blood (i.e. between the peak drug levels and the trough drug levels). They may also be used instead of intermittent bolus injections for the same reason, such as with furosemide. Infusions can also be intermittent, in which case the medication is administered over a period of time, then stopped, and this is later repeated. Intermittent infusion may be used when there are concerns about the stability of medicine in solution for long periods of time (as is common with continuous infusions), or to enable the administration of medicines which would be incompatible if administered at the same time in the same IV line, for example vancomycin.

Failure to properly calculate and administer an infusion can result in adverse effects, termed infusion reactions. For this reason, many medications have a maximum recommended infusion rate, such as vancomycin[30] and many monoclonal antibodies. These infusion reactions can be severe, such as in the case of vancomycin, where the reaction is termed "red man syndrome".

Secondary

Any additional medication to be administered intravenously at the same time as an infusion may be connected to the primary tubing; this is termed a secondary IV, or IV piggyback. This prevents the need for multiple IV access lines on the same person. When administering a secondary IV medication, the primary bag is held lower than the secondary bag so that the secondary medication can flow into the primary tubing, rather than fluid from the primary bag flowing into the secondary tubing. The fluid from the primary bag is needed to help flush any remaining medication from the secondary IV from the tubing. If a bolus or secondary infusion is intended for administration in the same line as a primary infusion, the molecular compatibility of the solutions must be considered. Secondary compatibility is generally referred to as "y-site compatibility", named after the shape of the tubing which has a port for bolus administration. Incompatibility of two fluids or medications can arise due to issues of molecular stability, changes in solubility, or degradation of one of the medications.

Methods and equipment

Access

A needle for intravenous access should be inserted at an approximately 25 degree angle.

The simplest form of intravenous access is by passing a hollow needle through the skin directly into a vein. A syringe can be connected directly to this needle, which allows for a "bolus" dose to be administered. Alternatively, the needle may be placed and then connected to a length of tubing, allowing for an infusion to be administered. The type and location of venous access (i.e. a central line versus peripheral line, and in which vein the line is placed) can be affected by the potential for some medications to cause peripheral vasoconstriction, which limits circulation to peripheral veins.

A peripheral cannula is the most common intravenous access method utilized in hospitals, pre-hospital care, and outpatient medicine. This may be placed in the arm, commonly either the wrist or the median cubital vein at the elbow. A tourniquet may be used to restrict the venous drainage of the limb and make the vein bulge, making it easier to locate and place a line in a vein. When used, a tourniquet should be removed before injecting medication to prevent extravasation. The part of the catheter that remains outside the skin is called the connecting hub; it can be connected to a syringe or an intravenous infusion line, or capped with a heplock or saline lock, a needleless connection filled with a small amount of heparin or saline solution to prevent clotting, between uses of the catheter. Ported cannulae have an injection port on the top that is often used to administer medicine.

The thickness and size of needles and catheters can be given in Birmingham gauge or French gauge. A Birmingham gauge of 14 is a very large cannula (used in resuscitation settings) and 24-26 is the smallest. The most common sizes are 16-gauge (midsize line used for blood donation and transfusion), 18- and 20-gauge (all-purpose line for infusions and blood draws), and 22-gauge (all-purpose pediatric line). 12- and 14-gauge peripheral lines are capable of delivering large volumes of fluid very fast, accounting for their popularity in emergency medicine. These lines are frequently called "large bores" or "trauma lines".

Peripheral lines

An arm board is recommended for immobilizing the extremity for cannulation of the hand, the foot or the antecubital fossa in children.

Peripheral venous catheter

A peripheral intravenous line is inserted in peripheral veins, such as the veins in the arms, hands, legs and feet. Medication administered in this way travels through the veins to the heart, from where it is distributed to the rest of the body through the circulatory system. The size of the peripheral vein limits the amount and rate of medication which can be administered safely. A peripheral line consists of a short catheter inserted through the skin into a peripheral vein. This is usually in the form of a cannula-over-needle device, in which a flexible plastic cannula comes mounted over a metal trocar. Once the tip of the needle and cannula are placed, the cannula is advanced inside the vein over the trocar to the appropriate position and secured. The trocar is then withdrawn and discarded. Blood samples may also be drawn from the line directly after the initial IV cannula insertion.

Central lines

Central venous catheter

A central line is an access method in which a catheter empties into a larger, more central vein (a vein within the torso), usually the superior vena cava, inferior vena cava or the right atrium of the heart. There are several types of central IV access, categorized based on the route the catheter takes from the outside of the body to the central vein output.

Peripherally inserted central catheter

A peripherally inserted central catheter (also called a PICC line) is a type of central IV access which consists of a cannula is inserted through a sheath into a peripheral vein and then carefully fed towards the heart, terminating at the superior vena cava or the right atrium. These lines are usually placed in peripheral veins in the arm, and may be placed using the Seldinger technique under ultrasound guidance. An X-ray is used to verify that the end of the cannula is in the right place if fluoroscopy was not used during the insertion. An EKG can also be used in some cases to determine if the end of the cannula is in the correct location.

Tunneled lines

A Hickman line, a type of tunneled catheter, inserted through the skin at the chest and tunneled to insert into the jugular vein in the throat.

A tunneled line is a type of central access which is inserted under the skin, and then travels a significant distance through surrounding tissue before reaching and penetrating the central vein. Using a tunneled line reduces the risk of infection as compared to other forms of access, as bacteria from the skin surface are not able to travel directly into the vein. These catheters are often made of materials that resist infection and clotting. Types of tunneled central lines include the Hickman line or Broviac catheter. A tunnelled line is an option for long term venous access necessary for hemodialysis in people with poor kidney function.

Port (medical)

An implanted port is a central line that does not have an external connector protruding from the skin for administration of medication. Instead, a port consists of a small reservoir covered with silicone rubber which is implanted under the skin, which then covers the reservoir. Medication is administered by injecting medication through the skin and the silicone port cover into the reservoir. When the needle is withdrawn, the reservoir cover reseals itself. A port cover is designed to function for hundreds of needle sticks during its lifetime. Ports may be placed in an arm or in the chest area.

Infusions

Equipment used to place and administer an IV line for infusion consists of a bag, usually hanging above the height of the person, and sterile tubing through which the medicine is administered. In a basic "gravity" IV, a bag is simply hung above the height of the person and the solution is pulled via gravity through a tube attached to a needle inserted into a vein. Without extra equipment, it is not possible to precisely control the rate of administration. For this reason, a setup may also incorporate a clamp to regulate flow. Some IV lines may be placed with "Y-sites", devices which enable a secondary solution to be administered through the same line (known as piggybacking). Some systems employ a drip chamber, which prevents air from entering the bloodstream (causing an air embolism), and allows visual estimation of flow rate of the solution.

Alternatively, an infusion pump allows precise control over the flow rate and total amount delivered. A pump is programmed based on the number and size of infusions being administered to ensure all medicine is fully administered without allowing the access line to run dry. Pumps are primarily utilized when a constant flow rate is important, or where changes in rate of administration would have consequences.

Techniques

To reduce pain associated with the procedure, medical staff may apply a topical local anaesthetic (such as EMLA or Ametop) to the skin of the chosen venipuncture area about 45 minutes beforehand.

If the cannula is not inserted correctly, or the vein is particularly fragile and ruptures, blood may extravasate into the surrounding tissues; this situation is known as a blown vein or "tissuing". Using this cannula to administer medications causes extravasation of the drug, which can lead to edema, causing pain and tissue damage, and even necrosis depending on the medication. The person attempting to obtain the access must find a new access site proximal to the "blown" area to prevent extravasation of medications through the damaged vein. For this reason it is advisable to site the first cannula at the most distal appropriate vein.

Adverse effects

Pain

Placement of an intravenous line inherently causes pain when the skin is broken and is considered medically invasive. For this reason, when other forms of administration may suffice, intravenous therapy is usually not preferred. This includes the treatment of mild or moderate dehydration with oral rehydration therapy which is an option, as opposed to parenteral rehydration through an IV line. Children in emergency departments being treated for dehydration have better outcomes with oral treatment than intravenous therapy due to the pain and complications of an intravenous line. Cold spray may decrease the pain of putting in an IV.

Certain medications also have specific sensations of pain associated with their administration IV. This includes potassium, which when administered IV can cause a burning or painful sensation. The incidence of side effects specific to a medication can be affected by the type of access (peripheral versus central), the rate of administration, or the quantity of drug administered. When medications are administered too rapidly through an IV line, a set of vague symptoms such as redness or rash, fever, and others may occur; this is termed an "infusion reaction" and is prevented by decreasing the rate of administration of the medication. When vancomycin is involved, this is commonly termed "Red Man syndrome" after the rapid flushing which occurs after rapid administration.

Infection and inflammation

As placement of an intravenous line requires breaking the skin, there is a risk of infection. Skin-dwelling organisms such as coagulase-negative staphylococcus or Candida albicans may enter through the insertion site around the catheter, or bacteria may be accidentally introduced inside the catheter from contaminated equipment. Infection of an IV access site is usually local, causing easily visible swelling, redness, and fever. However, pathogens may also enter the bloodstream, causing sepsis, which can be sudden and life-threatening. A central IV line poses a higher risk of sepsis, as it can deliver bacteria directly into the central circulation. A line which has been in place for a longer period of time also increases the risk of infection.

Inflammation of the vein may also occur, called thrombophlebitis or simply phlebitis. This may be caused by infection, the catheter itself, or the specific fluids or medication being given. Repeated instances of phlebitis can cause scar tissue to build up along a vein. A peripheral IV line cannot be left in the vein indefinitely out of concern for the risk of infection and phlebitis, among other potential complications. However, recent studies have found that there is no increased risk of complications in those whose IVs were replaced only when clinically indicated versus those whose IVs were replaced routinely.[46] If placed with proper aseptic technique, it is not recommended to change a peripheral IV line more frequently than every 72–96 hours.

Phlebitis is particularly common in intravenous drug users and those undergoing chemotherapy, whose veins can become sclerotic and difficult to access over time, sometimes forming a hard, painful "venous cord". The presence of a cord is a cause of discomfort and pain associated with IV therapy, and makes it more difficult for an IV line to be placed as a line cannot be placed in an area with a cord.

Infiltration and extravasation

Infiltration (medical) and Extravasation

Infiltration occurs when a non-vesicant IV fluid or medication enters the surrounding tissue as opposed to the desired vein. It may occur when the vein itself ruptures, when the vein is damaged during insertion of the intravascular access device, or from increased vein porosity. Infiltration may also occur if the puncture of the vein by the needle becomes the path of least resistance—such as a cannula which has been left inserted, causing the vein to scar. It can also occur upon insertion of an IV line if a tourniquet is not promptly removed. Infiltration is characterized by coolness and pallor to the skin as well as localized swelling or edema. It is treated by removing the intravenous line and elevating the affected limb so the collected fluids drain away. Injections of hyaluronidase around the area can be used to speed the dispersal of the fluid/drug. Infiltration is one of the most common adverse effects of IV therapy and is usually not serious unless the infiltrated fluid is a medication damaging to the surrounding tissue, most commonly a vesicant or chemotherapeutic agent. In such cases, the infiltration is termed extravasation, and may cause necrosis.

Others

If the solutions administered are colder than the temperature of the body, induced hypothermia can occur. If the temperature change to the heart is rapid, ventricular fibrillation may result. Furthermore, if a solution which is not balanced in concentration is administered, a person's electrolytes may become imbalanced. In hospitals, regular blood tests may be used to proactively monitor electrolyte levels.

Composition of commonly used intravenous fluids

Electrolytes ($meqL^{-1}$)	NS	Ringers lactate	Isolyte P	Plasmalyte A	D5	Albumin 5%	Hetastrach 6%
Na^+	154	130	26	140	-	145±15	154
K+	-	4	21	5	-	<2.5	-
Cl	154	109	21	98	-	100	154
Mg^{++}	-	-	3	-	-	-	-
Acetate	-	-	24	27	-	-	-
Lactate	-	28	-	-	-	-	-
Glucose (gm%)	-	-	5	-	5	-	-
Phosphate (mg%)	-	-	3	-	-	-	-
Osmolarity ($mOsmL^{-1}$)	308	274	-	295	252	330	310

Table 8

Normal saline fluid (NS 0.9%)

- (NS) is the commonly used term for a solu:on of 0.90% weight/volume of NaCl, about 300 mOsm/L or 9.0 g per liter
- 1 liter of normal saline contains 154 mmol/L of Na and 154 mmol/L of Cl only.

One litre of Hartmann's solution contains:
• 131 mEq of sodium ion = 131 mmol/L.
• 111 mEq of chloride ion = 111 mmol/L.
• 29 mEq of lactate = 29 mmol/L.
• 5 mEq of potassium ion = 5 mmol/L.
• 4 mEq of calcium ion = 2 mmol/L.
One litre of lactated Ringer's solution contains:
• 130 mEq of sodium ion = 130 mmol/L
• 109 mEq of chloride ion = 109 mmol/L
• 28 mEq of lactate = 28 mmol/L
• 4 mEq of potassium ion = 4 mmol/L
• 3 mEq of calcium ion = 1.5 mmol/L

Intravenous fluids are classified into two main types: Crystalloids and colloids. Each group has its very own characteristics and moreover, each particular solution has its unique properties.

Crystalloids

Crystalloids consist of glucose or sodium chloride (saline) solutions. Osmolarity of the solution determines if the solution is hypotonic, isotonic or hypertonic. Isotonic solutions have the closest osmolarity to plasma and the other solution types are named comparing to plasma osmolarity. Saline solution containing 0.9 g of NaCl in each liter of water is defined as isotonic saline, and it is the most popular intravenous fluid worldwide. Some widely used saline solutions also contain one or more of these components: potassium, calcium, bicarbonate, lactate, and glucose. Isotonic glucose solution contains 50 g glucose in each liter of water and it is defined as isotonic glucose. Glucose in these solutions is metabolized right after administration and solvent is mixed into total body water. On the other hand, saline solution's high NaCl concentration serves to keep its solvent water in the extracellular compartment. However, any crystalloid solution can freely pass through double barrier of endothelium. This condition causes up to four-fifth of the infused crystalloid to distribute directly into the interstitial compartment. Accordingly, crystalloid infusion in high amounts is related with serious complications, such as pulmonary edema, and hyperchloremic acidosis. Despite that, colloid solutions are generally imprisoned in intravascular compartment, unless double-barrier of endothelium is impaired. Major advantage of crystalloids to colloids is containing only ions or small sized molecules which can easily be metabolized in reasonable amounts.

Colloids

Colloids can be blood products, such as human albumin solution and fresh frozen plasma, or they can also be synthetic large molecules which are not able to distribute across vascular barrier such as gelatins, dextrans, and hydroxyethyl starches.

Colloids are, like crystalloids, widely used in fluid resuscitation. Although colloids are thought to be more useful than crystalloids for increasing intravascular volume and providing osmotic pressure, they are both shown to be similarly effective on mortality. Colloid solutions are prepared by dissolving colloid molecules in isotonic saline solutions, or more rarely in other crystalloids.

Endogenous albumin is primarily responsible for intravascular osmotic pressure in healthy subjects. Thus, albumin, as an intravenous colloid solution, makes perfect sense to maintain intravascular colloid pressure. However, like all blood products, it has significant disadvantages, like allergic reactions and (theoretically) infection risks, although it is generally considered safe. Molecular weight of albumin is around 69000 Dalton. Gelatins, dextrans and hydroxyethyl starches (HES) are other common colloid substances. Gelatins are products of biochemical processes executed on bovine collagen. Although there are some concerns about its relation with Creutzfeld-Jacob disease and bovine spongiform encephalitis, there is no solid evidence proving these concerns. Dextrans are polysaccharides that can vary in size. Most common types of dextrans are dextran 70 and dextran 40, which are named after their average molecular weights: 70000 and 40000 Dalton, respectively. Lastly, HES is a nonionic starch derivative, which is synthetized from amylopectin. HESs also vary in molecular weight, and can be classified as low (70000-130000 Dalton), medium, and high (450000-480000 Dalton) molecular weights. They are also classified by their molar substitution degree, which defines the proportion of glucose molecules that are replaced by hydroxyethyls. HESs are the most commonly used colloids in Europe. Commonly used examples of these colloids are Voluven® (Fresenius Kabi, Bad Homburg, Germany) which is a 130000 Dalton tetrastarch, dissolved in saline with substitution degree of 0.4 and HAES-steril® (Fresenius Kabi, Bad Homburg, Germany) which is a 200000 Dalton pentastarch, dissolved in saline with substitution degree of 0.5.

Each type of colloid solution has its unique features. Effect on plasma volume and plasma viscosity, adverse reactions, and side effects on the system are the main concerns while choosing colloid solutions. Every colloid substance has a concentration decrease rate (half-life) in plasma by being metabolized, or by a loss through endothelial barrier and glomerular filtration. Half-life of a colloid determines the amount and the duration of plasma volume expansion. Higher molecular weight colloids tend to stay longer in the intravascular compartment. Besides, some studies point that the dextrans and the HESs provide significantly better expansion of plasma volume than the gelatins. Whereas, some studies indicate that only albumin has significant advantage over other colloids and saline; and none of the other colloids is superior to others regarding plasma volume expansion.

All colloids provide a level of expansion in plasma volume and this leads to hemodilution. Hemodilution causes a decrease in plasma viscosity. However, it is known that some colloids cause a total increase in viscosity due to red cell aggregation. High molecular weight dextrans and HESs cause a significant increase in viscosity, while low molecular weight dextrans HESs and albumin solutions decrease both red cell aggregation and plasma viscosity. Colloids have various effects on hemostasis, such as impaired platelet function, decreased factor VIIIc and von Willebrand Factor levels, in addition to previously described hemodilution and altered red cell aggregation. Particularly, dextrans are known with their significant antithrombotic effects.

Accumulation of colloid substances in the body is possible. Dextrans and gelatins can be metabolized in humans. On the other hand, HESs may also accumulate. Metabolism and filtration of HES is relatively slow and storage in reticulo-endothelial system is not well recognized yet.

All colloids are large molecules and can trigger anaphylaxis of anaphylactoid events. Colloids also have minor anti-inflammatory effects.

Although it has been argued for a long time, there are still no definite rules on "crystalloid *vs* colloids" issue. There are studies that show crystalloid infusion is related with interstitial edema and worse anastomotic healing. On the other side, it is still arguable that colloid solutions are able to prevent consequences of these negative effects. In a study on pancreaticoduodenectomy patients, who are resuscitated with lactated Ringer's solution (isotonic crystalloid solution; including lactate, potassium and calcium in addition to sodium chloride), the significantly increased interstitial edema in jejunum was shown. However, colloid use has been reported to have an increasing effect on mortality, in some fairly criticized studies, especially on critically ill patients. On the other hand, CRISTAL trial, which is a multicenter randomized study on critically ill patients, failed to demonstrate this effect on mortality. In contrast, fewer death rates were found within 90 d in colloids group.

Moreover, although colloids are proved to be capable of maintaining efficient plasma volume, they do not appear to have positive effects on renal function. Contrarily, reports had shown significant harmful effects of dextran 40 use on kidney function in the second half of 20th century. Some of the subsequent studies on HESs also revealed negative effects of these solutions on kidneys. Schortgen et al also reported that the use of hyperoncotic colloids and human albumin is significantly associated with renal dysfunction. However, in a multicenter study on over 3000 intensive care patients, no significant relation was detected between HES use and renal dysfunction. Similarly, in a review of studies with different HES products, no adverse effects on kidneys were reported. In a randomized clinical multicenter trial, 6997 critically ill patients were randomized into two groups. One group was assigned to receive 4% of albumin and the other group was assigned to receive saline for intravenous resuscitation during 28 d. There was no significant difference between two groups, regarding to mortality, days spent in intensive care unit, days of mechanical ventilation, or days of renal replacement therapy. In addition to all of these results, it should be taken into consideration that none of the colloid solutions is proved to be directly toxic to the kidneys.

Considering all pros and cons of each solution family, it is still not possible to make a strict evidence based statement about how to use colloids and crystalloids. It should be kept in mind that, crystalloids have less negative effects on hemostasis, immune system and kidneys; whereas colloids may provide a better plasma volume expansion with less interstitial edema in elective surgery patients.

CHAPTER SIX

FLUID RESUSCITATION STRATEGIES

Although there has been various different strategies defined in literature in decades, none has been adopted alone by most of the clinicians as the superior strategy. We think that many clinicians tend to keep their accustomed strategy, despite the evidences in the literature. There are studies that compare outcomes of different strategies of fluid management. Lately, "crystalloids *vs* colloids" debates are fading, while recent studies mostly focus on the amount of fluid given perioperatively.

Traditional approach to determine the fluid amounts is more likely to generate formulas based on parameters such as patients' body weights and duration of surgeries. However, there is an evidence that each patient has his/her own body fluid status depending on the type of surgery, comorbid conditions, fluid already administered before, and various other factors. In addition, each patient should be considered as unique and his/her unique status should be monitored closely in the correct ways. As stated before, the main goal of fluid management is to maintain adequate tissue perfusion, with minimized risks of complications of over-hydration, such as pulmonary edema, cerebral edema, and intestinal edema. Both inadequate and excessive fluid administration may increase the stress on the circulatory system, and can affect tissue healing after surgery. From this perspective, without decent monitoring of patient's current status, any strategy may fail.

Debates about fluid management strategies are gathered around liberal strategy, restricted (conservative) strategy and goal-directed strategy so far. Liberal and restricted strategies are defined by different authors with variable volume ranges. For example, in one study, restricted fluid volume is defined as 1000 mL plus loss through drains, while in another study, patients in restricted fluid volume group were subjected to over 2000 mL fluid on the day of surgery. These variances make it difficult to consider these studies as a whole. Still, majority of authors studying this subject point out that restrictive strategy has positive effects on gastrointestinal function, wound healing and pulmonary function. Brandstrup et al stated that, excessive hydration with crystalloids is related with increased major complications, such as leakage, peritonitis, sepsis, pulmonary edema and bleeding in patients who underwent elective colorectal surgery. Also, intestinal edema is known to be related with increased bacterial translocation and multiple organ dysfunction syndrome rates. It can be concluded that, staying closer to the dehydration level is more reasonable, because it is safer and more efficient than administering large volumes to avoid dehydration. On the other hand, the liberal strategy is superior to the restricted strategy for reducing postoperative nausea, headache, dizziness and vomiting.

However, the goal directed strategy (GDS) is totally based on patient's current data, obtained from monitoring methods (See section: Monitoring body fluid status). Rivers and colleagues, one of the pioneers of this strategy, monitored CVP, mean arterial pressure, serum lactate, and mixed venous oxygen saturation in order to manage therapy in sepsis patients. Later studies were focused on monitoring hemodynamics, and the effects of administered fluids on patients. Now, GDS can be defined as an individualized fluid therapy, based on patient's fluid responsiveness; in other words, "fluid need". The extra volume, which won't be able to affect the left ventricle stroke volume is regarded as unnecessary; and as a matter of fact, hazardous. It makes perfect sense to totally evaluate patient's needs and replace what is needed. Still, efficiency of GDS is limited with the power of our monitoring tools, which is determined by accessibility, applicability of the tools and the quality of information we acquire from them.

PPV and SVV are defined to monitor the fluid need of the patient dynamically as it is stated above. Esophageal Doppler monitoring of cardiac volumes and aortic flow are also one of the helpful tools in GDS. In a systematic review of esophageal Doppler guided GDS studies; reduced hospital stay, fewer ICU admissions, and less inotropes usage were detected in GDS group. In a single center, blinded, prospective controlled trial, 128 patients who underwent colorectal resection were randomized into two groups. Each group was managed with esophageal Doppler or CVP guided fluid therapy during surgery. Intraoperative Doppler guided fluid management was associated with decrease in the duration of hospital stay. A randomized controlled study on 108 elective colorectal surgery patients also showed shorter hospital stay and decreased morbidity in GDS group. GDS is also advantageous in patients who undergo major surgery. A systematic review and meta-analysis studies by Hamilton on major surgery patients state that preemptive hemodynamic monitoring reduces mortality and morbidity. Similarly, Poeze et al showed that efforts to achieve an optimized hemodynamic condition resulted in a decreased mortality rate, in their meta-analysis study in 2005. Another meta-analysis also shows that GDS reduces both major and minor gastrointestinal complications after surgery.

In contrast with these studies, in a multicenter study, which included 762 high risk patients in 56 intensive care units, no significant effects of GDS were found. In this study, patients were randomly assigned to cardiac-index group, mixed venous oxygen-saturation group and standard therapy group. Predetermined hemodynamic targets were reached significantly better in the control group. There were no significant differences among the three groups, regarding mortality at six months. Even the subgroup analysis of patients, whose predetermined hemodynamic targets have been reached successfully, showed similar mortality rates among the three groups. Moreover, the number of dysfunctional organs and the duration of stay in the intensive care unit were similar in all groups.

Despite these evidences, low accessibility and applicability of esophageal Doppler are the major disadvantages of this method. This leads researchers to search for a more accessible and applicable method for common use in postoperative care unit, such as non-invasive pulse oximetry and invasive arterial pressure measurement. Thus, predictive value of pulse pressure variation, systolic pressure variation and stroke volume variation tests for fluid responsiveness are defined. All of these tests are applicable in an average postoperative care unit. However, the true value of these tests should be evaluated by larger studies. After that, optimization of patient monitoring devices should be done accordingly. Moreover, even PLR alone can provide important information about fluid responsiveness and lead the intensivists for GDS.

Since there is still insufficient number of randomized controlled trials with standardized criteria, the fluid management debates are going on. A consensus on criteria for each fluid management strategy should be made. We think that the related studies from all around the world with defined criteria are going to reveal the true value of each strategy.

Each surgeon should keep in mind that the patient is totally managed by the anesthesiologist during the surgery, so depending on the anesthesiologist's preference on fluid strategy, patient's fluid status after surgery may vary widely. Besides, intraoperative bleeding and other causes of surgical fluid loss should also be considered. During or after the surgery, the blood loss in patients with low hemoglobin levels is generally managed with erythrocyte suspensions. However, in patients with reasonable hemoglobin levels, appropriate fluid strategy should be chosen to avoid complications of transfusion. We think that determining the actual fluid status and the needs of a postoperative patient, by using monitoring tools and examining the report of the anesthesiologist, is of great importance.

When prescribing IV fluids, remember the 5 Rs: **Resuscitation, Routine maintenance, Replacement, Redistribution and Reassessment**.

The goal of IV fluid administration is to restore and maintain tissue fluid and electrolyte homeostasis and central euvolemia, while avoiding salt and water excess. This will in turn facilitate tissue oxygen delivery without causing harm. Achieving optimal IV fluid therapy should improve perioperative outcomes and is a key component in many perioperative guidelines and pathways.1,2 IV fluids, like other medications, should only be given in well-defined protocols according to individual needs.

There have been numerous studies of fluid and hemodynamic optimization over the past 20 yr. Most of these studies were very small single-center studies, sometimes with conflicting results. However, in recent years several large multicenter randomized controlled trials and observational studies using electronic medical records have been published on these topics in major medical journals.6–12 These efforts have greatly improved the evidence base and are a credit to our specialty.

This article reviews the latest evidence on perioperative IV fluid therapy for major surgery, focusing on the type and volume of fluids, and including suitable criteria to guide such therapy. Although a full review of hemodynamic optimization using advanced monitoring is beyond the scope of this review, it will be briefly covered as the two topics are interrelated.

Preoperative fluid management strategies aim to avoid the patient arriving in the operating room in a hypovolemic or dehydrated state. Multiple international guidelines, including those from the American Society of Anesthesiologists, allow unrestricted intake of clear fluids up to 2 h before elective surgery. The guidelines are based on a meta-analysis of randomized trials that reports a lower risk of aspiration (gastric volume less than 25 ml and pH greater than 2.5) when clear liquids are given 2 to 4 h before a procedure compared with fasting overnight. We continually produce saliva along with endogenous gastric secretions, and therefore after an 8-hr "fast," roughly 500 to 1,250 ml of fluid is added naturally to the stomach. This acidic fluid is diluted by whatever we drink. In other words, allowing unrestricted access to clear fluids up to 2 h before surgery is likely to improve patient comfort and safety as it reduces thirst and hunger, does not increase gastric volumes, and reduces the acidity of gastric contents. The most significant factor determining gastric emptying of fluids is its caloric content.

Some preoperative fasting guidelines have changed the wording from "allow" to "encourage" clear fluids up to 2 h before surgery ; this appears to be safe, but requires further scientific validation. Examples of clear liquids include, but are not limited to, water, fruit juices without pulp, carbonated beverages, carbohydrate-rich nutritional drinks, clear tea, and black coffee. Interestingly, some pediatric centers and adult day-case units have removed any restriction on clear fluids before surgery —that is, to allow patients to drink clear fluids right up until arrival in the operating suite. This appears to be safe, but it does require further large-scale research before such a practice can be recommended.

Many Enhanced Recovery After Surgery pathways also include the oral intake of a maltodextrin carbohydrate drink 2 h before surgery, which has a probable metabolic benefit of reducing insulin resistance in addition to improving patient satisfaction and reducing thirst, hunger, and postoperative nausea and vomiting. The metabolic benefits center around creating a fed, anabolic state before surgery. This in turn reduces hyperglycemia postoperatively, which is a risk factor for nosocomial infection.

Assessing Fluid Responsiveness

Preoperative IV fluids are needed for most emergency surgery and sometimes for elective surgery, because of extra fluid losses and typically longer fasting times. Accurate assessment of an individual patient's fluid status can be difficult, but a careful history and physical examination supported by simple beside tests should be sufficient to gauge fluid responsiveness in most cases —that is, circumstances when additional IV fluid will increase cardiac output and so improve tissue perfusion.

Additional IV fluids should only be given to patients with a predicted positive fluid response. This is best evaluated by taking advantage of the steep portion of the Frank–Starling curve, whereby small increases in preload will increase stroke volume (SV). The volume needed for a fluid challenge is typically 250 ml of a colloid, but crystalloids are probably equally effective and even smaller volumes (100 ml) can be used. Fluid responsiveness is typically defined as a 10% or greater increase in SV. Positive pressure mechanical ventilation induces a cyclic reduction in left ventricular preload mainly through a decrease in venous return, with this effect more pronounced in hypovolemia. Hence, changes in preload during the respiratory cycle will result in variations of SV and pulse pressure. Lung recruitment maneuvers can induce similar effects on preload to predict fluid responsiveness. The resultant SV variations and pulse pressure variations are estimated by analysis of the arterial waveform.

A systematic review of 50 studies (2,260 patients) evaluating techniques to assess adult patients with refractory hypotension or signs of organ hypoperfusion found that half of all the patients studied were fluid-responsive. Findings on physical examination were not predictive of fluid responsiveness, but a low central venous pressure (less than 8 mm Hg) was associated with fluid responsiveness (positive likelihood ratio, 2.6 [95% CI, 1.4 to 4.6]; pooled specificity, 76%). Respiratory variation in vena cava diameter measured by ultrasound (distensibility index greater than 15%) had similar benefits. But perhaps the most compelling, based in part on the simplicity and ready availability, was augmentation of blood pressure or SV after passive leg raising, which reliably predicted fluid responsiveness (positive likelihood ratio, 11 [95% CI, 7.6 to 17]; pooled specificity, 92%). Those with a negative passive leg raising test were very unlikely to be fluid-responsive (negative likelihood ratio, 0.13 [95% CI, 0.07 to 0.22]; pooled sensitivity, 88%). Central venous pressure monitoring is unlikely to be helpful in those who are hemodynamically stable. The passive leg raising maneuver transfers about 300 ml of venous blood into the right atrium, mimicking a fluid bolus. Ideally, passive leg raising should be done along with advanced monitoring of fluid responsiveness using a pulse contour device or esophageal Doppler to better reflect changes in SV; if unavailable, the effect on systolic blood pressure can be used. The passive leg raising maneuver can also be used during and after surgery to ascertain intravascular volume status at those times.

Intraoperative Fluid Management

Optimal intraoperative IV fluid management is important, with both under- and overresuscitation associated with harm. There are two main bodies of literature providing guidance on this subject: those studies comparing restrictive versus liberal fluid regimens, and those studies comparing goal-directed fluid therapy using advanced hemodynamic monitoring versus control. We consider each in turn.

Over the past 20 yr, the "sweet spot" for optimal IV fluid administration has shifted with evolving surgical techniques, patient pathways such as Enhanced Recovery After Surgery, evolving literature, and popular trends. Minimally invasive (and robotic) approaches have reduced evaporative fluid loss and gross anatomic manipulation during many operations. Historically, large amounts of IV fluids were given during and after surgery, particularly for abdominal surgery, because of perceived third space and insensible losses. Approximately 15 yr ago, Brandstrup et al.28 showed that the liberal use of IV fluid in abdominal surgery was associated with a significant increase in complications compared with a restrictive approach. Patients in the liberal group were given just more than 6 l of fluid on the day of surgery, and had a postoperative weight gain (reflecting tissue edema) of close to 4 kg. In contrast, patients in the restrictive group were given just under 4 l of fluid on the day of surgery and had a maximal weight gain of approximately 1 kg.

Over the years, the term "restrictive fluid management" has gained popularity, particularly with the widespread adoption of Enhanced Recovery After Surgery pathways, with recent guidelines advocating a restrictive approach. However, the amount of fluid given with restrictive fluid management has gradually decreased, and the term "zero balance" was introduced to describe a restrictive regimen aiming to avoid postoperative fluid retention (as indicated by weight gain).

There has been ongoing concern that an excessively restrictive fluid approach could be associated with an increase in adverse events, particularly acute kidney injury. This concern was supported by two large observational studies that showed worse outcomes, including acute kidney injury, with patients who had the most restrictive fluid regimen. This background, along with uncertainty as to how best to treat intraoperative hypotension, formed the rationale for the multicenter Restrictive versus Liberal Fluid Therapy for Major Abdominal Surgery (RELIEF) trial, which compared a restrictive IV fluid regimen (designed to achieve zero balance during surgery and the 24-hour postoperative period) with a liberal fluid regimen.

One of the key results of RELIEF was that patients in the restrictive fluid group had a significantly higher risk of acute kidney injury than those in the liberal fluid group (8.6% vs. 5%, $P < 0.001$). The median duration of surgery was 3.3 h in both groups, and the restrictive regimen led to a median of 1.7 l of fluid administered intraoperatively, compared with 3 l with the liberal regimen. These findings suggest that many perioperative physicians may have become too restrictive if using a zero-balance approach, and that a moderately liberal fluid regimen aiming for an overall positive fluid balance of 1 to 2 l at the end of surgery should be recommended30 —that is, an overall crystalloid fluid infusion rate of 10 to 12 ml · kg−1 · h−1 during major abdominal surgery, and 1.5 ml · kg−1 · h−1 in the 24-h postoperative period. Other types of major surgery not associated with such extensive fluid shifts are unlikely to need as much intraoperative IV fluid administration to achieve a moderate positive fluid balance at the end of surgery.

Enhanced Recovery After Surgery guidelines recommend early transition from IV to oral fluid therapy after surgery, and we see no reason to modify this. In many patients recovering from major surgery, the transition from

IV to oral fluids can occur within 24 h. Early transition to oral intake can help preserve gastrointestinal motility, thus limiting ongoing fluid loss into the bowel.

Advanced Hemodynamic Monitoring versus Control

There is a significant body of literature advocating individualized goal-directed fluid or hemodynamic therapy using advanced monitors to optimize SV and/or reduce SV variation. The physiologic rationale for optimizing SV on an individual patient basis is that there is no established definition of normovolemia and that blood pressure is widely accepted as having significant limitations as a monitor of intravascular volume status. In 1928, Jarisch is quoted as saying, "It is a source of regret that the measurement of flow [i.e., SV] is so much more difficult than the measurement of pressure. This has led to an undue interest in the blood pressure manometer. Most organs, however, require flow rather than pressure." In reality, organs need both, but a physiologic response to hypovolemia is to maintain pressure at the expense of flow (especially splanchnic flow) to maintain perfusion of vital organs. Thus, measuring blood flow can theoretically alert physicians to hypovolemia earlier than pressure monitoring can.

There have been many small studies showing benefit of fluid administration guided by advanced monitoring (goal-directed therapy) over the last 20 yr. However, within Enhanced Recovery After Surgery pathways, some of this additional benefit seems to have been diminished by overall improvements in patient care, so that the more recent small, single-center studies were unable to show significant reductions in length of stay or complications with implementation of goal-directed therapy pathways.

The first large, multicenter trial of goal-directed therapy, OPTIMISE, reported fewer complications with goal-directed therapy, but this finding did not reach statistical significance (P = 0.07). An updated meta-analysis (38 trials) accompanied this publication, showing that goal-directed therapy was associated with a lower risk of complications (31.5% vs. 41.6%; relative risk, 0.77 [95% CI, 0.71 to 0.83]) and mortality (8.3% vs. 10.3%; relative risk, 0.86 [95% CI, 0.74 to 1.00]). More recently, the multicenter FEDORA trial showed a significant reduction in complications and length of stay with implementation of a goal-directed hemodynamic strategy. There is increasing evidence that even a short duration of hypotension intraoperatively, defined as a mean blood pressure less than 65 mm Hg, is associated with myocardial and kidney injury. The INPRESS trial, recently published in Journal of the American Medical Association, was one of the first interventional studies aimed at individualizing perioperative blood pressure management. The study showed a reduction in complications in the intervention group that first had their fluid status optimized, followed by inclusion of a vasopressor to maintain blood pressure within 10% of normal.

Practical Considerations

How do we reconcile the two different areas of research—determining the optimal infusion rate or volume of IV fluids, and how best to identify an individual patient's need for extra boluses of IV fluid—into practical considerations for perioperative fluid management? Each patient should have a fluid management plan, in line with local department guidelines and then individualized to the patient.1 The selection, timing, and doses of IV fluids should be evaluated as carefully as they are for any other medication, with the aim of maximizing efficacy and minimizing iatrogenic toxicity. Institutions without any departmental fluid guidelines have been shown to have tremendous variation in how fluid is administered.

Intraoperative fluid requirements can be considered in two categories: maintenance therapy and volume therapy. Maintenance therapy is needed to cover insensible losses and urine output (from the beginning of preoperative fasting), and current evidence suggests that maintenance fluid requirements should be met with a basal crystalloid infusion rate of 1 to 1.5 ml/kg/h; more is needed for major surgeries associated with large fluid shifts. Volume therapy refers to the administration of boluses of IV fluid (typically 250 ml) to assess volume responsiveness and treat objective evidence of hypovolemia, with the goal of improving intravascular volume and oxygen delivery.

In general terms, based largely on the results of the RELIEF trial, the overall goal of fluid management for major surgery should now be considered to be a moderately liberal approach, with a positive fluid balance at the end of surgery of 1 to 2 l. This can typically be achieved with overall intraoperative fluid requirements of approximately 3 l for a 3- to 4-h procedure, but will obviously vary depending on blood loss and the surgical procedure and duration. Less extensive surgery, such as day-surgery procedures and laparoscopic cholecystectomy, require less IV fluid, with most needing no more than 1 to 2 l of crystalloid in total (i.e., net fluid balance, 0 to 1 l).

The timing of fluid administration is also important to avoid episodes of hypovolemia and hypotension. There is a significant body of evidence to show that the timing of fluid administration and management of high-risk patients when the "sweet spot" for fluid administration is harder to be consistently maintained can be aided by using goal-directed therapy with advanced monitoring of SV or SV variation.33,36,41 We therefore suggest a risk-adapted matrix for fluid and hemodynamic management, an update from previous versions following results of the RELIEF trial (fig. 1). If a patient is volume-optimized (not fluid responsive) and remains hypotensive (mean blood pressure greater than 65 mm Hg and possibly higher in patients with preexisting hypertension), a vasopressor infusion should be considered.

A suggested matrix for consideration of goal-directed therapy and postoperative admission to a surgical intensive care unit (SICU) in major surgery.

Postoperative Phase

Early oral intake is encouraged postoperatively in all patients whenever possible (fig. 2).2 In many Enhanced Recovery After Surgery pathways, this enables IV fluid administration to be discontinued, sometimes even before the patient leaves the postanesthesia care unit. In fact, Enhanced Recovery After Surgery pathways highlight the need to minimize postoperative continuation of intravascular lines (IV and arterial), nasogastric tube, urinary catheter, and drain tubes, which further limit a patient's ability to ambulate.

However, the results of the RELIEF study suggest that we should be cautious in patients recovering from major abdominal who are not able to obtain adequate oral intake.8 In RELIEF, the restrictive group were administered a postoperative IV crystalloid infusion at an average rate of 0.8 ml /kg/1/h (calculated with a maximum weight of 100 kg) or up to 80 ml/h for at least 24 h, and the liberal group were administered a crystalloid infusion of 1.5 ml/kg/h/1. There was a lower urine output and more oliguria during and after surgery, and a near doubling of the incidence of postoperative acute kidney injury, in the restrictive group. Therefore, although we don't know the overall contribution of the postoperative part of the protocol in RELIEF, it seems prudent to continue titrated IV fluid therapy in patients with impaired oral intake.

What IV Fluid Should Be Used?

The primary maintenance IV fluid for all major surgery should be an isotonic, balanced crystalloid,that is, an IV fluid that more closely aligns with plasma electrolytes and acid–base equilibrium (e.g., lactated Ringer's, Hartmann's, PlasmaLyte A [Baxter Healthcare Corp., USA], Normosol [Hospira Inc., USA]). Over the last few years, there has been increasing observational evidence suggesting that 0.9% saline should not be used during major surgery, because it is associated with hyperchloremia, metabolic acidosis, and acute kidney injury. This led to the two recent trials comparing the use of balanced crystalloids and 0.9% saline in critically and noncritically ill patients. The studies used a pragmatic, cluster-randomized, multiple-crossover design in which participating emergency departments and intensive care units were randomly assigned to use either balanced crystalloid or 0.9% saline in all patients for a month for each month of the trial. Both trials showed a lower incidence of acute kidney injury with balanced solutions, and in critically ill patients a lower incidence of death and new-onset renal replacement therapy. We therefore suggest that maintenance fluid therapy should be achieved with an isotonic, balanced crystalloid solution at a rate of 1 to 3 ml/kg/h.

The choice of fluid for volume therapy remains controversial. There is a physiologic rationale for using colloids for volume therapy because they tend to remain in the intravascular space longer, and in animal models of hemorrhage, resuscitation with colloids has also been shown to be significantly faster than with crystalloids. Indeed, most goal-directed therapy studies have used colloid boluses for volume therapy. However, there are only a handful of small studies that have compared crystalloids and colloids for volume therapy during major surgery. Although these studies have all demonstrated lower IV fluid volumes with colloid-based resuscitation (ratio around 1.6:1), most have not demonstrated any meaningful difference in clinical outcomes.However, a recent study did show a reduction in postoperative complications when using colloids for resuscitation in a closed-loop system. Nevertheless, the crystalloid versus colloid debate continues and is one of the unresolved questions in perioperative fluid management.

In major hemorrhage scenarios, there is often a necessity to quickly restore circulating blood volume, and this is probably best accomplished with red cell, plasma, and other blood product transfusion. Institutions should have a massive transfusion protocol in place.

Conclusions

One of the most common practices and areas of responsibility for anesthesiologists is perioperative IV fluid therapy. Variations in practice and clinical uncertainty have dogged this seemingly straightforward issue. Thankfully, many high-quality clinical studies have recently been published to guide our practice. Knowledge of these, and thoughtful inclusion of key findings in contemporary practice, should improve the care of patients undergoing major surgery. Perioperative patients with hypotension or evidence of inadequate tissue perfusion should first be fluid-optimized before implementation of vasopressor therapy.

CHAPTER SEVEN

PERIOPERATIVE FLUID MANAGEMENT

Perioperative maintenance of adequate intravascular volume status is important to achieve optimal outcomes after surgery, but there are controversies regarding optimal composition and volume of intraoperative fluid therapy. This topic will review derangements and monitoring of intravascular volume status in this setting, as well as strategies for choosing appropriate composition, amount, and timing of intraoperative fluid administration.

Intraoperative administration of fluids aims to maintain or restore effective circulating blood and hence assuring adequate organ perfusion. There is continuous debate about the optimum intraoperative fluid therapy. There is wide variability of practice, both among individuals and institutions in terms of the type of fluid used, the timing of administration and the volume administered. Over the last decade, this debate gave rise to three strategies of fluid management: the "liberal", "restricted", and "goal-directed" fluid therapy strategy.

Although administering large volume of fluids may expand intravascular space and improve organ perfusion, it may also increase the incidence of perioperative cardiopulmonary and tissue-healing complications. On the other hand, fluid restriction may reduce the length of hospital stay; however, it might increase the risks for postoperative acute kidney injury (AKI). Goal-directed therapy (GDT), in which individualized fluid administration based on reproducible end-points, have been associated with improved perioperative outcomes.

The present review aims to summarize the existing evidence supporting the different approaches of intraoperative fluid therapy.

Liberal versus Restrictive Fluid Management

Liberal strategy

Conventionally, infusion of large volumes of crystalloid was used for long decades to achieve a good blood volume. This concept assumed that surgical patients are hypovolemic due to prolonged fasting over the midnight, bowel preparation, and ongoing losses from perspiration and urinary output. There was also a widespread misconception that surgical exposure required aggressive replacement of nebulous insensible fluid loss, often termed "third space" losses. In addition, the 4-2-1 rule for perioperative fluid therapy was adopted for a long time without any supporting evidence base proofs. The latter can potentially lead for overzealous fluid administration and postoperative fluid-based weight gain which in turn might result in increased major morbidity.

The preoperative dehydration has been almost eliminated by reduced fasting times and use of oral fluids up to 2 h before operation. Studies have shown that in patients without significant cardiopulmonary diseases, blood volume is normal even after prolonged fasting. In addition, a transthoracic echocardiography study demonstrated that the preoperative fasting did not alter the dynamic and static preload indices in adult patients with the American Society of Anesthesiologists (ASA) I to III. Moreover, the mechanical bowel preparations can be overlooked because there is growing evidence showing the minimal difference in the surgical conditions where this is used.

The concept of "third space" fluid loss has been emphatically refuted. Previous studies have expanded our understanding of fluid movement across the endothelial vascular barrier. The endothelium barrier is a one-cell thickness and is coated on its luminal side with a fragile layer, the glycocalyx, which provides a first-line barrier to regulating cellular and macromolecule transport across the endothelium. The endothelial glycocalyx can be destroyed not only by ischemia and surgery but also by acute hypervolemia from large volume fluid loading. There are several systematic reviews, emphasizing the measurement of the extracellular volume changes, have concluded that a classic third space does not exist. They have considered the fluid shift to occur from the vascular to the interstitial space because of glycocalyx destruction. Hence, no need to flood the patient with unnecessary extra fluids which proportionately increased risk of morbidity and mortality.

In outpatient surgery, 1–2 L of balanced crystalloids reduces postoperative nausea and vomiting and improves well-being.

Restrictive fluid management

Fluid restrictive strategies are often used as a standard practice for special types of surgery like as lung surgery because of the inherent risk of postpneumonectomy pulmonary edema which is directly related to the amount of positive fluid balance. In addition, maintenance of low intraoperative central venous pressure (CVP) using restrictive fluid strategy was found to be associated with less intraoperative blood loss and need for blood transfusion in patients undergoing hepatic resection.

A "restrictive" intraoperative fluid regimen, avoiding hypovolemia but limiting infusion to the minimum necessary, initially reduced major complications after complex surgery, but inconsistencies in the type of fluid infused and in definitions of adverse outcomes have produced conflicting results in clinical trials.

Several protocols for restrictive fluid regimens have been described including (1) replacement of blood loss with colloids on a "1 mL per 1 mL" basis, (2) nonreplacement of intraoperative interstitial/third space loss or urine output, (3) nonfluid loading, and (4) administration of vasopressor for correcting intraoperative hypotension.

Where does evidence stand?

It has been noted that routine fluid prescription among anesthesiologists varies largely according to the individual habit as well as other independent factors such as differences in surgical types, trauma, preoperative hydration, anesthetic technique, comorbidity, gender, and age. Currently, there is not a clear consensus on the definition of liberal versus restrictive fluid therapy (i.e., how less is too less?).

In 2009, Bundgaard-Nielsen *et al.* performed a narrative synthesis including 705 patients from 7 retrieved randomized controlled trials (RCTs) comparing liberal versus restrictive fixed-volume regimens during the period from 1986 to 2008. Three RCTs only reported improved outcomes with a restrictive fluid regimen after major abdominal surgery in terms of improved gastrointestinal recovery and reduced length of stay (by −2 to −3 days). Contradictory, two RCTs found no difference between both fluid regimens in terms of wound infection (one RCT) or gastrointestinal recovery and length of stay (one RCT). This might be explained with the heterogeneity between the included RCTs in terms of the definition of liberal versus restricted fluid regimens and measured outcomes.

A retrospective cohort study, randomized 89 patients undergoing orthotopic liver transplantation into liberal fluid strategy and restrictive therapy. The restrictive strategy was associated with less need for intraoperative transfusion of packed red blood cells (5.02 ± 4.5 IU vs. 8.5 ± 7.02 IU, $P < 0.001$), fresh frozen plasma (8.7 ± 6.04 IU vs. 15.02 ± 8.2 IU, $P < 0.001$), and platelet concentrates transfusion (2.0 ± 1.08 IU vs. 2.05 ± 1.1 IU, $P = 0.014$), and less demonstration of colloids.

Similarly, an RCT focusing on the use of restrictive intraoperative fluid therapy combined with a concomitant administration of norepinephrine during radical cystectomy demonstrated reduced intraoperative blood loss, the need for blood transfusion, and morbidity.

In contrast, a small RCT including 16 patients undergoing esophageal cancer surgery found that the restrictive volume of intraoperative fluid (≤8 ml/kg/h) does not significantly affect pulmonary exchange function or tissue perfusion. That study included few patients. Patients in the restrictive group received 480 ml/h in 60 kg patient.

A recent retrospective study, including 553 patients who underwent pancreaticoduodenectomy at a tertiary hospital over 12-year-period, found that patients who received >6000 ml intraoperative fluid had more wound infections ($P = 0.049$), intra-abdominal abscesses ($P = 0.020$), and postoperative interventions ($P = 0.007$). In addition, patients who received >14,000 ml fluid until the 5th postoperative experienced all types of postoperative complications (infectious, fistula, delayed gastric emptying, and bleeding).

Straub *et al.* have randomly allocated 100 women undergoing gynecological laparoscopy to receive either 10 ml/kg or 30 ml/kg of intravenous compound sodium lactate during the intraoperative period. Pulmonary function (forced expiratory volume in 1 s, forced vital capacity, and peak expiratory flow rate) and oxygen saturation were similar between the two study groups. However, liberal administration of crystalloid was associated with a clinical modest reduction in pain scores. That study included only patients with ASA physical Class I and Class II who would not be affected with liberal fluid therapy. In addition, that study was powered to study the changes in pain scores, and the use of 10 ml/kg might be not considered as a restrictive regimen.

In a small pediatric study, Mandee *et al.* randomized 25 children (mean age <3 years) undergoing major abdominal surgery to receive maintenance plus deficit with or without interstitial space replacement. They reported higher heart rates ($P = 0.012$) and more negative base excess ($P = 0.049$) in the restrictive group, despite there were no differences between the groups in terms of the total volume requirement, postoperative kidney function, chest X-ray, variation of body weight, and the postoperative outcomes. That study included few patients to study the more important postoperative clinical outcomes.

In another small RCT, Niescery *et al.*, including 45 patients undergoing posterior scoliosis surgery, who received crystalloids at a rate of 5.5 ml/kg/h or 11 ml/kg/h. Patients received 5.5 ml/kg/h of crystalloids had a less frequent reintubation rate ($P = 0.015$) and better postoperative oxygen saturations ($P = 0.043$). That study included few patients, and 5.5 ml/kg/h cannot be considered as a restrictive regimen.

A multicenter prospective study in the intensive care settings included 479 patients (mean age 61.2 ± 17.0 years) who needed postoperative admission to the Intensive Care Unit (ICU) after major surgery in three tertiary hospitals. Fluid balance was calculated as sum of (the preoperative fasting, insensible losses from surgeries, and urine output) minus fluid replacement intraoperatively. They found that an intraoperative fluid balance of + 550 ml might distinguish between from nonsurvivors and survivors ($P < 0.001$). Patients with fluid balance above 2000 ml intraoperatively had a longer ICU stay (4.0 vs. 3.0 days, $P < 0.001$) and higher incidence of infectious (41.9% vs. 25.9%, $P = 0.001$), neurological (46.2% vs. 13.2%, $P < 0.001$), cardiovascular (63.2% vs. 39.6%, $P < 0.001$), and respiratory complications (34.3% vs. 11.6%, $P < 0.001$). Interestingly, the multivariate analysis showed that the fluid balance was an independent factor for death (odds ratio [odds ratio] per 100 ml = 1.024; $P = 0.006$; 95% confidence interval [CI] 1.007–1.041). Of note, in that study, patients who underwent palliative surgery and whose fluid balance could change in outcome were excluded from the study. We think that study could help our understanding for the difference between the liberal and restrictive fluid therapy regimen as being a positive balance of 550 ml (550 ml in 70 kg patient equals approximately 7.9 ml/kg). This can potentially reduce the heterogeneity in the methodology of the future RCTs.

A recent systematic review and meta-analysis included patients with reported ASA physical classes from 1 to 3 in three RCTs. The primary outcome was the total number of patients with a complication and the complication rate. They analyzed data of 1397 patients (693 restrictive protocol and 704 liberal protocol). Compared with the liberal group, they found that fewer patients in the restrictive group experienced a complication (−35%) (relative risk [RR], 0.65; 95% CI, 0.55–0.78) and the total complication rate (RR, 0.57; 95% CI, 0.52–0.64), risk of infection (RR, 0.62; 95% CI, 0.48-0.79), and transfusion rate (RR, 0.81; 95% CI, 0.66–0.99) were also lower.

There is an alerting question: Does the evidence support the concept of the associated increased incidence of the acute kidney injury with the use of restrictive fluid therapy? A systematic review and meta-analysis included 15 RCTs (1966 to present) with a total of 1594 adult patients undergoing surgery comparing restrictive fluid management with a conventional fluid management protocol and reporting the occurrence of postoperative AKI. Interestingly, there was insufficient evidence to associate restrictive fluid management with an increase in oliguria or more frequent occurrence of the AKI. There was no statistically significant difference in acute renal failure occurrence between studies targeting oliguria reversal and not targeting oliguria reversal (OR 0.31; 95% CI, 0.08–1.22; $P = 0.088$).

Goal-Directed Fluid Therapy

The concept of individualized goal-directed cardiovascular optimization and finally assessed on a procedure-specific basis. GDT utilizes monitoring techniques to help guide clinicians with administering fluids, vasopressors, inotropes, or other treatments to patients in various clinical settings. It depends on individual intravascular volume optimization to get a maximum cardiac stroke volume.

Kimberger *et al.* investigated the underlying tissue mechanisms during GDT management with crystalloids or colloids for abdominal surgery with a colonic anastomosis in 27 pigs. Three types of fluid management were instituted at the end of surgery: restricted Ringer lactate (RL) versus GDT RL or GDT colloid to achieve a mixed venous oxygen saturation greater than 60%. The results show no significant differences between the groups in conventional cardiovascular functional parameters or urinary output, but an increased oxygen tension in healthy colonic tissue compared with RL and a further increase with GDT colloid compared with GDT RL. Interestingly, compared with lactated ringers (LR), oxygen tension in perianastomotic tissue (245% with GDT colloid vs. 147% in the GDT RL group vs. 116% in the restricted RL group) and microcirculatory flow were significantly higher with the administration of colloids.

It has been shown in several RCTs that the GDT strategy improved outcome compared with the fixed volume regimens as it can offer a state of normovolemia.

The advent of individualized goal-directed fluid therapy, facilitated by minimally invasive, flow-based cardiovascular monitoring, for example, esophageal Doppler monitoring, has improved outcomes in colorectal surgery, and this monitor has been approved by clinical guidance authorities.

In elective major abdominal surgery, a "zero-balance approach" intraoperative fluid strategy aiming at avoiding fluid overload and comparable to the so-called restrictive approach, has shown to reduce postoperative complications and is easily applied for most patients. It is less expensive and simpler than the zero-balance GDT approach and therefore recommended in this review.

Goals used to guide fluid administration in goal-directed therapy

Table 7 shows the parameters used to monitor fluid administration in the perioperative period. Classic static preload measurement, by whatever technique, is still commonly used to guide fluid therapy but can fail to estimate the response to fluids in one-half of the patients, thus rendering them exposed to the hazards of unnecessary fluid therapy. A systematic review of the role of CVP measurement in fluid therapy concluded that neither CVP nor the rate of change of CVP have been shown to be accurate markers of right ventricular and left ventricular end-diastolic volumes or in predicting the response to a fluid challenge. Therefore, caution should be exercised in interpreting CVP data to guide fluid administration. Dynamic parameters of fluid responsiveness relying on cardiopulmonary interactions in patients under general anesthesia and mechanical ventilation. Studies have demonstrated the higher value of dynamic parameters (analyzing cardiopulmonary interactions) compared with classic static preload indicators in predicting fluid responsiveness.

Table 7: Parameters used to guide fluid administration in the perioperative period

Parameters used to guide fluid administration in the perioperative period

Static parameters
- HR, BP, urine output
  - Lack specificity in identifying volume deficit
  - Do not correlate with cardiac output
  - Lead to over or under-transfusion
- CVP, RAP, PAOP
  - Lack specificity in identifying volume deficit
  - Do not correlate with cardiac output
  - Lead to over or undertransfusion

Dynamic parameters (fluid responsiveness)
- Fluid challenge tests
  - Heterogeneous: Volume and type of fluid, duration of the trial, definition of fluid response
  - Not able to predict the effects of volume expansion before performing volume expansion
  - Not suitable in the OR
- Ventilatory variability
  - SVV
  - SPV
  - PPV
  - Aortic blood flow variation by esophageal laser Doppler
  - Change in PWV amplitude
  - PVI

SVV: Stroke volume variation; SPV: Systolic pressure variation; PPV: Pulse pressure variation; PWV: Plethysmographic waveform variation; PVI: Plethysmographic variability index; CVP: Central venous pressure; RAP: Right atrial pressure; PAOP: Pulmonary artery occlusive pressure; BP: Blood pressure; HR: Heart rate; OR: Odds ratio

Table 8

In patients under general anesthesia, positive pressure ventilation induces cyclic changes in vena cava blood flow, pulmonary artery flow, and aortic blood flow. During inspiration, vena cava blood flow (venous return) decreases and according to the Frank-Starling relationship, pulmonary artery flow decreases. Depending on the position of the patient on the Frank-Starling relationship mechanical ventilation is going to induce either high respiratory variations in the left ventricular stroke volume (when the patient is on the steep portion and more likely to be a responder to volume expansion) or low respiratory variations in the left ventricular stroke volume (when the patient is on the plateau and more likely to be a nonresponder to volume expansion).

Fig 9: Cardiopulmonary interactions during general anesthesia and mechanical ventilation

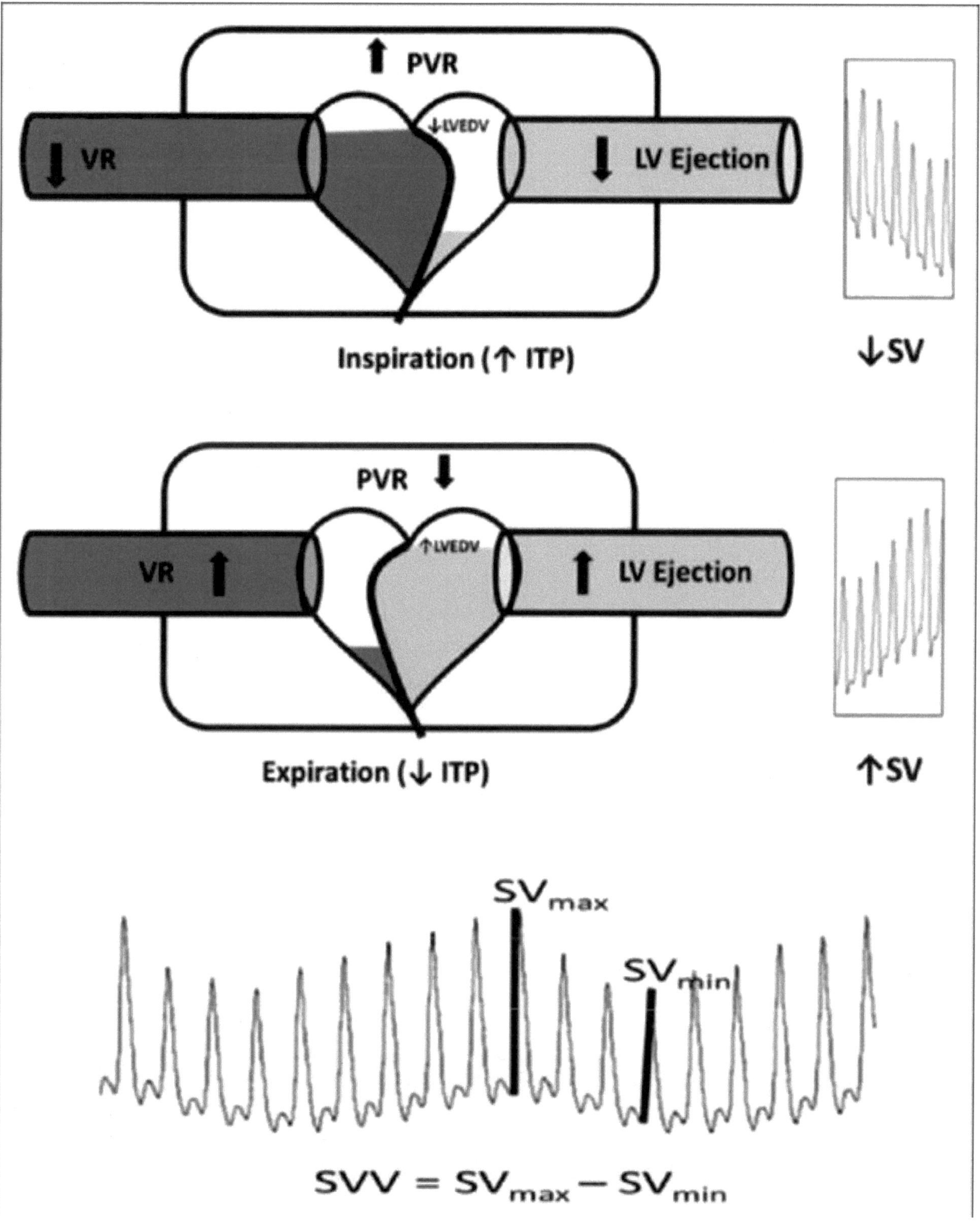

Fig. 9

Fig.10: Relation between stroke volume variability and position of the patient on Frank–Starling law predicts fluid responsiveness.

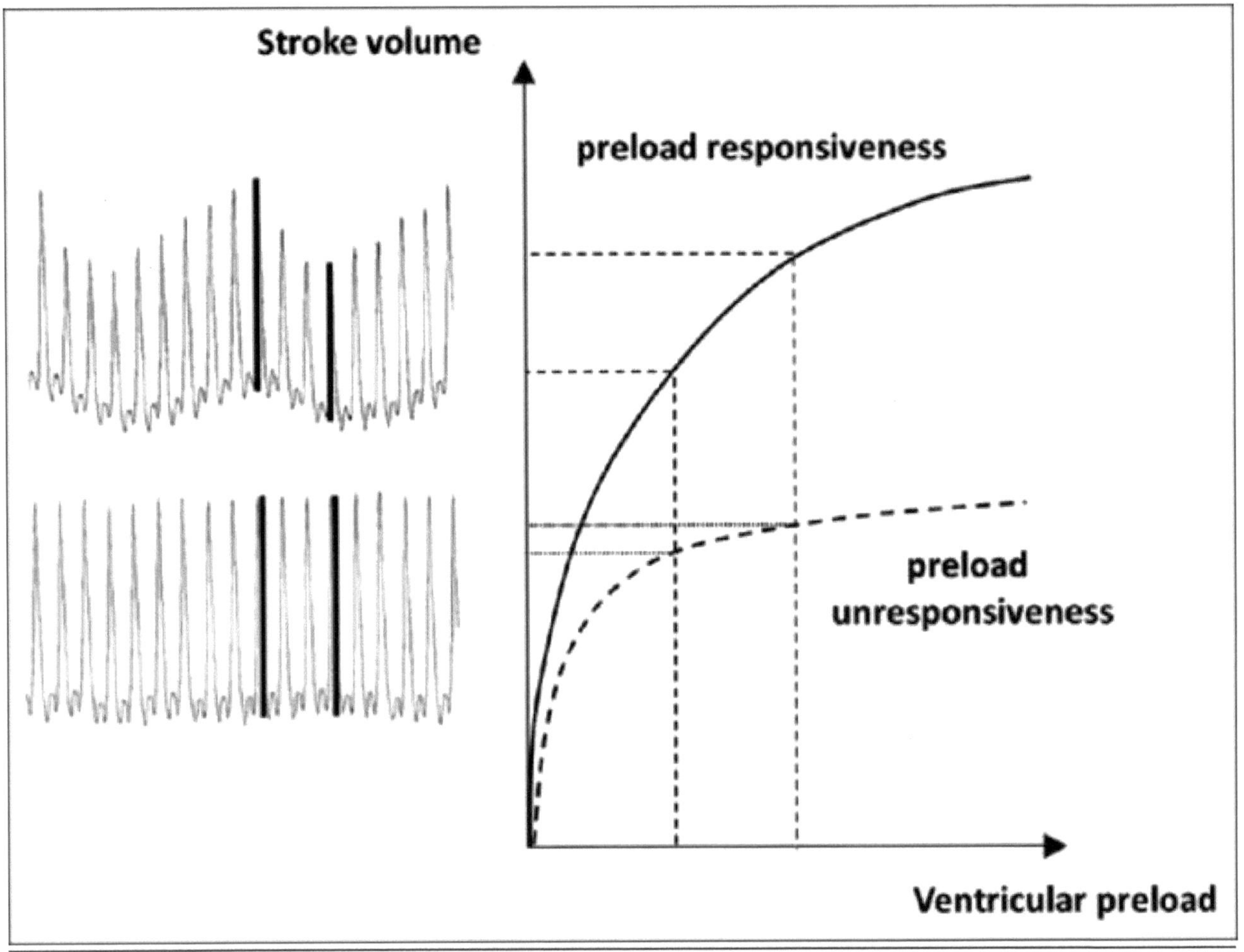

Fig. 10

Currently used dynamic indices include systolic pressure variation, pulse pressure variation (PPV), stroke volume variation (SVV), and plethysmographic waveform variation. The clinical utility of dynamic parameters is limited by many confounding factors that must be clearly understood by the clinician utilizing them.

The role of echocardiography, both transthoracic and transesophageal, can be critical when evaluating both fluid responsiveness and cardiac function. In addition, echocardiography is of particular use when assessing volume responsiveness in patients undergoing open-chest surgery where the predictive ability of dynamic indices is also reduced.

Where does evidence stand?

A recent multicenter RCT in four high volume hepatobiliary-pancreatic surgery centers randomly assigned 52 consecutive adult patients with or without a cardiac output GDT algorithm. Compared with the non-GDT group, patients in the GDT group received less volume of fluid administered intraoperatively (2050 ml vs. 4088, $P < 0.0001$) and more frequent administration of vasoactive medications and shorter median length of hospital stay (9.5 days vs. 12.5 days, $P = 0.002$).

A recent RCT, including 80 adult patients undergoing elective supratentorial brain tumor resection randomly divided into a low SVV and a high SVV group, found that the former had a shorter ICU stay (1.4 vs. 2.6 days, $P = 0.03$), fewer postoperative neurological events (17.5% vs. 40%, $P = 0.05$), and lower intraoperative serum lactate (P <

0.05).

Similarly, the use of the fluid protocol based on PPV assessed using continuous noninvasive arterial pressure measurement during total knee, and hip replacement was associated with a reduction in postoperative complications and transfusion needs as compared to standard no protocol treatment.

A retrospective comparative study, including 145 consecutive patients undergoing pancreaticoduodenectomy in a high-volume center, found that the GDT was associated with fewer cardiorespiratory complications, shorter median hospital stays (10 days vs. 13 days, $P \leq 0.01$), and median total volume of administered fluid intraoperatively.

Conclusion

Whatever the intravenous fluid replacement strategy used, the anesthesiologist must be prepared to adjust the composition and rate of the fluids administered to provide sufficient intravascular fluid volume for adequate perfusion of vital organs without overwhelming the glycocalyx function with fluid overloads. The GDT or zero-balance strategies can potentially improve the patients' outcomes.

Further larger longitudinal studies are needed to test the reliability of different perioperative dynamic fluid therapy monitors.

Postoperative paediatric patients are a different population from medical inpatients. The important differences regarding their fluid management are: Intra-operative fluid losses – blood and insensible Potential for ongoing losses – "maintenance" fluids and replacement for ongoing losses need to be considered and calculated separately. Increased circulating antidiuretic hormone due to multiple factors including surgical stress, pain, nausea, and episodes of hypovolaemia. Potential for ileus due to abdominal/spinal surgery or analgesic infusions. Care should be taken when prescribing maintenance fluids, with consideration of patient selection fluid type rate of administration strict fluid balance. Patients are given fluids in theatre and recovery to replace their deficit from fasting and intra-operative blood loss. Only those who are still not drinking for a period of hours to days post-op will need ongoing maintenance IV fluid for their metabolic requirements. Some postoperative patients will also require replacement fluid for their ongoing losses which can be measured in drains or estimated (in the case of concealed losses) from vital signs, urine output and serum biochemistry. Example patients: after major bowel or spinal surgery (likely to develop ileus), surgery to the head and neck, or patients requiring large doses of intravenous analgesics. Patients with cirrhosis, renal impairment, or congestive cardiac failure are at extra risk of fluid retention and electrolyte imbalances. These groups should be managed by medical specialists or in PICU after major surgery. Fluid Type: Evidence is emerging that isotonic fluids are preferable in postoperative patients, due to their increased risk of free water retention and hyponatraemia. Postoperative patients can also be at risk of hyperglycaemia if excessive glucose is administered. Blood glucose and electrolytes should be monitored closely regardless of fluid choice. Appropriate maintenance fluids readily available on RCH wards are:

0.9% NaCl with 5% dextrose

0.45% NaCl with 5% dextrose (Plasmalyte with 5% dextrose is currently being compared in the PIMS study and will hopefully become available for routine use if benefit is shown)

0.9% NaCl (mainly used for fluid boluses to replace ongoing losses or correct hypovolaemia), but also an appropriate maintenance fluid.

Hartmann's solution = Compound Sodium Lactate Potassium should be added after >24hours of fasting.

Rate of administration: Standard maintenance rates according to the 4-2-1 rule* may deliver excessive fluid to postoperative patients. ½ to 2/3 standard maintenance rates may be more appropriate. Ongoing losses should be replaced like for like. e.g;

nasogastric losses are replaced with 0.9% NaCl with 20mmol/L KCl

ongoing bleeding should trigger Hb monitoring and consideration of blood products

Hypovolaemia or dehydration, as evidenced by decreased urine output, weight loss, tachycardia, decreased perfusion, should be corrected with boluses of 0.9% NaCl - give 20ml/kg and reassess.

Keep vein open infusions running purely to "piggyback" IV drug infusions can be any compatible fluid, run at a low rate. For example a total of 2ml/hour for small babies 40kg patients. These infusions only need to run if there is no other maintenance through that particular lumen\cannula or if there is only an infusion at such a low rate that it is not adequate to keep the vein open (eg morphine or PCA).

Monitoring: In order to avoid iatrogenic complications of intravenous fluid regimes, all patients on maintenance fluid should ideally have: Frequent vital signs Daily weight Strict input and output charts, including drain and nasogastric losses

Note: Urine output should be greater than 0.5-1.0ml/kg/hour (depending on age) At least daily serum biochemistry and glucose monitoring At least daily medical review to determine ongoing need for intravenous therapy.

Special Groups:

Neurosurgical patients – more likely to be prescribed 0.9% saline maintenance, to maintain serum sodium in the high-normal range. Neonates - managed according to neonatal unit maintenance fluid protocol.

Craniofacial surgery – at particular risk of SIADH and anaemia. This guideline applies but particular care is required. Blood tests on the evening of surgery and the following morning are recommended.

Scoliosis surgery – older children who rarely require additional glucose. Should receive 0.9% saline or Hartmann's for postoperative day 1 at 2/3 – 3/4 maintenance with a rescue order of 10mL/kg if urine output declines below 0.5mLs/kg/hr for 2 consecutive hours or systolic BP is low.

* 4/ 2/ 1 rule for maintenance fluid calculations:

i.e. 4mls/kg/hr for any part of the first 10 kilos

2mls/kg/hr for any part of the second 10 kilos

1ml/kg/hr for the remaining kilos e.g. 8 kg 4x 8 = 32mls/hr

17kg (4x10) + (2x7) = 54mls/hr

25kg (4x10) + (2x10) + (1x5) = 65mls/hr

43kg (4x10) + (2x10) + (1x23) = 83mls/hr

CAUSES AND CONSEQUENCES OF INTRAVASCULAR VOLUME DERANGEMENTS

Normovolemia/euvolemia should be maintained throughout the perioperative period to maintain adequate tissue perfusion. Both hypovolemia and hypervolemia are associated with postoperative morbidity.

Hypovolemia

Causes

•**Preoperative factors** – Preoperative hypovolemia may increase the risk of significant decreases in blood pressure during induction of anesthesia.

•Although preoperative fasting overnight for approximately 10 hours does not significantly reduce intravascular volume, the fasting period is limited to avoid preoperative dehydration. Patients are encouraged to consume clear oral liquids up to two hours before surgery.

•Mechanical bowel preparation is associated with fluid loss from the gastrointestinal tract, which may reduce preoperative intravascular volume. Newer bowel preparations are designed to minimize this loss.

•Disorders such as bowel obstruction or pancreatitis may cause intravascular volume loss due to inflammation and interstitial edema.

•Ongoing bleeding typically requires surgical hemostasis to allow adequate volume repletion.

•**Surgery-related factors**

•Surgical bleeding

•Coagulopathy due to hemodilution and/or hypothermia, which aggravates blood loss

•Decreased venous return due to:

-Abdominal insufflation during laparoscopy.

-Compression of the inferior vena cava (eg, in the supine position during pregnancy) or other major veins (eg, portal vein)

•Positive pressure mechanical ventilation with large tidal volumes, high positive end-expiratory pressure, or lung recruitment maneuvers to reverse atelectasis.

•Prolonged duration of surgery with evaporation and insensible fluid loss from exposed body cavities or wounds, particularly with an open abdominal cavity resulting in bowel edema and sequestration of fluid in tissues. Conversely, minimal fluid losses occur during short less invasive surgical procedures.

•Any other factors preventing early transition (within 24 hours of surgery) from intravenous (IV) to oral fluid therapy.

Consequences — Hypovolemia results in reduced cardiac output and tissue perfusion. Persistent hypovolemia can lead to shock and multiorgan failure.

Hypervolemia

Causes — Development of hypervolemia is generally due to excessive volume administration. In many cases, intraoperative fluid is administered to treat hemodynamic instability due to vasodilation, surgical bleeding, myocardial dysfunction, or vascular permeability. This often results in postoperative fluid overload.

•Anesthesia-related factors

•General anesthetic agents – Most IV and inhalation anesthetic and adjuvant drugs including opioids cause dose-dependent vasodilation and myocardial depression that may lead to hypotension that is treated with fluid administration. Unnecessarily deep anesthesia with hypotension may lead to excessive fluid administration.

Hypotension that persists after reducing anesthetic depth (if appropriate), administration of appropriate amounts of fluid to replace surgical losses, and exclusion of other causes of hypotension should be treated with IV vasopressor/inotropic agents such as phenylephrine rather than continuing administration of large amounts of fluid alone.

•Neuraxial anesthesia – Sympathetic blockade during neuraxial anesthesia increases venous capacitance and dilates arteriolar resistance vessels, with resultant hypotension. However, rather than preloading with IV fluid to prevent hypotension, we use a vasopressor such as phenylephrine or norepinephrine.

•Surgery-related factors

•Treatment of surgical bleeding – Excessive administration of crystalloid or colloid together with transfusion of red blood cells results in dilution of coagulation factors, which may exacerbate bleeding and lead to additional transfusions and administration of fluid.

•Patient-related factors

•Congestive heart failure (CHF) with compensatory fluid retention

•Renal insufficiency, particularly if renal replacement therapy is inadequate

Consequences — Hypervolemia can result in reduced tissue perfusion due to tissue edema, with clinically significant postoperative fluid retention (ie, weight gain >10 percent above preoperative baseline). Postoperative fluid overload is associated with increased morbidity, length of stay in the intensive care unit, and mortality. Specific systemic effects include the following:

•Respiratory effects – Increased extravascular fluid in lung tissue impairs oxygen exchange and increases risk for postoperative respiratory failure and pneumonia. Some patients develop frank pulmonary edema, particularly those with a history of heart failure.

•Gastrointestinal effects – Increased extracellular fluid in the bowel can lead sequentially to gastrointestinal edema, decreased gastrointestinal motility, and possibly ileus. In patients undergoing bowel surgery, intestinal edema can increase tension at bowel anastomoses contributing to anastomotic dehiscence.

Occasionally, massive fluid resuscitation is associated with acute ascites. Ascites and bowel edema can contribute to development of abdominal compartment syndrome

•Effects on hemostasis – Excess intravascular fluid dilutes clotting factors, which can contribute to or cause coagulation abnormalities.

•Effects on wound healing – Marked tissue edema impairs wound healing.

MONITORING INTRAVASCULAR VOLUME STATUS

Intraoperative monitoring challenges — Intravascular fluid status is monitored to maintain euvolemia with adequate tissue perfusion. Standard hemodynamic monitors include noninvasive blood pressure (BP) cuff and heart rate (HR) monitoring. In selected cases, one or more invasive monitors of dynamic hemodynamic parameters may be used to predict fluid responsiveness (ie, an increase in stroke volume [SV] and cardiac output [CO] following intravenous fluid administration.

Challenges in estimating intravascular volume status during the intraoperative period include:

- Preoperative volume status may be suboptimal or unknown.
- Surgical volume losses may be continuously changing, but are difficult to quantify.
- Cardiovascular responses to anesthetic agents and dosing are occurring.
- Measured laboratory values do not reflect contemporaneous changes in intravascular volume status.
- Clinical methods routinely used to assess volume status in awake patients (eg, thirst, postural dizziness, lethargy, confusion) are unavailable in the anesthetized patient.

Traditional static parameters — Static parameters (eg, measurements of BP, HR, urine output [UO], central venous pressure [CVP]) have been traditionally used to provide supplemental data regarding intravascular volume status.However, sole use of these parameters to guide fluid therapy may result in either hypovolemia or hypervolemia. Even with continuous monitoring of these static parameters, significant intraoperative reduction in tissue perfusion may not be recognized.

- **Blood pressure and heart rate** – BP and HR responses to changes in intravascular volume status are not predictable in individual patients. Examples include:
  - There is no correlation between BP and CO in patients undergoing major abdominal surgery.
  - Healthy young patients with subclinical hypovolemia often have normal BP and HR because the stress response to surgery activates the sympathetic nervous system and the renin-angiotensin system, with release of vasoconstrictor hormones that increase BP. Although the resulting peripheral vasoconstriction favors maintenance of adequate perfusion to the heart and the brain, perfusion to other organs (eg, kidneys, gastrointestinal tract, skin) are reduced. Notably, general or neuraxial anesthesia may blunt these compensatory vasoconstrictive responses to decreased perfusion.
  - Patients treated with beta-blockers may not manifest tachycardia as a compensatory response to hypovolemia.
- **Central venous pressure** – CVP measured from a central venous catheter (CVC) or pulmonary artery occlusion pressure (PAOP) measured from a pulmonary artery catheter (PAC) are sometimes used to provide supplemental data regarding intravascular volume status, but these parameters are inaccurate surrogates to determine cardiac preload, fluid responsiveness, or impending pulmonary edema.
- **Urine output** – Oliguria (UO <0.5 mL/kg per hour) is a commonly used indicator of hypovolemia. However, oliguria alone is not a sufficient indication for fluid administration in patients undergoing anesthesia and surgery. For example, inhalation anesthetics, as well as surgical stress, may reduce UO in patients who are actually euvolemic, leading to fluid overload if fluid is administered to treat oliguria.

Notably, intraoperative oliguria does not predict acute kidney injury (AKI). Data suggest that traditional targets that attempt to continuously maintain UO >0.5 mL/kg per hour are not warranted, although sustained oliguria may be associated with increased risk of renal injury, particularly if <0.3 mL/kg per hour.

- **Mixed venous oxygen saturation** – Measurements intended to track global oxygen (O_2) delivery have limited utility to guide fluid therapy. These include measurements of mixed venous O_2 saturation from a PAC (SvO_2) or central venous O_2 saturation ($ScvO_2$) from a CVC. Although SvO_2 and $ScvO_2$ are proportional to CO, tissue perfusion, and tissue O_2 delivery, these measurements are also inversely proportional to tissue O_2 consumption. Thus, values do not reflect changes in tissue perfusion during the perioperative period when O_2 consumption is variable.

Dynamic parameters to assess volume responsiveness — Dynamic hemodynamic indices are used to assess fluid responsiveness and guide goal-directed fluid therapy in patients undergoing major invasive surgery, particularly for procedures with large expected blood losses or fluid shifts. Compared with traditional static parameters, dynamic parameters provide superior assessment of response to a fluid challenge (ie, volume responsiveness)

The following parameters are examples:

Respiratory variations in arterial pressure waveform

- **Measured variables** – Variations in the intra-arterial pressure waveform that occur during respiration can be observed or measured to assess responses to fluid challenges. These include pulse pressure variation (PPV), SV variation (SVV), systolic blood pressure variation (SPV), or change in inferior vena cava diameter. These variations occur during controlled mechanical ventilation because inspiration increases intrathoracic pressure, which reduces venous return, right ventricular (RV) filling volume, and SV. The opposite effects occur during expiration. If arterial vasomotor tone and cardiac function remain constant. these changes in venous return and SV create variations in pulse pressure and systolic BP. Normal respiratory variations in these dynamic parameters are <10 percent. Greater variations suggest fluid responsiveness and the likely need for fluid administration.

•**Limitations** – Each of the dynamic indices based on respiratory variation has advantages and disadvantages. Although generally superior to static parameters for assessment of fluid responsiveness

•During spontaneous ventilation

•During mechanical ventilation with low tidal volumes <8 mL/kg or high positive end-expiratory pressure >15 cm H_2O

•During open chest procedures

•Patients with clinical abnormalities such as elevated intra-abdominal pressure, cardiac tamponade, significant auto-PEEP, nonsinus rhythm or other cardiac arrhythmias, right heart failure, or a requirement for vasoactive infusions

Also, there are limitations in sensitivity and specificity. A 2018 systematic review calculated the pooled area under the curve (AUC) for PPV and for SVV (5017 patients; 68 studies)

•For PPV, AUC was 0.86 (95% CI 0.80-0.92), with a sensitivity of 80 percent (95% CI 74-85 percent) and specificity of 83 percent (95% CI 73-91 percent)

•For SVV, AUC was 0.87 (95% CI 0.81-0.93), with a sensitivity of 82 percent (95% CI 75-89 percent) and specificity of 77 percent (95% CI 71-82 percent)

Thus, indices based on respiratory variations are interpreted with caution and should consider the clinical setting and clinical data such as the physical examination and static parameters such as filling pressures, UO, or SvO_2 or $ScvO_2$

Notably, although hemodynamic indices of respiratory variation can be computed (manually or automatically), visual estimation is often adequate to guide fluid therapy. In one study, determination of the need for a fluid bolus based on visual estimation of SPV in the intra-arterial waveform was compared with computed values; only 1 percent of treatment decisions were incorrect when based solely on visual estimation.

Changes in mean arterial pressure and/or SV induced by lung recruitment maneuvers (eg, ventilation with positive pressure held at 30 cm H_2O for 30 seconds) can also be used to predict volume responsiveness.

Ultrasound technologies

Esophageal doppler technology — Esophageal Doppler devices use a flexible transesophageal Doppler ultrasound probe to measure blood flow velocity in the descending thoracic aorta to derive estimates of SV. Such devices may be useful when indices based on respiratory variation in the intra-arterial waveform cannot be used.

Echocardiography — Left ventricular (LV) size and intravascular volume status can be quickly estimated using transesophageal echocardiography (TEE) or transthoracic echocardiography (TTE). This is typically accomplished in the transgastric midpapillary short-axis view by qualitative visual assessment of LV cavity size. Underfilling of the left ventricle caused by acute hypovolemia is easily recognized in a patient with hyperdynamic systolic function and decreased end-diastolic and end-systolic LV cavity dimensions. Quantitative measurements of the internal diameter or cross-sectional area of the LV at end-diastole can also be made. Changes from baseline (normovolemia) are monitored using these qualitative and/or quantitative assessments.

Point-of-care ultrasound (POCUS) transthoracic echocardiography can also be used to assess left and right atrial and ventricular chambers to estimate intravascular volume status. One study noted good correlation between pulse pressure variation (PPV) during the respiratory cycle and the collapsibility index and distensibility index of the inferior vena cava measured using transthoracic echocardiography during mechanical ventilation.

Noninvasive technologies — Several types of noninvasive commercially available technologies that measure CO and/or assess fluid responsiveness have been studied (eg, pleth variability index, pulse wave analysis [pulse wave transit time or pulse contour analysis], carbon dioxide rebreathing, and thoracic electrical bioimpedance or bioreactance devices). A 2017 meta-analysis concluded that the percentage error of these devices for measurements of CO can be significant compared with standard thermodilution techniques.

Measurement of laboratory values — Increased serum lactate levels or lactic acidosis on sequential arterial blood gases can be an important indicator of reduced global tissue perfusion. However, these laboratory values do not provide information regarding contemporaneous clinical intravascular volume status since they are measured intermittently and do not immediately reflect acute changes.

CHOOSING FLUID: CRYSTALLOID, COLLOID, OR BLOOD

Crystalloid solutions — Crystalloids are solutions of electrolytes and sterile water that may be isotonic, hypotonic, or hypertonic with respect to plasma. Balanced electrolyte solutions (also termed buffered crystalloid solutions) that have an electrolyte composition similar to plasma with the addition of a buffer (eg, lactate) are most widely used. Examples include lactated Ringer's solution (also termed Hartmann's solution) or Plasmalyte.

We typically select a balanced electrolyte crystalloid solution for routine perioperative fluid administration to maintain intraoperative normovolemia. During major surgical procedures, we administer approximately 3 mL/kg per hour to replace sensible and insensible losses and support basal metabolic rate, and we administer fluid boluses (typically 250 mL) in volume responsive patients to optimize intravascular volume, and replacement of lost blood with crystalloid on a 1.5:1.0 volume basis until a blood transfusion threshold is met. We avoid dextrose-containing solutions due to the putative adverse effects of hyperglycemia.

We avoid administration of a large volume of normal saline (NS; 0.9 percent), as this has been associated with hyperchloremic acidosis. Risk for other adverse outcomes, particularly acute kidney injury (AKI), has been associated with NS in several observational and randomized studies. However, results are not consistent in patients who do not receive large volumes of NS or are not critically ill. A 2017 meta-analysis of randomized trials that included 1096 surgical patients noted that perioperative administration of buffered (ie, balanced) electrolyte solutions was associated with a lower incidence of minor metabolic derangements, particularly mild metabolic acidosis compared with NS, but did not demonstrate an effect on mortality or renal replacement therapy (RRT); however, most of these patients were not critically ill. Another 2018 meta-analysis of randomized trials in more than 3700 unselected critically ill or perioperative adult patients did not find a significant reduction in mortality (odds ratio [OR] 0.90, 95% CI 0.69-1.17) or incidence of RRT (OR 1.12, 95% CI 0.80-1.58) with administration of balanced electrolyte solutions rather than NS; however, most of these patients received a low fluid volume. Similarly, a 2020 single-center alternating cohort trial of infusion of large volumes of saline versus lactated Ringer's solution noted comparable outcomes including renal, respiratory, infectious, and hemorrhagic complications in 8616 patients undergoing major noncardiac surgical procedures.

Colloid solutions — Colloids are human plasma derivatives (eg, human albumin, fresh frozen plasma [FFP]) or semisynthetic preparations (eg, hydroxyethyl starch [HES], gelatins). Colloids may be dissolved in isotonic saline or in a solution with a balanced electrolyte concentration similar to plasma.

Some clinicians prefer to use colloids in selected patients or situations in attempts to expand microvascular volume with minimal capillary leakage in fluid responsive patients, thereby minimizing the total quantity of administered fluid and edema formation. For example, during blood loss, colloids may be administered on a 1:1 volume basis until a transfusion threshold is met. Administration of 20 percent albumin results in a long-lasting plasma volume expansion lasting into the postoperative period. In one study of patients undergoing open abdominal surgery, the intravascular half-life of 20 percent albumin was 9.1 (5.7 to 11.2) hours.

However, evidence that colloid solutions are superior to balanced electrolyte crystalloid solutions is scant. A study using closed loop administration of balanced HES for open abdominal surgery noted lower morbidity on postoperative day two and better disability-free survival at follow-up one year after surgery, compared with closed loop administration of balanced crystalloid solution. A small study of administration of 20 percent albumin in the postoperative period after cardiac surgery noted less positive fluid balance and volume of fluid boluses and lower requirements for a vasopressor (norepinephrine).

Overall, we minimize use of colloids since they do not provide significant hemodynamic benefits over crystalloids. When we do select a colloid to expand microvascular volume, we use albumin rather than HES.

Albumin — Human serum albumin is available in both 5 and 25 percent solutions. In some parts of the world, human serum albumin is available as 4 and 20 percent solutions. Human albumin 5 percent has a volume effect (ie, the percent of fluid administered that remains intravascular) of 70 percent, while albumin 25 percent solution is isosmotic with plasma. Human albumin is pasteurized and does not transmit any known infectious diseases.

Notably, albumin is more expensive than other solutions, and may not be safer or more efficacious than synthetic colloids (eg, HES) or balanced crystalloid solutions.

Hydroxyethyl starches — HES solutions are synthetic colloids, identified by three numbers corresponding to concentration, molecular weight, and molar substitution (ie, the average hydroxyethyl groups per one glucose unit). As an example, Hespan is HES 6 percent (600/0.75) with a volume effect of 100 percent and a high molar substitution of 0.75. Due to concerns regarding renal toxicity and effects on hemostasis, administration of HES solutions is restricted in Europe and North America.

A 2018 systematic review in critically ill patients with medical and surgical diagnoses noted a higher incidence of RRT in those receiving HES solutions compared with those receiving crystalloids (risk ratio [RR] 1.30, 95% CI 1.14-1.48; 8527 participants, nine studies). Also, a 2010 systematic review in mixed surgical and nonsurgical patient populations found an overall increased risk of author-defined kidney failure in surgical and medical patients receiving HES solutions (including some who received highly substituted HES products) compared with those receiving various other types of fluid therapy. Furthermore, administration of HES solutions in cardiac surgical patients increased risk of postoperative bleeding and transfusion compared with albumin .

However, data are not consistent. A 2022 meta-analysis of randomized trials (seven trials; 2398 patients) noted that intraoperative intravascular volume replacement with 6 percent hetastarch 130/.04 during open abdominal surgery was not associated with increased risk of AKI after 30 postoperative days compared with using crystalloid solutions (eg, lactated Ringers, Plasmalyte, NS) . Furthermore, randomized trials comparing outcomes after administration of 6 percent hetastarch 130/.04 versus 5 percent albumin noted similar risk for AKI and other serious postoperative complications with either colloid. Notably, risk of HES-induced renal toxicity and other complications is likely influenced by the molar substitution level in the specific product, with less risk for more recently developed low substituted HES products such as 6 percent hetastarch 130/.04. Nevertheless, in 2021, the FDA required additional warnings about the risk of death, bleeding, and AKI.

Since HES products impair platelet reactivity and decrease circulating plasma concentrations of coagulation factor VIII and von Willebrand factor, administration may result in weakening of clot formation and more transfusions of blood products including FFP, cryoprecipitate, and platelets compared with other fluid choices. A 2018 systematic review of randomized trials in critically ill patients noted a higher incidence of transfusion in those receiving starch solutions compared with those receiving crystalloids (RR 1.19, 95% CI 1.02-1.39; 1917 participants, eight studies). HES products with low molar substitution (eg, pentastarch and tetrastarch) may have less effect on hemostasis. One 2008 meta-analysis of randomized trials compared HES solutions with low (0.4) versus a somewhat higher (0.5) molar substitution, noting significantly less blood loss (404 mL) and red blood cell (RBC) transfusion (137 mL) in patients receiving the low substituted product (seven trials; 449 patients). Subsequently, a 2020 randomized trial noted similar coagulation, platelet count, and platelet function parameters with use of 6 percent hetastarch 130/.04 for plasma volume replacement compared with 5 percent albumin. Furthermore, a multicenter retrospective study noted that bleeding rates did not change after switching from HES solution to albumin for musculoskeletal surgical procedures (3078 total patients).

Gelatins — Gelatins are not used in the United States because of their short duration of action (two to three hours) due to rapid excretion in the urine, possible effects on coagulation, and a relatively high incidence of anaphylaxis

Gelatins are used in some countries because they are inexpensive and have a volume effect of 70 to 80 percent.

Blood transfusion

- **Red blood cells** – RBCs are used to replace intraoperative blood loss when a transfusion threshold is met, as discussed separately.

•**Plasma** – Decisions regarding transfusion of plasma derivatives of human blood (eg, fresh frozen plasma [FFP], cryoprecipitate) are based on estimates of the amount of current and expected ongoing blood loss and evidence of intractable microvascular bleeding indicating abnormal hemostasis, ideally with confirmation by diagnostic test results. In patients with disseminated intravascular coagulation, administration of colloid lacking coagulation factors may exacerbate depletion of natural anticoagulants needed to prevent microthrombosis; thus, plasma rather than albumin is typically preferred for volume replacement in these patients. Further discussions regarding transfusion are available in a separate topic.

CHOOSING A FLUID MANAGEMENT STRATEGY Our intraoperative fluid management strategy and selection of noninvasive or invasive monitoring is based on the expected blood loss and the likelihood of nonhemorrhagic fluid shifts (eg, from open body cavities and wounds) during the planned surgical procedure. Other factors influencing these decisions include patient comorbidities (eg, anemia, congestive heart failure [CHF], chronic obstructive pulmonary disease [COPD]) and planned postoperative disposition (eg, home, hospital ward, intensive care unit).

Minimally/moderately invasive surgery — For most relatively brief minimally or moderately invasive surgery with planned early postoperative ambulation, we administer 1 to 2 L of a balanced electrolyte solution for procedures that will not incur significant fluid shifts or blood loss. This volume of fluid is typically administered during surgery over a period of 30 minutes to two hours. Such empiric but limited fluid administration for less invasive surgery in ambulatory patients addresses the mild dehydration caused by preoperative fasting and is associated with less risk for postoperative nausea and vomiting (PONV) or pain compared with controls receiving minimal fluids. In patients with a history of CHF or COPD, fluid is administered cautiously (eg, in increments), with a total volume in the lower end of this range.

Major invasive surgery — For adult patients undergoing major invasive surgical procedures, we select one of the following strategies:

Restrictive (zero-balance) strategy — For invasive major surgery with expected blood loss <500 mL, we typically employ a restrictive zero-balance approach that minimizes fluid administration, particularly if no invasive monitoring of dynamic hemodynamic parameters is planned (eg, intra-arterial catheter, transesophageal echocardiography [TEE] or esophageal Doppler probe). With this approach, only the fluid that is lost during surgery is replaced, including the following strategies:

•During the intraoperative period, patients receive a balanced electrolyte crystalloid solution administered at a rate of approximately 3 mL/kg per hour to replace sensible and insensible losses and support metabolic rate.

•For blood loss, additional fluid may be administered. Studies suggest that the optimal crystalloid-to-blood volume ratio is approximately 1.5:1.0, and that the optimal colloid-to-blood ratio is 1:1, until a threshold for red blood cell (RBC) transfusion is reached.

•We avoid "preloading" of crystalloids prior to a neuraxial block or induction of general anesthesia.

•We avoid replacement of nonanatomic "third space" losses since evidence suggests that this practice has no benefit and may cause morbidity.

•We avoid extremely deep anesthesia (eg, bispectral index values <40) that may result in hypotension treated with unnecessary additional fluid. If necessary, vasopressor agents such as phenylephrine or ephedrine may be employed to treat hypotension caused by administration of anesthetic agents and/or neuraxial block.

•Administration of a total volume of balanced electrolyte solutions that modestly exceeds zero fluid balance is appropriate in patients with evidence of hypovolemia.

A potential disadvantage of this approach is that hypovolemia may not be clinically appreciated. Also, if hypotension occurs, it may be difficult to determine the etiology (eg, surgical volume losses or other causes such as cardiovascular responses to anesthetic agents). However, in most studies, restrictive fluid therapy has been associated with better outcomes than traditional liberal or fixed-volume approaches for major elective surgical procedures.

A modified approach was described in a 2014 randomized trial in 166 patients undergoing radical cystectomy employing a restrictive approach (1 mL/kg/hour) combined with low-dose norepinephrine infusion during the initial portion of the surgery, subsequently followed by hydration (3 mL/kg/hour) during the last part of the surgical procedure. This so-called "restrictive deferred hydration" approach was associated with fewer complications (RR 0.70, 95% CI 0.55-0.88) and a lower median duration of hospital stay (15 days, range 11 to 27) than a liberal approach with 6 mL/kg/hour (17 days, range 11 to 95).

Notably, variability in study design has resulted in inconsistent results. A randomized trial in 3000 patients undergoing major abdominal surgery noted that a restrictive (zero-balance) fluid regimen was associated with a higher rate of acute kidney injury (AKI) compared with a liberal fluid regimen (8.6 versus 5 percent; RR 1.71, 95% CI 1.29-2.27). A limitation of this study was its pragmatic design in that perioperative care was not standardized and there was a wide variation in the anesthetic and analgesic techniques, including the use of epidural analgesia, variable intraoperative hemodynamic management, and variable postoperative care. The total fluid volume administered (balanced electrolyte solutions in both groups) during and up to 24 hours after surgery was 3.7 versus 6.1 L in the restrictive and liberal groups, respectively. These volumes were lower than traditional liberal fluid strategy totals. A retrospective observational study also noted an association between use of a restrictive strategy with AKI in patients undergoing cystectomy (odds ratio [OR] 0.79, 95% CI 0.68-0.91).

Taken together, these studies suggest that hypovolemia should be recognized and appropriately treated with fluid to avoid hemodynamic compromise and organ ischemia. However, excessive perioperative fluid administration should also be avoided since this can cause tissue and organ edema.

Goal-directed fluid therapy — For invasive major surgery with anticipated significant blood losses (eg, >500 mL) and/or fluid shifts, we typically employ a goal-directed approach to fluid administration using one or more invasive dynamic hemodynamic parameters to achieve a prespecified goal. With this approach, we ensure that intravascular volume status is optimal before adding vasopressor therapy to achieve optimal blood pressure. Clinical questions regarding goal-directed therapy (GDT) that remain unanswered include which types of patients are most likely to benefit, optimal timing of the use of GDT (preoperative, intraoperative, and/or postoperative), which outcome measures or endpoints are optimal, which combinations of therapies constitute the best approach (eg, fluids with or without vasopressors or inotropic agents), and how long the regimen should be maintained during the postoperative period.

Specific techniques

●As with a restrictive strategy, patients receive balanced electrolyte crystalloid solution administered at a rate of approximately 3 mL/kg per hour during the intraoperative period to replace sensible and insensible losses and support metabolic rate.

●A disadvantage of GDT is that it requires invasive monitoring of dynamic hemodynamic parameters. We consider the following factors in selection of monitoring modalities:

•In most patients undergoing major surgery, we use the intra-arterial waveform tracing for automated measurements of pulse pressure variations (PPV) or stroke volume variation (SVV), or visually estimated or manually calculated PPV or systolic pressure variations (SPV), in order to determine responses to fluid boluses (typically 250 mL increments). For some patients, fluid boluses are administered in 100 mL increments to avoid excessive fluid administration and consequent hypervolemia.

•For high-risk patients undergoing a surgical procedure with expected blood loss >1000 mL, significant nonhemorrhagic fluid losses, and/or likely prolonged duration, we typically use a commercially available device that provides automated calculation of PPV, SVV, or SPV by analyzing the intra-arterial waveform tracing to assess responses to fluid challenges. An alternative is use of an esophageal Doppler device to estimate stroke volume (SV). TEE is another option, allowing visual qualitative evaluation or quantitative measurements of the left ventricular (LV) cavity size to monitor fluid responsiveness.

●For a GDT approach, fluid is administered to achieve a prespecified goal:

•If respiratory variations in the arterial pressure waveform (PPV or SPV) are >10 to 15 percent, then the patient is assumed to be fluid responsive and we administer fluid boluses of a balanced electrolyte crystalloid solution (typically in 250 mL increments). Once change in the monitored dynamic parameter is <10 percent, fluid administration is stopped to avoid hypervolemia.

•If SV estimates are used for dynamic hemodynamic monitoring, the typical goal of therapy is to achieve and maintain optimal intravascular volume with maximum SV. The new SV value after fluid administration has resulted in <10 percent change is recorded as the new baseline goal value (representing the maximum SV to be maintained).

•If TEE is employed, hypovolemic and hypervolemic states can be quickly assessed by visual qualitative evaluation or quantitative measurements of LV cavity size. Fluid administration is stopped once normovolemia has been achieved.

•Although most studies evaluating GDT have used boluses of colloid fluid, we typically select a balanced crystalloid solution for fluid boluses. Randomized trials in patients undergoing elective abdominal surgery have found little difference in postoperative complications or any clinical benefit with use of a 6 percent hydroxyethyl starch (HES) colloid solution for fluid boluses compared with a balanced crystalloid solution to provide GDT.

Comparison with other strategies — Variable benefits have been noted in comparisons of GDT with other fluid management strategies. Numerous limitations in study design may account for variable benefits of GDT compared with other fluid management strategies. These include clinical heterogeneity among trials with differing definitions for GDT, lack of well-defined endpoints, different types of fluid therapy, different devices used to monitor dynamic hemodynamic parameters, variations in management of the control group, different types of surgery, and small sample sizes. In addition, most studies have included only limited information regarding anesthetic techniques and perioperative surgical care.

•**Comparison with traditional liberal fluid strategies** – GDT appears to be superior to traditional fixed-volume or liberal fluid approaches. A 2022 meta-analysis of randomized trials in noncardiac surgical patients noted a trend toward reduced mortality with GDT (OR 0.84, 95% CI 0.64-1.09) and shorter length of hospital stay (mean difference -0.72 days, 95% CI -1.10 to -0.25 days), with low certainty evidence for these primary outcomes compared with standard of care (76 trials; 9081 patients). In subgroup analyses, GDT was also favored for other outcomes (pneumonia, acute respiratory distress syndrome, surgical site infection, anastomotic leakage, and delirium) compared with standard of care, but with low or moderate certainty of evidence. A 2018 meta-analysis noted similar results with GDT compared with standard care (eg, lower risk of respiratory, renal, wound, and gastrointestinal complications, with shorter time to hospital discharge).

However, data are not consistent. In particular, GDT does not appear to offer additional benefits over a restrictive fluid approach for patients managed with protocols to achieve enhanced recovery after surgery (ERAS). The likely reason is that ERAS protocols implement multiple processes that each reduce the risk of perioperative fluid imbalances (eg, avoidance of preoperative dehydration, use of an intraoperative restrictive fluid approach, emphasis on early postoperative alimentation and ambulation). One meta-analysis assessing GDT in this setting found no benefit (or harm) with its use.

In some studies, administration of optimal fluid volume using a GDT approach was combined with attempts to achieve optimal hemodynamic management, thereby ensuring optimal tissue and organ perfusion in individual patients. A 2018 meta-analysis of GDT (defined as fluid and/or vasopressor therapy titrated to hemodynamic goals (eg, cardiac output [CO]) was associated with lower risk of mortality (OR 0.66, 95% CI 0.50-0.87), pneumonia (OR 0.69, 95% CI 0.51-0.92), AKI (OR 0.73, 95% CI 0.58-0.92), wound infection (OR 0.48, 95% CI 0.37-0.63), and shorter length of hospital stay (-0.9 days; 95% CI -1.3 to -0.5 days), compared with fluid management at the discretion of treating clinicians (11,659 patients; 95 randomized trials). Another 2018 meta-analysis noted that studies using dynamic hemodynamic parameters to optimize intravascular volume and achieve optimal cardiac output (CO) or index (CI) reported less short-term mortality (OR 0.45, 95% CI 0.24-0.85) and less overall morbidity (OR 0.41, 95% CI 0.28-0.58), compared with standard fluid therapy (13 trials; 1100 total patients). Notably, data from other trials in this meta-analysis that employed GDT without attempts to optimize CO or CI that were analyzed separately did not note differences between GDT versus standard fluid management strategies (six trials; 524 patients). Similarly, a 2020 network meta-analysis noted that studies employing GDT aimed at optimizing intravascular volume as well as stroke volume and CO most effectively reduced the incidence of surgical site infections and other postoperative complications compared with usual care (43 trials; 8100 patients). One 2021 randomized trial employed computer-assisted individualized hemodynamic management that included a fluid management support system for GDT combined with a closed-loop system to titrate norepinephrine. The investigators reported higher mean CI at the end of the procedure as well as lower total requirements for norepinephrine and lower fluid balances in patients receiving computer-assisted management, compared with those receiving manually directed GDT and manually titrated norepinephrine.

•**Comparison with restrictive fluid strategies** – Whether GDT is superior to a restrictive fluid strategy is less certain as there are limited data comparing GDT to this approach. In a 2019 meta-analysis of randomized trials in patients undergoing major noncardiac surgery, very low-certainty evidence suggested that restrictive fluid therapy does not affect the risk of complications (RR 1.61, 95% CI 0.78-3.34; five studies; 484 participants), but may increase the risk of all-cause mortality (risk difference [RD] 0.03, 95% CI 0.00-0.06).

Avoid traditional liberal or fixed-volume approaches — Traditional liberal or fixed-volume approaches have been abandoned. Evidence suggests that these approaches resulted in administration of a large volume of crystalloid solution with likely fluid overload. Specifically, traditional fixed-volume approaches were based upon:

•Predetermined calculations that included administration of fluid to account for presumed preoperative deficits, as well as intraoperative blood and urinary losses.

•Additional fluid administered to compensate for calculated non-anatomic "third space" fluid losses during the surgical procedure. This practice is inappropriate, as it has been well-established that such third space losses do not exist.

•Large volumes of fluid as preloading before a neuraxial block.

•Replacement of initial blood loss with crystalloid volume that was three times the amount of lost blood. For example, if blood loss was estimated to be 500 to 1000 mL, then 1500 to 3000 mL of crystalloid was typically administered. This calculation is not supported by available data. Rather, optimal volume ratios to compensate for lost blood are estimated to be 1.5:1.0 for crystalloid and 1:1 for colloid, as discussed above.

These traditional fixed volume calculations for fluid administration resulted in a higher incidence of perioperative tissue and organ edema, and were associated with increased risk for adverse outcomes compared with restrictive or goal-directed approaches.

SUMMARY AND RECOMMENDATIONS

•**Causes and consequences of intravascular volume derangements** – Normovolemia/euvolemia should be maintained throughout the perioperative period to maintain adequate tissue perfusion. Both hypovolemia and hypervolemia are associated with postoperative morbidity.

•**Hypovolemia** – Hypovolemia is common due to preoperative, anesthesia-related, and surgery-related factors. Hypovolemia results in reduced cardiac output and tissue perfusion. Persistent hypovolemia can lead to shock and multiorgan failure.

•**Hypervolemia** – Development of hypervolemia is generally due to excessive volume administration (eg, to treat hemodynamic instability). Hypervolemia can result in reduced tissue perfusion due to tissue edema and clinically significant postoperative fluid retention.

•**Monitoring intravascular volume status**

•**Traditional static parameters** – Static physiological parameters such as blood pressure, heart rate, central venous pressure, and urine output are monitored during surgery to provide supplemental data regarding intravascular volume status. However, significant reduction in tissue perfusion may not be recognized.

•**Dynamic hemodynamic parameters** – Dynamic hemodynamic indices are used to assess responses to a fluid challenge (ie, volume responsiveness) and guide goal-directed fluid therapy in patients undergoing major invasive surgical procedures, particularly if large blood losses or fluid shifts are anticipated. These include:

-Respiratory variation using the intra-arterial waveform tracing for estimates or calculations of pulse pressure variations (PPV), stroke volume variation (SVV), systolic pressure variations (SPV) or stroke volume (SV).

-Ultrasound technologies including esophageal Doppler measurements of blood flow velocity in the descending thoracic aorta to estimate SV, or transesophageal echocardiography (TEE) or transthoracic echocardiography (TTE) for visual qualitative assessment or measurements of left ventricular cavity size.

•**Laboratory measurements** – Increased serum lactate levels or lactic acidosis indicate reduced global tissue perfusion, but are measured intermittently and do not reflect acute changes.

●**Selection of fluid**

•**Balanced crystalloid solutions** – We suggest a balanced electrolyte solution (eg, Ringer's lactate, Plasmalyte) rather than normal saline or colloid to maintain intraoperative normovolemia, including replacement of sensible and insensible losses, fluid boluses (typically 250 mL) in volume responsive patients, and replacement of lost blood on a 1.5:1.0 volume basis until a transfusion threshold is met.

•**Colloid solutions** – During blood loss, some clinicians prefer to administer colloid (eg, albumin) on a 1:1 volume basis until a transfusion threshold is met. We minimize colloid use due to insignificant hemodynamic benefits compared with crystalloids. We administer albumin rather than hydroxyethyl starch (HES) when a colloid is selected.

•**Blood transfusion** – Red blood cells (RBCs) are used to replace blood loss when a transfusion threshold is met. Decisions regarding transfusion of plasma derivatives (eg, fresh frozen plasma [FFP]) are based on estimates of blood loss and evidence of abnormal hemostasis.

●**Selection of a fluid management strategy**

•**Minimally or moderately invasive procedures** – For most adult patients undergoing minimally or moderately invasive surgical procedures, we administer 1 to 2 L of a balanced electrolyte solution to provide adequate intravascular hydration.

•**Major invasive procedures** – For major invasive surgical procedures, we suggest a restrictive (zero-balance) or a goal-directed therapy (GDT) approach to fluid administration (Grade 2B).

-**Restrictive strategy** – For procedures without significant anticipated blood loss (eg, <500 mL) and/or other fluid shifts, we use a restrictive approach replacing only fluid lost during the procedure (approximately 3 mL/kg per hour to replace sensible and insensible losses).

Goal-directed fluid therapy – For procedures with significant anticipated blood losses (eg, >500 mL) and/or fluid shifts, we use GDT with invasive dynamic hemodynamic parameters to achieve a pre-specified goal.

•**Avoid liberal fixed-volume strategies** – We avoid traditional liberal or fixed-volume approaches that lead to administration of large volumes of crystalloid solution, tissue edema, and associated adverse outcomes.

Debates about fluid management strategies are gathered around liberal strategy, restricted (conservative) strategy and goal-directed strategy so far. Liberal and restricted strategies are defined by different authors with variable volume ranges. For example, in one study, restricted fluid volume is defined as 1000 mL plus loss through drains, while in another study, patients in restricted fluid volume group were subjected to over 2000 mL fluid on the day of surgery. These variances make it difficult to consider these studies as a whole. Still, majority of authors studying this subject point out that restrictive strategy has positive effects on gastrointestinal function, wound healing and pulmonary function. Brandstrup et al stated that, excessive hydration with crystalloids is related with increased major complications, such as leakage, peritonitis, sepsis, pulmonary edema and bleeding in patients who underwent elective colorectal surgery. Also, intestinal edema is known to be related with increased bacterial translocation and multiple organ dysfunction syndrome rates. It can be concluded that, staying closer to the dehydration level is more reasonable, because it is safer and more efficient than administering large volumes to avoid dehydration. On the other hand, the liberal strategy is superior to the restricted strategy for reducing postoperative nausea, headache, dizziness and vomiting.

However, the goal directed strategy (GDS) is totally based on patient's current data, obtained from monitoring methods (See section: Monitoring body fluid status). Rivers and colleagues, one of the pioneers of this strategy, monitored CVP, mean arterial pressure, serum lactate, and mixed venous oxygen saturation in order to manage therapy in sepsis patients. Later studies were focused on monitoring hemodynamics, and the effects of administered fluids on patients. Now, GDS can be defined as an individualized fluid therapy, based on patient's fluid responsiveness; in other words, "fluid need". The extra volume, which won't be able to affect the left ventricle stroke volume is regarded as unnecessary; and as a matter of fact, hazardous. It makes perfect sense to totally evaluate patient's needs and replace what is needed. Still, efficiency of GDS is limited with the power of our monitoring tools, which is determined by accessibility, applicability of the tools and the quality of information we acquire from them.

PPV and SVV are defined to monitor the fluid need of the patient dynamically as it is stated above. Esophageal Doppler monitoring of cardiac volumes and aortic flow are also one of the helpful tools in GDS. In a systematic review of esophageal Doppler guided GDS studies; reduced hospital stay, fewer ICU admissions, and less inotropes usage were detected in GDS group. In a single center, blinded, prospective controlled trial, 128 patients who underwent colorectal resection were randomized into two groups. Each group was managed with esophageal Doppler or CVP guided fluid therapy during surgery. Intraoperative Doppler guided fluid management was associated with decrease in the duration of hospital stay. A randomized controlled study on 108 elective colorectal surgery patients also showed shorter hospital stay and decreased morbidity in GDS group. GDS is also advantageous in patients who undergo major surgery. A systematic review and meta-analysis studies by Hamilton on major surgery patients state that preemptive hemodynamic monitoring reduces mortality and morbidity. Similarly, Poeze et al showed that efforts to achieve an optimized hemodynamic condition resulted in a decreased mortality rate, in their meta-analysis study in 2005. Another meta-analysis also shows that GDS reduces both major and minor gastrointestinal complications after surgery.

In contrast with these studies, in a multicenter study, which included 762 high risk patients in 56 intensive care units, no significant effects of GDS were found. In this study, patients were randomly assigned to cardiac-index group, mixed venous oxygen-saturation group and standard therapy group. Predetermined hemodynamic targets were reached significantly better in the control group. There were no significant differences among the three groups, regarding mortality at six months. Even the subgroup analysis of patients, whose predetermined hemodynamic targets have been reached successfully, showed similar mortality rates among the three groups. Moreover, the number of dysfunctional organs and the duration of stay in the intensive care unit were similar in all groups.

Despite these evidences, low accessibility and applicability of esophageal Doppler are the major disadvantages of this method. This leads researchers to search for a more accessible and applicable method for common use in postoperative care unit, such as non-invasive pulse oximetry and invasive arterial pressure measurement. Thus, predictive value of pulse pressure variation, systolic pressure variation and stroke volume variation tests for fluid responsiveness are defined. All of these tests are applicable in an average postoperative care unit. However, the true value of these tests should be evaluated by larger studies. After that, optimization of patient monitoring devices should be done accordingly. Moreover, even PLR alone can provide important information about fluid responsiveness and lead the intensivists for GDS.

Since there is still insufficient number of randomized controlled trials with standardized criteria, the fluid management debates are going on. A consensus on criteria for each fluid management strategy should be made. We think that the related studies from all around the world with defined criteria are going to reveal the true value of each strategy.

Each surgeon should keep in mind that the patient is totally managed by the anesthesiologist during the surgery, so depending on the anesthesiologist's preference on fluid strategy, patient's fluid status after surgery may vary widely. Besides, intraoperative bleeding and other causes of surgical fluid loss should also be considered. During or after the surgery, the blood loss in patients with low hemoglobin levels is generally managed with erythrocyte suspensions. However, in patients with reasonable hemoglobin levels, appropriate fluid strategy should be chosen to avoid complications of transfusion. We think that determining the actual fluid status and the needs of a postoperative patient, by using monitoring tools and examining the report of the anesthesiologist, is of great importance. Management of postoperative fluid therapy should be done considering both patients' unique status and intraoperative events. Thus, surgeons must be aware of pros and cons of current fluid management strategies and their effects on surgical outcome. Although there has been a significant progress on fluid status monitoring and fluid management strategies, most clinicians still prefer their traditional approaches for postoperative fluid management. This tendency towards empirical fluid management can be replaced by evidence based strategies, only if significant benefits of new strategies are proved with multicenter randomized controlled trials which use standardized criteria. GDS is the most rational approach to assess the patient and maintain optimum fluid balance. However, accessible and applicable monitoring tools for determining patient's actual fluid need should be further studied and universalized.

The debate around colloids and crystalloids should also be considered with goal directed therapies. Advantages and disadvantages of each solution must be evaluated with the patient's specific condition.

CHAPTER EIGHT

CALCULATION OF FLUID AND ELECTROLYTES

Fluid and electrolyte balance should not only be considered as the external balance between the body and its environment, but also the internal balance between the extracellular and the intracellular compartments, and between the intravascular and interstitial compartments of the extracellular fluid. The sodium intake of an adult varies with diet, but the UK Reference Nutrient Intake suitable for maintenance in normal adult males and females is 70 mmol/24 hours, which should be accompanied by about 1.5 to 2.5 litres (25 to 35 mL/kg/24h) of water. Despite a wide variation in salt and water intake, in normal subjects the kidneys are able to maintain the extracellular fluid sodium concentration and osmolality within a narrow range. This is mainly achieved via the osmoreceptors and appropriate changes in vasopressin secretion affecting urinary concentration and free water clearance. In the presence of salt depletion the reninangiotensin-aldosterone system (RAAS) is activated with consequent reduction in urinary sodium to 5 mmol/L or less. Perhaps, due to the fact that our physiology has evolved in an environment with wide variations in water availability but a relative paucity of salt, the response to changes in water intake or to a low sodium intake is both rapid and efficient. In contrast, we have not been exposed during evolution to excessive salt intake or infusion until recent times, so that the response to sodium excess is sluggish and even normal subjects are slow to excrete an excess sodium load. The excretion of excess sodium appears to be dependent on the passive and permissive suppression of the RAAS rather than any positive action of natriuretic hormone and is, therefore, slow. In addition, studies have revealed that chloride ions cause renal vasoconstriction and reduce glomerular filtration rate resulting in sodium retention. Overview of fluid and electrolyte therapy in injury, illness and starvation It is important to distinguish between fluid and electrolytes required for normal existence (daily maintenance) and for resuscitation or replacement of abnormal losses. Crystalloid solutions contain low molecular weight salts or sugars which dissolve completely in water and pass freely between the intravascular and interstitial compartments. Colloid solutions contain larger molecular weight substances that do not dissolve completely and, depending on their molecular size, structure and the permeability of the capillaries of the patient, remain for a longer period in the vascular compartment than crystalloid solutions. Several times more crystalloid than colloid is required to achieve the same degree of vascular filling, and because crystalloid solutions move rapidly into the interstitial compartment, a side effect of crystalloid resuscitation is more interstitial oedema than in colloid treated patients. There have been many studies attempting to compare outcomes using 'colloids' or 'crystalloids' for volume replacement therapy. Unfortunately, there is widespread ignorance among doctors of the content and clinical properties of different colloids and crystalloids and it is incorrect to assume that all crystalloids and all colloids have similar properties. Colloids in common use are gelatines, albumin and hydroxyethyl starches and all have a significant sodium and chloride content. In general gelatines have a low molecular weight and are rapidly excreted through the kidneys giving short term volume expansion. In health, 40% of albumin is in the intravascular space and leaks through the capillary pores at a rate of 5%/h, being returned to the circulation via the lymphatic system. This flux increases in inflammatory conditions including sepsis and surgery which, together with the cost, has led to a decreased use of albumin as a volume expander for resuscitation. Hydroxyethyl starch preparations have widely differing properties depending on their average molecular weight, the degree of hydroxyethyl group substitution of the starch polymer and the C2 to C6 substitution ratio. There are well recognized and documented differences in the pharmacokinetic properties of these colloids.88 Because the choice of colloid is controversial, where recommendation is made in these guidelines for a 'suitable colloid,' the choice is left to the practitioner based on their own judgement and experience. However, it must be emphasized that because of the widely differing properties of colloids, care must be taken to ensure that sufficient water is given to avoid hyperoncotic states which may lead to acute kidney injury. No intravenous solution is without risk, and it is essential that the practitioner reads and follows the product instructions carefully and understands its limitations. With the exception of 5% dextrose solutions, almost all intravenous solutions contain sodium and chloride – some in near physiological concentrations of 140 mmol/L for sodium and 95 mmol/L for chloride, and others in 16 supranormal amounts e.g. 154 mmol/L Na and 154 mmol/L Cl in 0.9% (so-called "normal") saline. Several studies have demonstrated that, in comparison with more physiological solutions such as Hartmann's, even healthy subjects find it difficult to excrete solutions with a high chloride content such as 0.9% saline, which can cause hyperchloraemic acidosis and reduced glomerular filtration rate (GFR). For the injured or surgical patient it is even more difficult to excrete a salt and water load and to maintain normal serum osmolarity for several reasons.

1. The stress response to the injury or surgery causes anti-diuresis and oliguria mediated by vasopressin, catecholamines and the RAAS. Water and salt are therefore retained even in the presence of overload. The role of natriuretic peptides in this situation is unclear.

2. Following surgery, even when the serum osmolarity is reduced by administration of hypotonic fluid, the ability to excrete free water is limited because the capacity of the kidney to dilute, as well as to concentrate the urine, is impaired. Thus, excess free water infusion risks dilutional hyponatraemia.

3. If saline is infused, chloride overload accompanies sodium overload, and hyperchloraemia causes renal vasoconstriction and reduced GFR, further compromising the ability of the kidney to excrete sodium and water.

4. In more seriously ill surgical catabolic patients with significant co-morbidities and increased urea production, there is a reduced ability to concentrate urine. As a consequence, it requires two or more times the normal volume of urine to excrete a sodium and chloride load given in the perioperative period. Sodium and chloride excretion competes with excretion of nitrogen mobilized by the inflammatory response to surgery; a large proportion of the administered sodium, chloride and water is therefore retained as interstitial oedema.

5. Potassium depletion, due both to RAAS activity and the cellular loss of potassium which accompanies protein catabolism, reduces the ability to excrete a sodium load.

6. Acute kidney injury may occur due to abdominal compartment syndrome compressing the kidney externally and increased intra-capsular pressure due to oedematous renal tissue.

7. A sustained increase in systemic capillary permeability allows albumin and its attendant fluid (18 ml for every gram of albumin) to leak into the interstitial space into the interstitial space, thereby worsening interstitial oedema. This also causes intravascular hypovolaemia and further sodium and water retention by activation of the RAAS and secretion of vasopressin.

8. Intracellular sequestration of sodium and fluid due to lack of intracellular energy and failure of the cellular Na/K ATPase pump may occur in trauma, shock and fasting/malnutrition. In severe cases this gives rise to the so-called sick cell syndrome. In recent years there has been major concern expressed in the context of paediatric practice about the risks of dilutional hyponatraemia when hypotonic solutions are infused, but even in children where the risks of hyponatraemia appear to be greatest, it seems best to stress that intravenous fluids should be used with care and knowledge, rather than denounce any particular solution entirely and risk over-infusion of sodium.

9. In postoperative adults hyponatraemia can still occur when near-isotonic solutions are used.

10. In the absence of complications, oliguria occurring soon after operation is usually a normal physiological response to surgery. However, at the bedside a falling urine output is commonly interpreted as indicating hypovolaemia and prompts infusion of yet more sodium-containing fluids. This not only expands the blood volume (often unnecessarily) but also over-expands the interstitial fluid volume, causing oedema and weight gain, as well as causing haemodilution, resulting in reduced serum albumin concentration and reduced haematocrit.

The response to injury impairs the patient's ability to excrete the additional saline load, making interstitial oedema worse, compromising organ function and increasing the risk of morbidity and mortality. Confusion may also arise in the common context of dilutional hypoalbuminaemia and dilutional or euvolaemic hyponatraemia, both of which are erroneously taken as indications for more saline. The key question is whether or not the oliguric patient has significant intravascular hypovolaemia which needs treatment. That can usually be decided on clinical grounds, but in more severe cases, and particularly intra-operatively, it may necessitate more invasive monitoring. Clinical signs reflecting intravascular volume include capillary refill, jugular (central) venous pressure, and the trend in pulse and blood pressure. Urine output should be interpreted in the light of these clinical signs, bearing in mind the normal short term physiological effects of surgery on urine output.

Recommendation 1 Because of the risk of inducing hyperchloraemic acidosis in routine practice, when crystalloid resuscitation or replacement is indicated, balanced salt solutions e.g. Ringer's lactate/acetate or Hartmann's solution should replace 0.9% saline, except in cases of hypochloraemia e.g. from vomiting or gastric drainage.

Recommendation 2 Solutions such as 4%/0.18% dextrose/saline and 5% dextrose are important sources of free water for maintenance, but should be used with caution as excessive amounts may cause dangerous hyponatraemia, especially in the elderly. These solutions are not appropriate for resuscitation or replacement therapy except in conditions of significant free water deficit e.g. diabetes insipidus. There follow guidelines for managing the common haemodynamic and fluid and electrolyte problems associated with the pre-, peri- and post-operative periods. For many surgical procedures, the assessment of fluid requirements will be straightforward, relying on the usual clinical parameters. Although the gold standard for volume replacement is invasive cardiac monitoring, especially in high dependency patients, in most cases fluid requirements have to be assessed and monitored using the usual clinical approach of history, clinical examination and investigations. No symptom or sign is pathognomonic in isolation so that a proper assessment can only be made using a combination of different variables interpreted in the light of an understanding of the underlying pathophysiology. Changes over time in any variable or the response to an appropriate fluid challenge are usually more significant than any isolated measurement.

Before any intravenous fluid is prescribed, whether for resuscitation, replacement of ongoing losses, or just maintenance, the following should be considered:

a. Clinical assessment of the patient's fluid status, i.e. is there a deficit requiring replacement or does the patient need maintenance fluids only.

b. Where a fluid deficit is identified (e.g. haemorrhage or vasodilatation, diarrhoea or vomitus, insensible or renal losses), the nature of the fluid deficit must be identified.

c. The type of fluid which will best treat the deficit or maintain euvolaemia.

d. The appropriate rate of fluid administration guided by clinical assessment and safety limits.

e. The proposed clinical endpoint.

f. Continued monitoring of fluid and electrolyte status. Flow guided fluid therapy.

Historically, intravenous fluid administration to treat hypovolaemia has been guided by measurements of pulse rate, arterial pressure and central venous pressure. However, this approach seems to lack sensitivity and specificity in identifying volume deficit, leading to both inadequate and excessive fluid administration. Thus while the pattern of change in heart rate, arterial pressure and central venous pressure remain helpful markers of the effects of fluid administration on vascular filling they are influenced by other factors and do not have a linear relationship with cardiac output or tissue perfusion. The absolute values of these parameters may therefore fail to provide a reliable indication of the need for intravenous fluid administration. Because of the Frank-Starling relationship between cardiac filling pressure and stroke volume, the latter more reliably reflects vascular filling and hence fluid requirement. With the availability of minimally invasive techniques for measurement of stroke volume and cardiac output, using trans-oesophageal Doppler or pulse contour analysis, it has been possible to tailor fluid requirements more precisely to the needs of the individual patient. Clinical trials have demonstrated that fluid therapy guided by measurements of stroke volume and cardiac index result in significantly better clinical outcomes than those associated with traditional intraoperative monitoring. The beneficial effect is likely to relate to the early tailoring of fluid administration to the requirements of the individual patient rather than the blanket administration of extra fluid.

Maintenance requirements

In the adult, daily maintenance requirements are usually the reference nutrient intake (RNI) 70mmol sodium, and 1500-2500 ml water. In the absence of kidney disease or hyperkalaemia potassium needs to be provided in amounts close to the RNI for adults (40-80 mmol/day) – bearing in mind that in the unfed, low insulin state potassium may equilibrate more slowly with the intracellular space than when insulin or nutritionally significant amounts of carbohydrate are being administered.

Recommendation 3 To meet maintenance requirements, patients should receive sodium 50-100 mmol/day, potassium 40-80 mmol/day in 1.5-2.5 litres of water by the oral, enteral or parenteral route (or a combination of routes). Additional amounts should be given to correct deficit or continuing losses. Careful monitoring should be undertaken using clinical examination, fluid balance charts and regular weighing, when possible.

Recommendations for preoperative fluid management

a) *Euvolaemia* - maintenance Although most patients undergoing elective surgery will derive their preoperative fluids from normal oral intake, those undergoing emergency surgery may require fluid and electrolytes parenterally for both replacement and maintenance. Judgements in practice will be based on clinical parameters such as, jugular (central) venous pressure, pulse, blood pressure, capillary refill, the presence of oedema – and on fluid balance charting.

b) *Preoperative fasting* Intra-and postoperative complications of fluid and electrolyte balance often have their origins in the preparation of patients for theatre. It is important that, where possible, patients are brought to theatre in a state of normal and stable fluid and electrolyte balance. Where appropriate and possible, fluid retention caused by cardiac, renal or hepatocellular disease should be corrected prior to surgery. Patients should be screened nutritionally preoperatively and if malnourished consideration should be given to perioperative nutritional support. It is also important that patients are adequately hydrated prior to surgery. The traditional axiom of the need to withhold all oral diet and fluids overnight prior to induction of anaesthesia has been reviewed and expert guidance, issued both in North America12 and in the UK14 now considers it unnecessary and undesirable to restrict access to clear, non-particulate fluids for more than two hours prior to induction of anaesthesia. These guidelines have since been supported by a Cochrane collaboration review13 reporting the results of 22 trials in which a relaxation of the period of preoperative fasting, as indicated above, failed to alter significantly the volume or pH of gastric secretions (although aspiration and regurgitation were seldom reported and studies excluded patients at particular risk of morbidity related to aspiration).

Recommendation 4 In patients without disorders of gastric emptying undergoing elective surgery clear non-particulate oral fluids should not be withheld for more than two hours prior to the induction of anaesthesia.

c) *Preoperative administration of carbohydrate-rich beverages*

Relaxation in the required duration of preoperative fasting has led to studies of the effect of nutrients upon patient well-being and outcome after surgery. Preoperative oral administration of solutions of carbohydrate oligomers has been shown in several trials to attenuate preoperative thirst, anxiety and postoperative nausea and vomiting. It also substantially reduces postoperative insulin resistance, thereby improving the efficacy of postoperative nutritional support.

Recommendation 5 In the absence of disorders of gastric emptying or diabetes, preoperative administration of carbohydrate rich beverages 2-3 h before induction of anaesthesia may improve patient well-being and facilitate recovery from surgery. It should be considered in the routine preoperative preparation for elective surgery.

d) Bowel preparation

Many patients undergoing colonic surgery receive agents designed to empty the colon of solid faeces. Although mechanical bowel preparation was previously considered the cornerstone of safe colorectal surgery, the use of powerful laxative agents to empty the colon has significant adverse effects on perioperative fluid balance and the benefits may be less clear than previously thought. Although surveys have shown that the majority of colorectal surgeons in the UK, USA and Scandinavia continue to use mechanical bowel preparation, this results in dehydration and derangement of plasma electrolyte concentrations, even in previously healthy patients. Unless corrected preoperatively, these fluid and electrolyte derangements may complicate intra- and postoperative fluid management. This may exacerbate hypovolaemia after induction of anaesthesia, necessitating intraoperative over-replacement and causing retention of fluid in the extravascular space and postoperative oedema. Since mechanical bowel preparation may actually increase anastomotic leak rates and has failed to show any benefit in terms of reducing postoperative complication rates, consideration should be given to avoiding mechanical bowel preparation in routine colorectal surgery. In those cases in which mechanical bowel preparation is deemed appropriate, simultaneous intravenous fluid therapy should be administered to minimize the resulting fluid and electrolyte derangement.

Recommendation 6 Routine use of preoperative mechanical bowel preparation is not beneficial and may complicate intra and postoperative management of fluid and electrolyte balance. Its use should therefore be avoided whenever possible.

Recommendation 7 Where mechanical bowel preparation is used, fluid and electrolyte derangements commonly occur and should be corrected by simultaneous intravenous fluid therapy with Hartmann's or Ringer-Lactate/acetate type solutions.

e) *Replacement of Fluid Losses*

Fluid replacement should be appropriate to the fluid deficit (e.g. pure dehydration, lack of salt and water, or intravascular hypovolaemia). Replacement is also needed in salt losing renal, or endocrine disease. Increased evaporation, for example from hyperventilation, non-humidified face masks, open wounds or excessive sweating, results in proportionately greater need for free water replacement. Thus, after correction of any current intravascular hypovolaemia, the patient's daily infusion should comprise: i) Maintenance requirements for water and electrolytes ii) Replacement of water and electrolytes to correct external losses of body fluids from gastric aspirate, vomitus, diarrhoea, intestinal stoma output or enterocutaneous fistulae; or internally e.g. from pooling of fluid in the gut from ileus or obstruction. iii) Correction of any continuing intravascular fluid loss, e.g. from serous losses into wounds or increased albumin escape rate due to inflammation. It is sometimes forgotten that, in the presence of hypovolaemia, the efficient mechanism for maintaining serum osmolality in normal subjects is superseded by the need to preserve volume, so that the kidney retains whatever volume or composition of fluid is infused. If that fluid is hypotonic there is a risk, particularly in the elderly, of causing hyponatraemia and its clinical consequences.

Recommendation 8 Excessive losses from gastric aspiration/vomiting should be treated preoperatively with an appropriate crystalloid solution which includes an appropriate potassium supplement. Hypochloraemia is an indication for the use of 0.9% saline, with appropriate additions of potassium and care not to produce sodium overload. Losses from diarrhoea/ileostomy/small bowel fistula/ileus/obstruction should be replaced volume for volume with Hartmann's or Ringer-Lactate/acetate type solutions. "Saline depletion," for example due to excessive diuretic exposure, is best managed with a balanced electrolyte solution such as Hartmann's.

f) *High risk surgical patients*

It is now well recognized that around 15% of patients undergoing in-patient surgical procedures are at particular risk of complications and death. Factors which place such patients at increased risk relate both to the patient and to the surgical procedure and include advanced age, the presence of co-morbid disease, major and emergency procedures. At present only a minority of such patients are admitted to critical care in the perioperative period. Optimal perioperative fluid management is of great importance in improving outcomes for the high-risk surgical patient. There is also a growing body of evidence to suggest that the use of low dose inotropic therapy may also be of benefit in selected cases. Preoperative 'goal directed haemodynamic therapy' using protocols incorporating fluid and inotropic therapy to achieve predetermined goals for cardiac output and systemic oxygen delivery in very high-risk surgical patients has been shown to improve outcome. However, such an approach in high-risk surgical patients has not been widely implemented, mainly because of the problems associated with arranging preoperative admission to intensive care. In the UK current practice focuses on the optimal fluid management of patients during surgery. In addition, for high-risk patients the use of early postoperative Goal Directed Haemodynamic Therapy may also offer additional benefit.

Recommendation 9 In high-risk surgical patients preoperative treatment with intravenous fluid and inotropes should be aimed at achieving predetermined goals for cardiac output and oxygen delivery as this may improve survival.

g) Fluid resuscitation prior to urgent or emergency surgery

Patients requiring urgent or emergency surgery may present with a widely differing pattern of fluid and electrolyte deficit or redistribution e.g. from haemorrhage, sequestration of fluid within the gut and widespread capillary leak due to sepsis. Although the primary aim of preoperative preparation is to ensure adequate tissue perfusion and oxygenation, there may be little time for detailed assessment and fluid resuscitation. The initial fluid and blood product requirement may have to be based on clinical criteria alone. These include pulse rate, respiratory rate, arterial pressure, urine output, conscious level (Glasgow coma score), capillary refill time and the presence of peripheral cyanosis. Under these circumstances, clinical measures of end-organ function such as urine output and Glasgow coma score are particularly important and although less sensitive than flow-based assessments of vascular filling, should be carefully assessed in the context of the individual patient. Arterial (or venous) blood gas analysis allows confirmation of a clinical impression of hypoperfusion as evidenced by an increasing base deficit or increased plasma lactate concentration. These biochemical markers are easily assessed and of great prognostic value. It is important to make regular adjustments based on changes in the clinical parameters which first indicated hypovolaemia. Infusion of boluses of 250 ml of hypertonic crystalloid or colloid has been shown to have some benefit in trauma patients, especially those with head injuries. *Recommendation 10* Although currently logistically difficult in many centres, wherever possible preoperative or operative hypovolaemia should be diagnosed by flow-based measurements. The clinical context should also be taken into account as this will provide an important indication of whether hypovolaemia is possible or likely. When direct flow measurements are not possible, hypovolaemia will be diagnosed clinically on the basis of pulse, peripheral perfusion and capillary refill, venous (JVP/CVP) pressure and GCS together with acid-base and lactate measurements. A low urine output can be misleading and needs to be interpreted in the context of the patient's cardiovascular parameters above. Diagnosis of hypovolaemia.

Recommendation 11 Hypovolaemia due predominantly to blood loss should be treated with either a balanced crystalloid solution or a suitable colloid until packed red cells are available. Hypovolaemia due to severe inflammation such as infection, peritonitis, pancreatitis or burns should be treated with either a suitable colloid or a balanced crystalloid. In either clinical scenario, care must be taken to administer sufficient balanced crystalloid and colloid to normalise haemodynamic parameters and minimise overload. The ability of critically ill patients to excrete excess sodium and water is compromised, placing them at risk of severe interstitial oedema. The administration of large volumes of colloid without sufficient free water (e.g.5% dextrose) may precipitate a hyperoncotic state.

Recommendation 12 When the diagnosis of hypovolaemia is in doubt and the central venous pressure is not raised, the response to a bolus infusion of 200 ml of a suitable colloid or crystalloid should be tested. The response should be assessed using the patient's cardiac output and stroke volume measured by flow-based technology if available. Alternatively, the clinical response may be monitored by measurement/estimation of the pulse, capillary refill, CVP and blood pressure before and 15 minutes after receiving the infusion. This procedure should be repeated until there is no further increase in stroke volume and improvement in the clinical parameters.

Volume to be given: The basic principle of maintaining adequate tissue perfusion must continue to be followed during surgery. However, this is influenced by a number of factors including the vasodilatory effects of anaesthesia, blood loss, the hormonal response to surgery, increased capillary permeability and albumin escape rate, and increased insensible losses. A number of single centre trials have evaluated flow guided intra-operative fluid therapy for patients undergoing orthopaedic and abdominal surgery. Recent meta-analyses suggest this approach is associated with reductions in the duration of postoperative hospital stay and complication rates, although not mortality. Those studies of patients undergoing abdominal surgery have identified an earlier return to enteral feeding associated with flow directed fluid therapy. This observation may be explained by a reduction in mesenteric hypoperfusion and therefore postoperative ileus.

Recommendation 13 In patients undergoing some forms of orthopaedic and abdominal surgery, intraoperative treatment with intravenous fluid to achieve an optimal value of stroke volume should be used where possible, as this is likely to reduce postoperative complication rates and duration of hospital stay. Very few published data are available to guide fluid management of patients undergoing urgent and emergency surgery. However, in some studies of goal directed haemodynamic therapy a subgroup of patients recruited underwent emergency surgery and appeared to benefit from this approach. This is also supported by related research which describes significant improvements in survival when goal directed haemodynamic therapy is utilised early in the management of medical and surgical patients presenting to hospital with severe sepsis and septic shock. Further research is required to confirm this impression. *Recommendation 14* Patients undergoing non-elective major abdominal or orthopaedic surgery should receive intravenous fluid to achieve an optimal value of stroke volume during and for the first eight hours after surgery. This may be supplemented by a low dose dopexamine infusion. It is essential that the haemodynamic state of the patient is assessed when they arrive on the ward, HDU or ICU. Before deciding the postoperative fluid regimen, adjustment must be made for the volume and content of fluids given pre operatively and perioperatively together with perioperative fluid losses. A frequent mistake is to implement a standard postoperative fluid regimen instead of tailoring it to the individual patient's needs. This is partly because details of fluid balance are often poorly recorded on several different documents. It is important to recognize the point where adequate replacement or resuscitation has been achieved and the goal changes to fluid and sodium mobilisation. Overloading with fluids is frequently caused by continuing a replacement regime for longer than necessary. Postoperatively almost all patients will be in positive sodium and fluid balance often reflected by interstitial oedema, and the aim should be to restore the patient to their normal weight and extracellular volume status. Provided the patient is euvolaemic, the aim should be to allow cautious net excretion of the excess salt and water. The postoperative fluid regime should be considered in relation to the current balance due to prior fluid treatment pre- and intra-operatively. Adjustment should also be made for perioperative fluid losses and the haemodynamic state of the patient when they arrive on the ward, HDU or ICU.

Recommendation 15 Details of fluids administered must be clearly recorded and easily accessible.

Recommendation 16 When patients leave theatre for the ward, HDU or ICU their volume status should be assessed. The volume and type of fluids given perioperatively should be reviewed and compared with fluid losses in theatre including urine and insensible losses.

Recommendation 17 In patients who are euvolaemic and haemodynamically stable a return to oral fluid administration should be achieved as soon as possible.

Recommendation 18 In patients requiring i.v. maintenance fluids, these should be sodium poor and of low enough volume until the patient has returned their sodium and fluid balance over the peri operative period to zero. When this has been achieved the i.v. fluid volume and content should be those required for daily maintenance and replacement of any on-going additional losses. *Recommendation 19*

The haemodynamic and fluid status of those patients who fail to excrete their peri operative sodium load, and especially whose urine sodium concentration is < 0.5 ml/kg/hr. Isolated oliguria soon after surgery does not necessarily reflect hypovolaemia and should be evaluated in the context of the patient's volume status. Treatment of hypovolaemia in surgical patients with AKI should follow similar principles to those outlined for patients with normal renal function. However, there are some provisos; it must be recognised that patients developing pre- kidney AKI secondary to hypovolaemia will try to conserve salt and water resulting in a reduced urine output. In this setting there will be reduced capacity to excrete fluid and electrolytes. Excessive administration of salt and water will result in interstitial oedema and a greater risk of developing hyperkalaemia. Early referral to the renal team is recommended to help with clinical evaluation of the patient's volume status and appropriate fluid management. Traditionally there has been concern in prescribing fluids containing potassium to patients with AKI due to the risks of precipitating hyperkalaemia. Ringer's lactate has been demonstrated to be safe for plasma volume expansion in patients undergoing renal transplantation.1 In this small study patients receiving 0.9% saline had an increased incidence of metabolic acidosis and hyperkalaemia compared with patients receiving Ringer's lactate. The question has been raised as to whether different colloid solutions may pose a risk of AKI. It is certainly important to prescribe adequate crystalloid when administering colloid solutions to avoid inducing a hyperoncotic state. However, there are data that have demonstrated higher molecular weight hydroxyethyl starch (hetastarch and pentastarch MW ≥ 200 kDa), is associated with an increased risk of AKI in critically ill patients with sepsis. A further study has reported that kidneys retrieved from brain-dead organ donors who received hydroxyethyl starch (MW 200 kDa), developed osmotic-nephrosis-like lesions and had impaired immediate kidney function. In contrast a large multicentre observational study of critically ill patients showed administration of HES had no influence on renal function or the need for renal replacement therapy in the ICU, and there is evidence of improved renal function with low molecular weight HES (6% 130/0.4) compared with gelatine in vascular surgery. Rhabdomyolysis (Crush Syndrome) has many causes including direct muscle trauma and compartment syndrome. Cell lysis results in release of myoglobin which is freely filtered by the kidneys and in the setting of hypovolaemia and acidosis can cause AKI. Effective management requires aggressive fluid resuscitation with a crystalloid solution. There is limited clinical evidence to support the common practice of alkalinising the urine through the administration of sodium bicarbonate solution.

Recommendation 24 Based on current evidence higher molecular weight hydroxyethyl starch (hetastarch and pentastarch MW ≥ 200 kDa) should be avoided in patients with severe sepsis due to an increased risk of AKI. *Recommendation 25* Higher molecular weight hydroxyethyl starch (hetastarch and pentastarch MW ≥ 200 kDa) should be avoided in brain-dead kidney donors due to reports of osmoticnephrosis-like lesions.

Recommendation 26 Balanced electrolyte solutions containing potassium can be used cautiously in patients with AKI closely monitored on HDU or ICU in preference to 0.9% saline. If free water is required 5% dextrose or dextrose saline should be used. Patients developing hyperkalaemia or progressive AKI should be switched to non potassium containing crystalloid solutions such as 0.45% saline or 4%/0.18 dextrose/saline Ringer's lactate versus 0.9% saline for patients with AKI.

Recommendation 27 In patients with AKI fluid balance must be closely observed and fluid overload avoided. In patients who show signs of refractory fluid overload, renal replacement therapy should be considered early to mobilize interstitial oedema and correct extracellular electrolyte and acid base abnormalities.

Recommendation 28 Patients at risk of developing AKI secondary to rhabdomyolysis must receive aggressive fluid resuscitation with an isotonic crystalloid solution to correct hypovolaemia. There is insufficient evidence to recommend the specific composition of the crystalloid.

Normal water and electrolyte balance

- Intravenous fluid is the giving of fluid and substances directly into a vein.
- Water forms about 60% of total body weight in men and 55% in women.
- Men will therefore contain about 42 litres, and a 70 kg. woman nearer 38 litres. The reason for this difference between the sexes is that women contain an extra 5% adipose tissue.
- Extracellular water is distributed between the plasma and the interstial space.

➲ To calculate total body water (TBW) need:

↳ Male TBW = body weight (BW) × 0.6

↳ Female TBW = body weight (BW) × 0.5

Example 1:

In a 70 kg male:

TBW= 70x 0.6 = 42 L

Intracelular volume = 0.66 x 42 = 28 L

Extracelular volume = 0.34 x 42 =14 L

↳ Interstitial volume = 0.75 x 14 = 10.5 L

↳ Intravascular volume = 0.25 x 14 = 3.5 L

Serum	Na^+	K^+	Cl^-	$HCO3^-$	Ca^{2+}
Normal value (mmol/L)	135-145	3.5-5	98-108	20-28	2.2-2.6

Table 9: Normal values of serum electrolytes

II. Assessing losses in the surgical patients

➲ Requirements of fluid and electrolytes

First: Fluid requirements

- the normal daily fluid requirement is ~30–35 ml/kg (~2500 ml/day).
- Normal adult requires approximately 35 cc/kg/d
- After the first month of life, fluid requirements decrease and the '4/2/1'formula can be used to estimate maintenance fluid requirements:

↪ the first 10 kg of body weight requires 4 ml/kg/h

↪ the next 10 kg 2ml/kg/h

↪ thereafter each kg of body requires 1ml/kg/h.

The estimated maintenance fluid requirements of a 35 kg child would therefore be: (10 x 4) + (10 x 2) + (15 x 1) = 75 ml/hr

- Hypovolemia, when TBW is deficit, it's not compatible with normal organ perfusion. Its causes are:

↪ GI: diarrhoea, vomiting, etc.

↪ renal: diuresis

↪ vascular: haemorrhage

↪ skin: burns

- Hypervolemia, when TBW is in excess it's necessary for organ perfusion, but usually harmful. Its causes are:

↪ Iatrogenic.

↪ Heart / Liver / Kidney failure.

➲ How to calculate fluid requirements (total requirement of fluids for a patient per day):

➲ Normal daily losses and requirements for fluids and electrolytes

Fluid requirements =of lost fluids per day + insensible loss

- **Normal fluid needed** = body weight x 35
- **Lost fluids:** Know if the patient has diarrhea, any disease or abnormal GI loss (e.g nasogastric tube suctioning) to measure the lost fluids
- **Insensible water loss** makes up about 500 ml a day. It is the amount of fluids lost on a daily basis from the lungs, skin, respiratory tract and water excreted in the faeces.

↪ Pyrexia increases water loss from the skin by approximately 200 ml/day for each 1°C rise in temperature.

↪ sweating and use of non-humidified oxygen increase insensible water loss as well.

	Volume (ml)	Na+ (mmol)	K+ (mmol)
Urine	2000	80	60
Insensible losses(skin and respiratory tract)	700	--	--
Faeces	300	--	10
Minus endogenous water	300	--	--
Total	2700	80	70

Table 10

How to measure fluid requirements per hour: (3 methods)

1. Find out the normal fluid requirement and divide it by 24 hours.
2. Apply the '4/2/1'formula
3. Body weight (kg) + 40 = IVF rate

- Assumes no significant renal or cardiac disease and NPO {nil per os (nothing by mouth)}
- This is the maintenance IVF rate, it must be adjusted for any dehydration or ongoing fluid loss.
- Conversely, if the patient is taking fluids PO (by mouth), the IVF rate must be decreased accordingly.
- Daily electrolytes, BUN (Blood urea nitrogen), Creatinine, Input/Output, and if possible, weight should be monitored in patients receiving significant IVF.

Example 2

Fluid requirements of a 70kg man = 70 + 40 = 110 cc/hr

Second: Electrolytes requirement

Sodium

- **1-3 meq/kg/day**
- 70 kg male requires 70-210 meq NaCl in 2600 cc fluid per day.

- 0.45% saline contains 77 meq NaCl per liter.
- 2.6 L x 77 = 200 meq

Thus, 0.45% saline is usually used as maintenance of IV fluid assuming no other volume or electrolyte issues.

Potassium

- **1 meq/kg/day**
- K can be added to IV fluids. Remember this increases osm load.
- 20 meq/L is a common IVF additive.
- This will supply basal needs in most pa:ents who are NPO.

- If significantly hypokalemia, order separate K supplementation.
- Oral potassium supplementation is always preferred when feasible.
- Should not be administered at rate greater than 10-20 mmol/hr

Calculation of osmolality

↪ Difficult: measure and add all active osmoles (molecules)

↪ Easy = [sodium in blood x 2] + urea + glucose (1)

↪ Normal = 280 - 290 mosm / kg

- We measure it to know if the fluid is isotonic, hypotonic or hypertonic

- In conditions such as hypernatremia, renal failure (raised urea) or hyperglycemia, osmolality is raised.

(1) As sodium is the major extracellular cation, the majority of extracellular anions will be equal to its concentration. Urea and glucose make up the remaining significant osmoles,

Example 3

70 kg male requires 70 - 210 mEq NaCl in 2600 cc fluid per day.

- In such case, you give the patient half normal saline. Why?
- The pa:ent needs 70 – 210 mEq NaCl in 2.6 L a day,

The half normal saline contains 77 mEq NaCl per liter
When you measure it: 77 x 2.6 = 200 mEq, It meets the daily requirement of the patient.

- Unlike giving normal saline which contains 154 mEq NaCl per liter.

- Intravenous fluid is the giving of fluid and substances directly into a vein.

CHAPTER NINE

GIBBS – DONNAN EQUILIBRIUM

Gibbs – Donnan Equilibrium: refers to movement of chargeable particles through a semi permeable membrane against its natural location to achieve equal concentrations on either side of the semi permeable membrane. For example, movement of Cl- from extra cellular space (natural location) to intracellular space (unusual location) in case of hyperchloremic metabolic acidosis because negatively charged proteins (natural location in intravascular space) are large molecules that cannot cross the semi permeable membrane for this equilibrium.

Sodium moves freely between the vascular and interstitial spaces, but is actively extruded from the intracellular space; it is therefore the principle extracellular cation. It is also the cation that we most frequently administer by giving intravenous saline (NaCl). When we do this, we increase extracellular tonicity and water must move from the intracellular space to normalise osmolality.

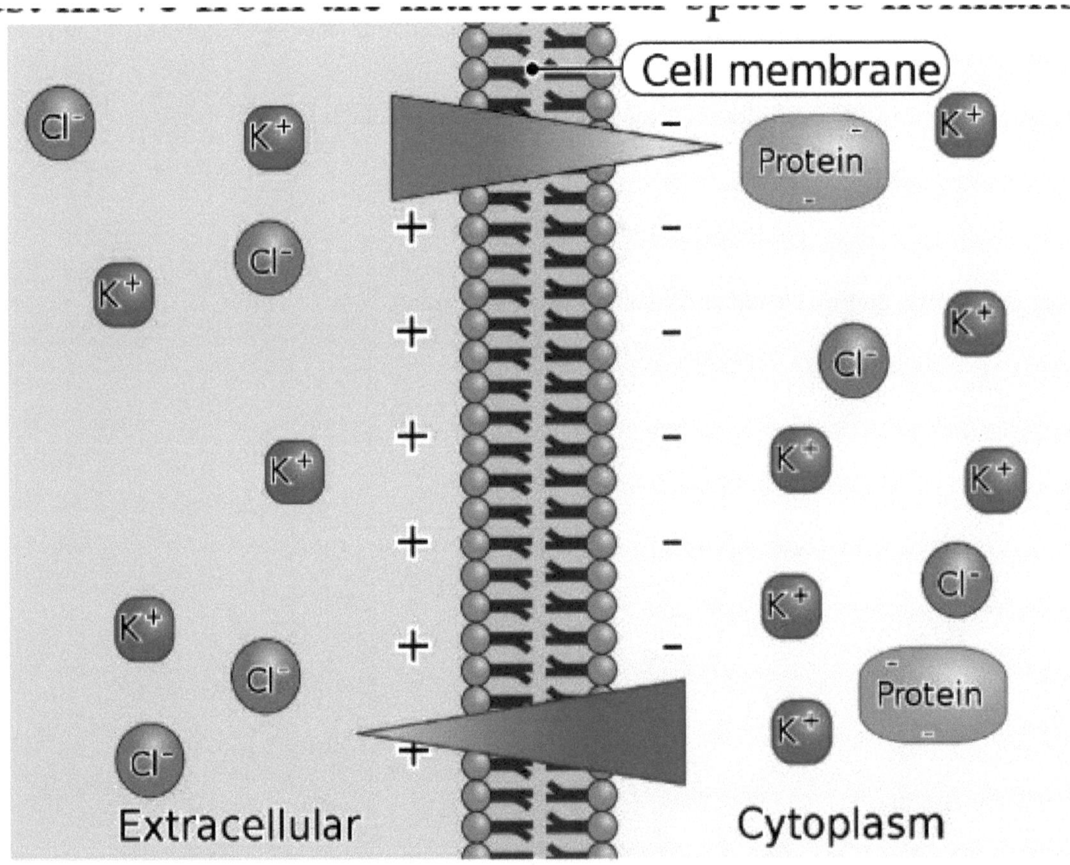

Fig. 11

- The Gibbs-Donnan effect describes the unequal distribution of permeant charged ions on either side of a semipermeable membrane which occurs in the presence of impermeant charged ions.
- At Gibbs-Donnan equilibrium,

  - On each side of the membrane, each solution will be electrically neutral
  - The product of diffusible ions on one side of the membrane will be equal to the product of diffusible ions on the other side of the membrane
  - The electrochemical gradients produced by unequal distribution of charged ions produces a transmembrane potential difference which can be calculated using the Nernst equation
  - The presence of impermeant ions on one side of the membrane creates an osmotic diffusion gradident attracting water into that compartment.

- The mechanisms which maintain the resting membrane potential and the mechanisms of the Gibbs-Donnan effect are different phenomena:

  - The Donnan equlibrium is a completely passive process: i.e. no active transporters are involved in maintaining this equilibrium.
  - A Donnan equilibrium is an *equilibrium,* i.e. ion concentrations on either side of the barrier are static.
  - If the Donnan equilibrium were to become fully established, the increase in intracellular ions would cause cells to swell due to the osmotic influx of water.
  - At a Donnan equilibrium, the resting membrane potential would be only about -20 mV. This potential would exist even if the membrane permeability for all ions was the same.
  - The resting membrane potential, in contrast, requires different permeabilities for potassium and for sodium, and is maintained actively by constant Na^+/K^+ ATPase activity.
  - Because biological membranes (especially of exciteable tissues) are never at equilibrium, the Goldman-Hodgkin-Katz equation is usually a better choice for explaining their electrochemical behaviour.

Explanation of the Gibbs-Donnan effect

The **Gibbs–Donnan effect** (also known as the **Donnan's effect**, **Donnan law**, **Donnan equilibrium**, or **Gibbs–Donnan equilibrium**) is a name for the behaviour of charged particles near a semi-permeable membrane that sometimes fail to distribute evenly across the two sides of the membrane. The usual cause is the presence of a different charged substance that is unable to pass through the membrane and thus creates an uneven electrical charge. For example, the large anionic proteins in blood plasma are not permeable to capillary walls. Because small cations are attracted, but are not bound to the proteins, small anions will cross capillary walls away from the anionic proteins more readily than small cations.

Thus, some ionic species can pass through the barrier while others cannot. The solutions may be gels or colloids as well as solutions of electrolytes, and as such the phase boundary between gels, or a gel and a liquid, can also act as a selective barrier. The electric potential arising between two such solutions is called the Donnan potential.

The effect is named after the American physicistJosiah Willard Gibbs who proposed it in 1878 and the British chemistFrederick G. Donnan who studied it experimentally in 1911.

The Donnan equilibrium is prominent in the triphasic model for articular cartilage proposed by Mow and Lai, as well as in electrochemical fuel cells and dialysis.

Thc Donnan effect is tactic pressure attributable to cations (Na^+ and K^+) attached to dissolved plasma proteins.

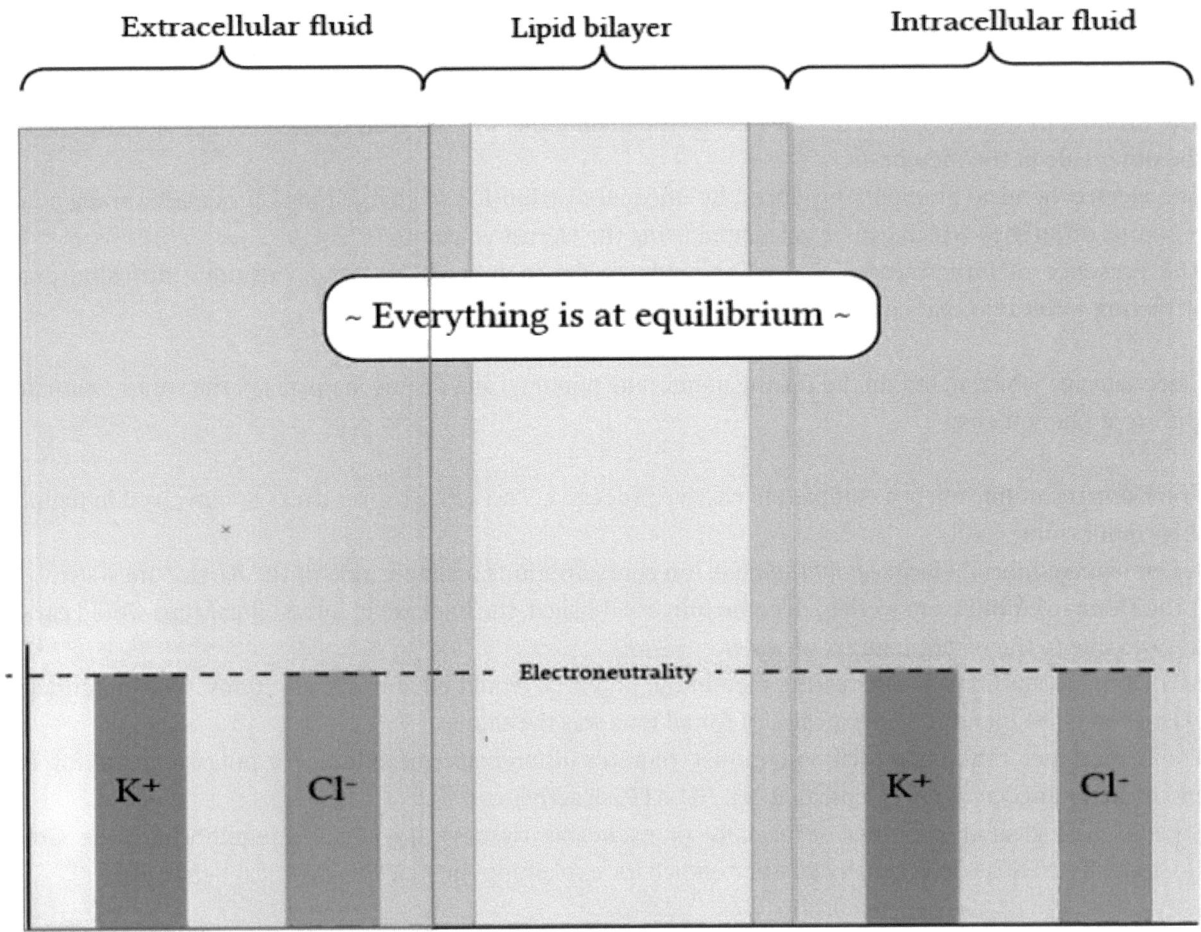

Fig. 12

- The concentration of electrolytes in each compartment is equal, and electroneutrality of each compartment is maintained. If one were that way inclined, one might be able to represent this equilibrium as an equation, where *"int"* means intracellular and *"ext"* means extracellular.
- $[K^+]_{ext} \times [Cl^-]_{ext} = [K^+]_{int} \times [Cl^-]_{int}$
- Now, let's replace the KCl in the intracellular compartment with a potassium proteinate, i.e. a molecule where the potassium comes with some negatively charged protein (Pr^-) as its conjugate. The protein is not diffusible, and so it does not participate in the equation above (i.e. $[Pr^-]_{ext}$can never be the same as $[Pr^-]_{int}$). Now, intracellular and extracellular concentrations of potassium remain the same (and so the potassium is not inclined to diffuse anywhere), but now there is a concentration gradient for the chloride ions. Let's say the original concentration was 100 mmol/L; the concentration gradient is now from 100 mmol/L to 0 mmol/L.

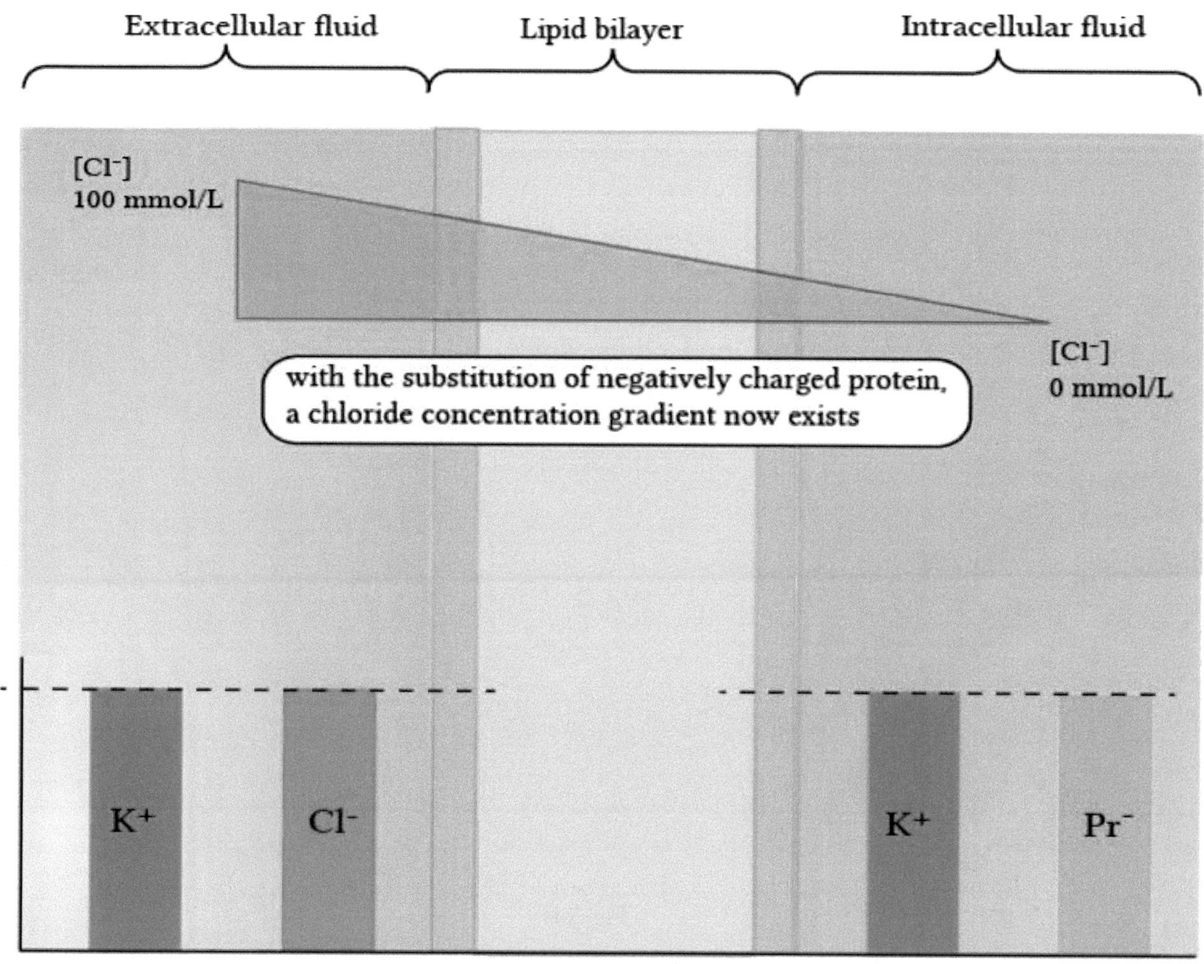

Fig. 13

- So, because the membrane is permeable to chloride ions and now there's a concentration gradient, some of the chloride ions diffuse into the intracellular compartment. By necessity, they are accompanied by some potassium ions, so that electroneutrality is preserved.

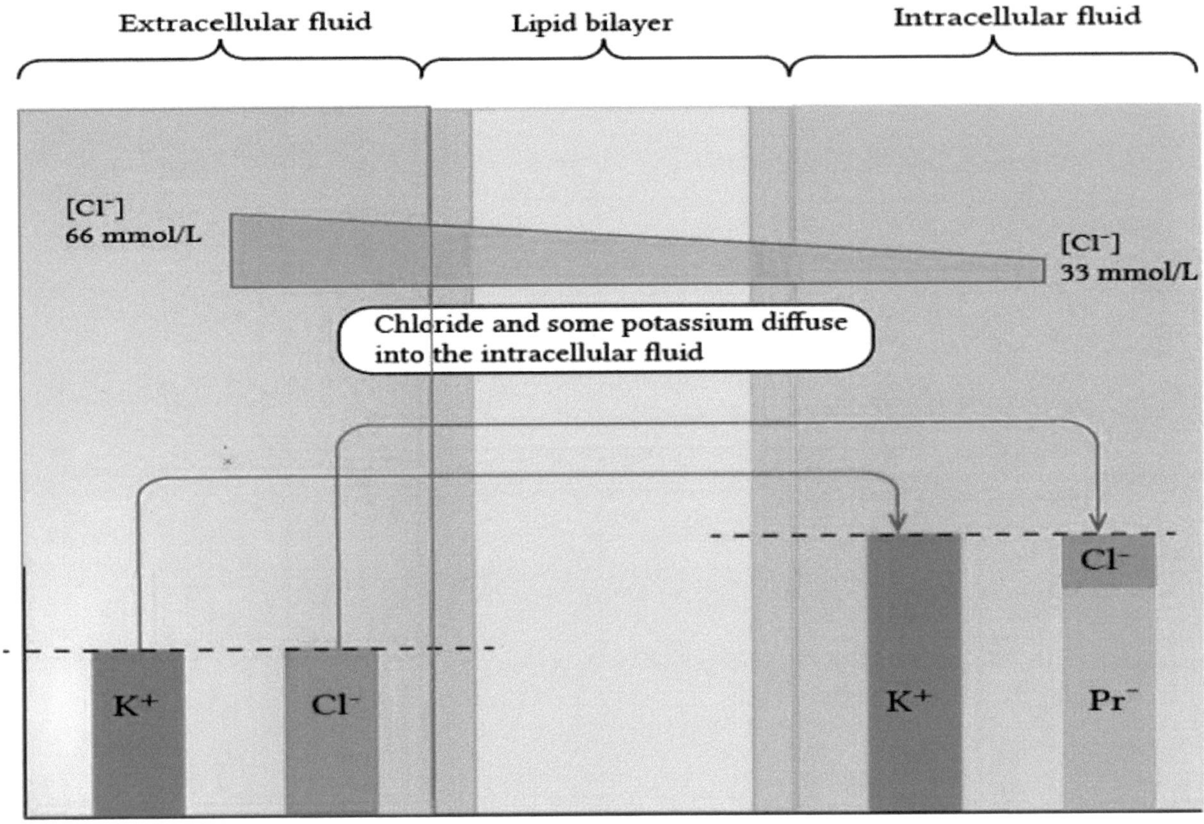

Fig. 14

- The chloride ions are also repelled by the negatively charged protein in the intracellular compartment, and so the bulk of the chloride remains on the extracellular side of the membrane.

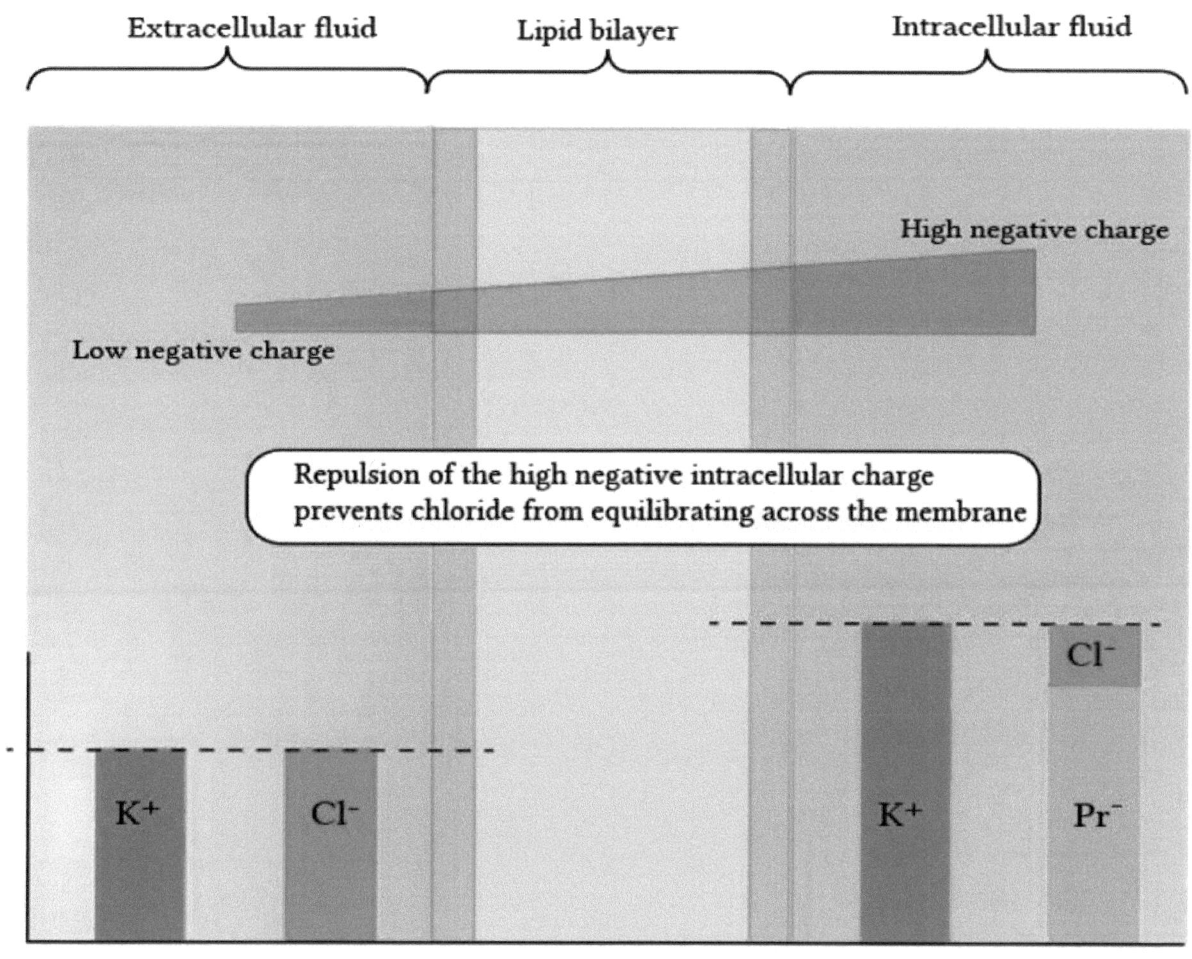

Fig. 15

- So; electroneutrality is preserved. So is the total concentration balance of diffusible ions, such that the product of extracellular diffusable ion concentrations is the same as the product of intracellular diffusible ion concentrations:
- $[K^+]_{ext} \times [Cl^-]_{ext} = [K^+]_{int} \times [Cl^-]_{int}$
- Without falling into a rabbit hole of quadratic equations, it will suffice to say that if we started with concentrations of 100 mmol/L on either side, once protein is added we end up with about 33 mmol/L of chloride on the intracellular side, as well as 133 mmol/L of potassium; the extra ion molecules came from the extracellular fluid, and therefore that compartment becomes relatively ion-poor, with about 66.6 mmol/L of each species.
- Now, of course, because there is an electrical gradient as well as a chemical diffusion gradient acting on the ions, there will be a slightly unequal distribution of charge across the membrane, leading to a potential difference. This is a familiar concept discussed at great lengths in the chapter on the resting membrane potential. It will suffice to say that for each ion the balance between the concentration gradient and the electrical gradient is described by the Nernst equation, and the total potential difference across the membrane which results from the combined effect of all the ion movements can be described by the Goldman–Hodgkin–Katz equation, taking into account the fact that for each ion the membrane permeability will be different. In short, the Gibbs-Donnan effect sets up a transmembrane potential difference because the distribution of charged ions across the membrane is uneven.

This potential difference is apparently quite small. Sperelakis (2011) gives a value of -20 mV, though it is not clear where that number comes from.

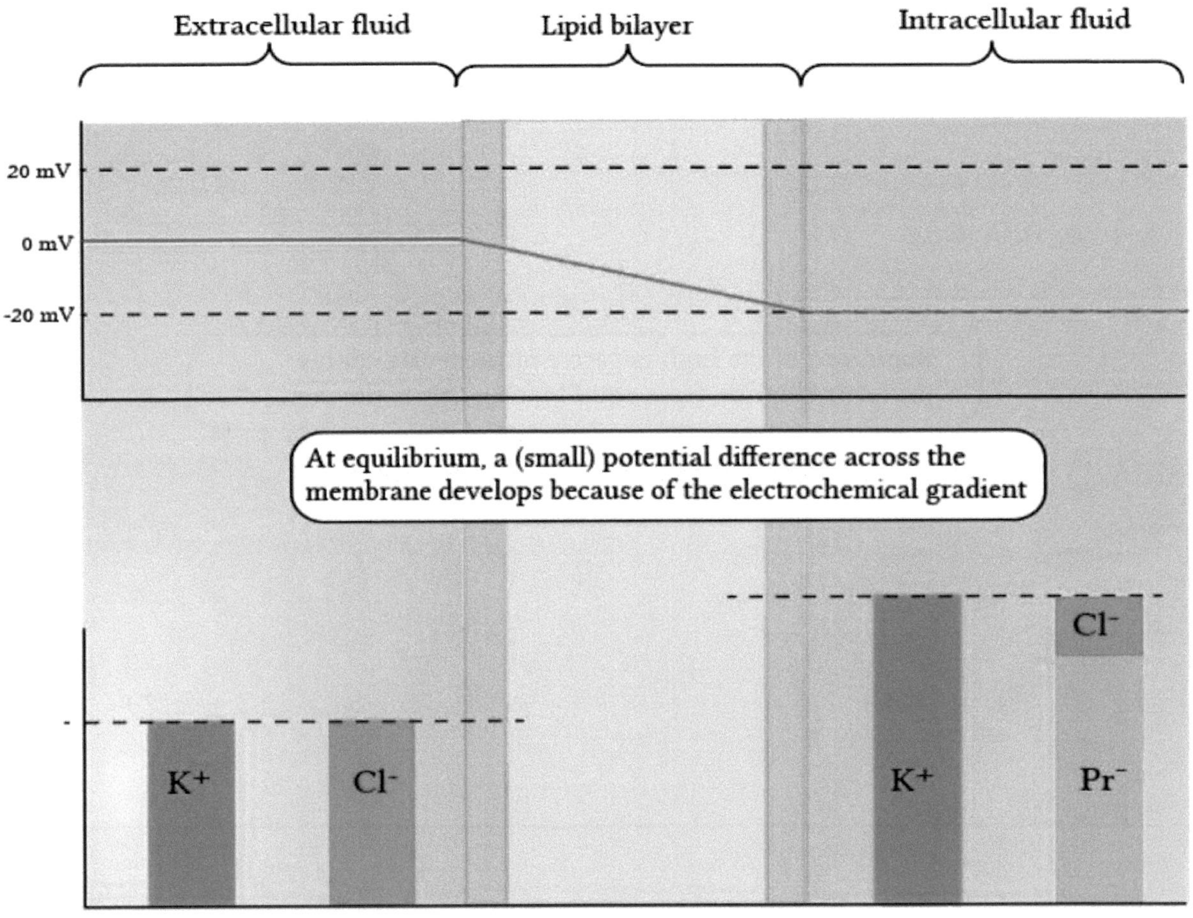

Fig. 15

- So, we are now at the Gibbs-Donnan equilibrium: the products of *diffusible* ion concentrations must be the same on both sides, and on each side of the membrane electrical neutrality is preserved. However, the presence of non-diffusible protein makes the total concentration of intracellular molecules much higher than the concentration of extracellular molecules:
- Intracellular concentration = $[K^+]_{int} + [Cl^-]_{int} + [Pr^-]_{int}$
- Extracellular concentration = $[K^+]_{ext} + [Cl^-]_{ext}$

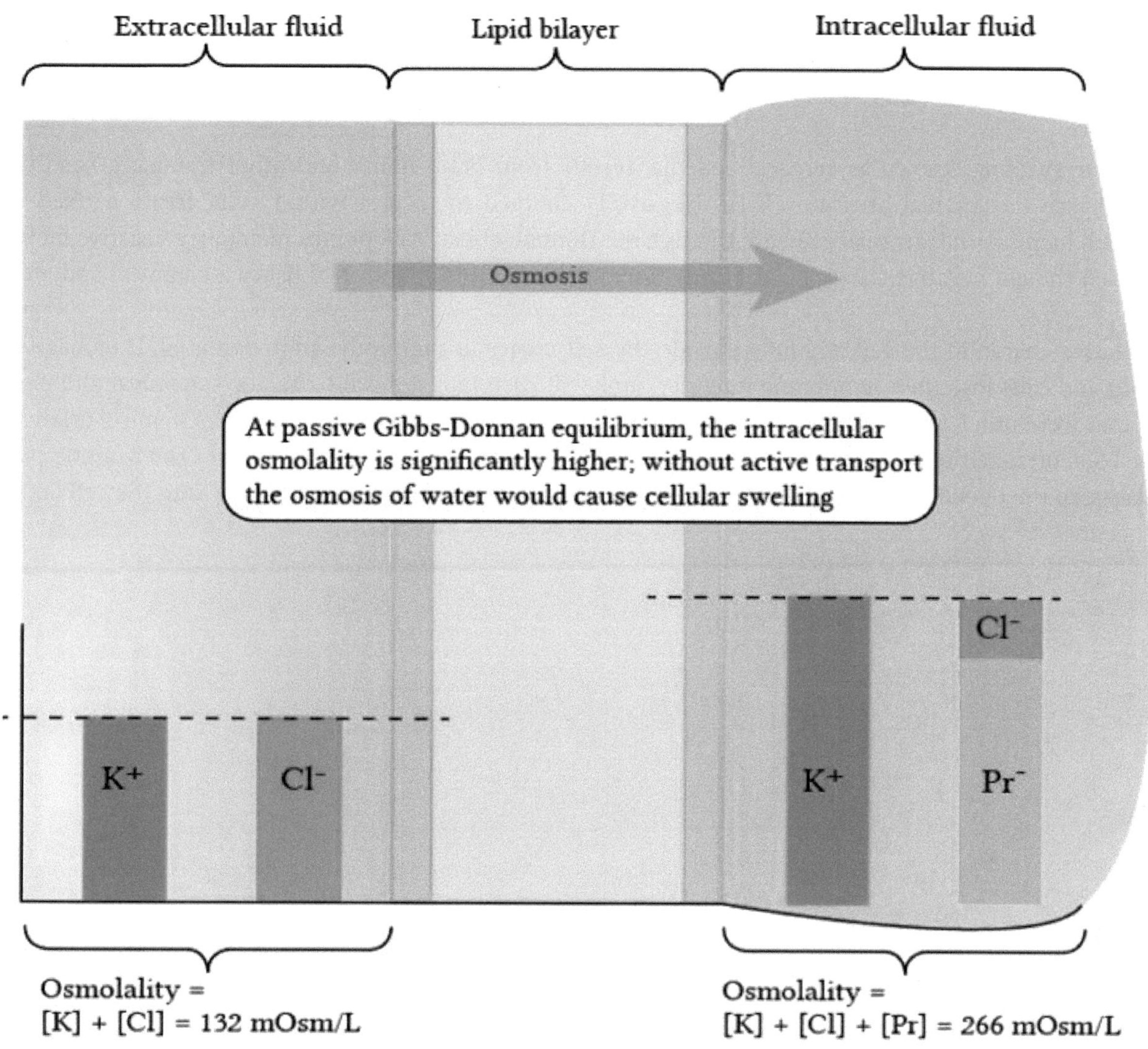

Fig. 16

- In fact, in this (wildly physiologically inaccurate) thought experiment, the difference in osmolality is quite stark (there's about 134 mOsm/L difference). With this sort of osmotic gradient, water would surge across the membrane, causing the cell to swell hideously and explode.
- Obviously, that does not happen *in vivo*. The Na^+/K^+ ATPase plays a major role in preventing cellular osmoexplosion by pumping three sodium ions out of the cell in exchange for two potassiums. The terrible sodium permeability of the cell membrane means that the sodium generally keeps to the extracellular compartment, maintaining the osmolality there. As a result, a second Donnan effect (this time with the non-diffusible ions being extracellular sodium) is established across the membrane, which maintains an osmotic counter-gradient for water movement. Thus, there is a "double Donnan effect" in action at every cell membrane.

Physiological applications

Red blood cells

When tissue cells are in a protein-containing fluid, the Donnan effect of the cytoplasmic proteins is equal and opposite to the Donnan effect of the extracellular proteins. The opposing Donnan effects cause chloride ions to migrate inside the cell, increasing the intracellular chloride concentration. The Donnan effect may explain why some red blood cells do not have active sodium pumps; the effect relieves the osmotic pressure of plasma proteins, which is why sodium pumping is less important for maintaining the cell volume .

Neurology

Brain tissue swelling, known as cerebral oedema, results from brain injury and other traumatic head injuries that can increase intracranial pressure (ICP). Negatively charged molecules within cells create a fixed charge density, which increases intracranial pressure through the Donnan effect. ATP pumps maintain a negative membrane potential even though negative charges leak across the membrane; this action establishes a chemical and electrical gradient.

The negative charge in the cell and ions outside the cell creates a thermodynamic potential; if damage occurs to the brain and cells lose their membrane integrity, ions will rush into the cell to balance chemical and electrical gradients that were previously established. The membrane voltage will become zero, but the chemical gradient will still exist. To neutralize the negative charges within the cell, cations flow in, which increases the osmotic pressure inside relative to the outside of the cell. The increased osmotic pressure forces water to flow into the cell and tissue swelling occurs.

CHAPTER TEN

FLUID AND ELECTROLYTE ABNORMALITIES

WATER IMBALANCE

Causes

- inappropriate use of hypotonic solu:ons (e.g. D5%Water) leading to hypo-osmolar hyponatremia
- Syndrome of inappropriate antidiuretic hormone secretion (SIADH)
- **SIADH causes** :malignant tumors, CNS diseases, pulmonary disorders, medications, and severe stress.

Symptoms develop slowly and if not recognized and treated promptly, they become evident by convulsions and coma due to cerebral edema

Signs Hypertension, Tachycardia, Raised JVP / gallop, edema, Pleural effusions, Pulmonary edema, Ascites, Organ failure

Diagnosis of SIADH secre:on is established when **urine sodium > 20 mEq/L when there is no renal failure, hypotension, and edema.**

Treatment

- water restriction and infusion of isotonic or hypertonic saline solution
- use of ADH- Antagonist (Demeclocycline 300-600 mg b.i.d).

Antidiuretic Hormone (ADH):

- ADH is released from the posterior pituitary gland in response to high osmolality in plasma or in response to low volume.
- ADH secretion is influenced by volume receptors so that hypovolemia s:mulates ADH secretion and water reabsorption. In the paradoxical situa:on where hypovolemia is accompanied by a fall in osmolality, ADH secre:on will increase because the major stimulan is hypovolemia.
- Human vasopressin, also called antidiuretic hormone (ADH), arginine vasopressin (AVP) or argipressin, is a hormone synthesized from the AVP gene as a peptide prohormone in neurons in the hypothalamus, and is converted to AVP. It then travels down the axon terminating in the posterior pituitary, and is released from vesicles into the circulation in response to extracellular fluid hypertonicity (hyperosmolality). AVP has two primary functions. First, it increases the amount of solute-free water reabsorbed back into the circulation from the filtrate in the kidney tubules of the nephrons. Second, AVP constricts arterioles, which increases peripheral vascular resistance and raises arterial blood pressure.

  A third function is possible. Some AVP may be released directly into the brain from the hypothalamus, and may play an important role in social behavior, sexual motivation and pair bonding, and maternal responses to
- stress.

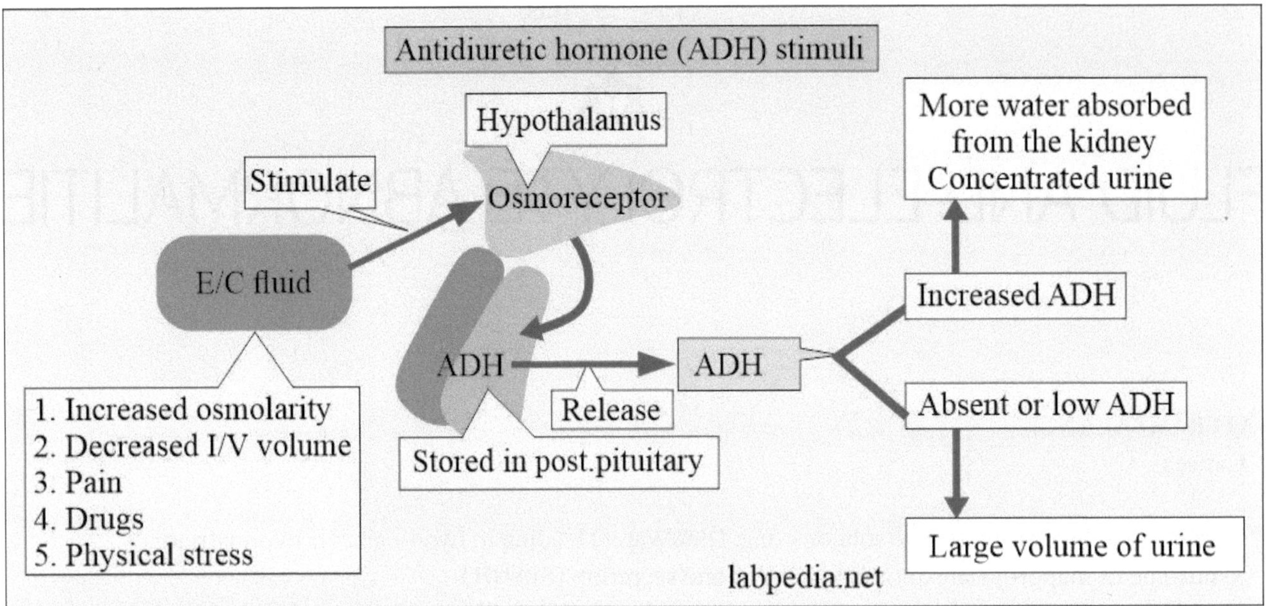

Vasopressin induces differentiation of stem cells into cardiomyocytes and promotes heart muscle homeostasis. It has a very short half-life, between 16 and 24 minutes.

- **Function**

Vasopressin regulates the tonicity of body fluids. It is released from the posterior pituitary in response to hypertonicity and causes the kidneys to reabsorb solute-free water and return it to the circulation from the tubules of the nephron, thus returning the tonicity of the body fluids toward normal. An incidental consequence of this renal reabsorption of water is concentrated urine and reduced urine volume. AVP released in high concentrations may also raise blood pressure by inducing moderate vasoconstriction.

AVP also may have a variety of neurological effects on the brain. It may influence pair-bonding in voles. The high-density distributions of vasopressin receptor AVPr1a in prairie vole ventral forebrain regions have been shown to facilitate and coordinate reward circuits during partner preference formation, critical for pair bond formation.

A very similar substance, lysine vasopressin (LVP) or lypressin, has the same function in pigs and its synthetic version was used in human AVP deficiency, although it has been largely replaced by desmopressin.

Kidney

Vasopressin has three main effects which are:

Increasing the water permeability of distal convoluted tubule (DCT) and cortical collecting tubules (CCT), as well as outer and inner medullary collecting duct (OMCD & IMCD) in the kidney, thus allowing water reabsorption and excretion of more concentrated urine, i.e., antidiuresis. This occurs through increased transcription and insertion of water channels (Aquaporin-2) into the apical membrane of collecting tubule and collecting duct epithelial cells.[15] Aquaporins allow water to move down their osmotic gradient and out of the nephron, increasing the amount of water re-absorbed from the filtrate (forming urine) back into the bloodstream. This effect is mediated by V2 receptors. Vasopressin also increases the concentration of calcium in the collecting duct cells, by episodic release from intracellular stores. Vasopressin, acting through cAMP, also increases transcription of the aquaporin-2 gene, thus increasing the total number of aquaporin-2 molecules in collecting duct cells.

Increasing permeability of the inner medullary portion of the collecting duct to urea by regulating the cell surface expression of urea transporters, which facilitates its reabsorption into the medullary interstitium as it travels down the concentration gradient created by removing water from the connecting tubule, cortical collecting duct, and outer medullary collecting duct.

Acute increase of sodium absorption across the ascending loop of Henle. This adds to the countercurrent multiplication which aids in proper water reabsorption later in the distal tubule and collecting duct.

- 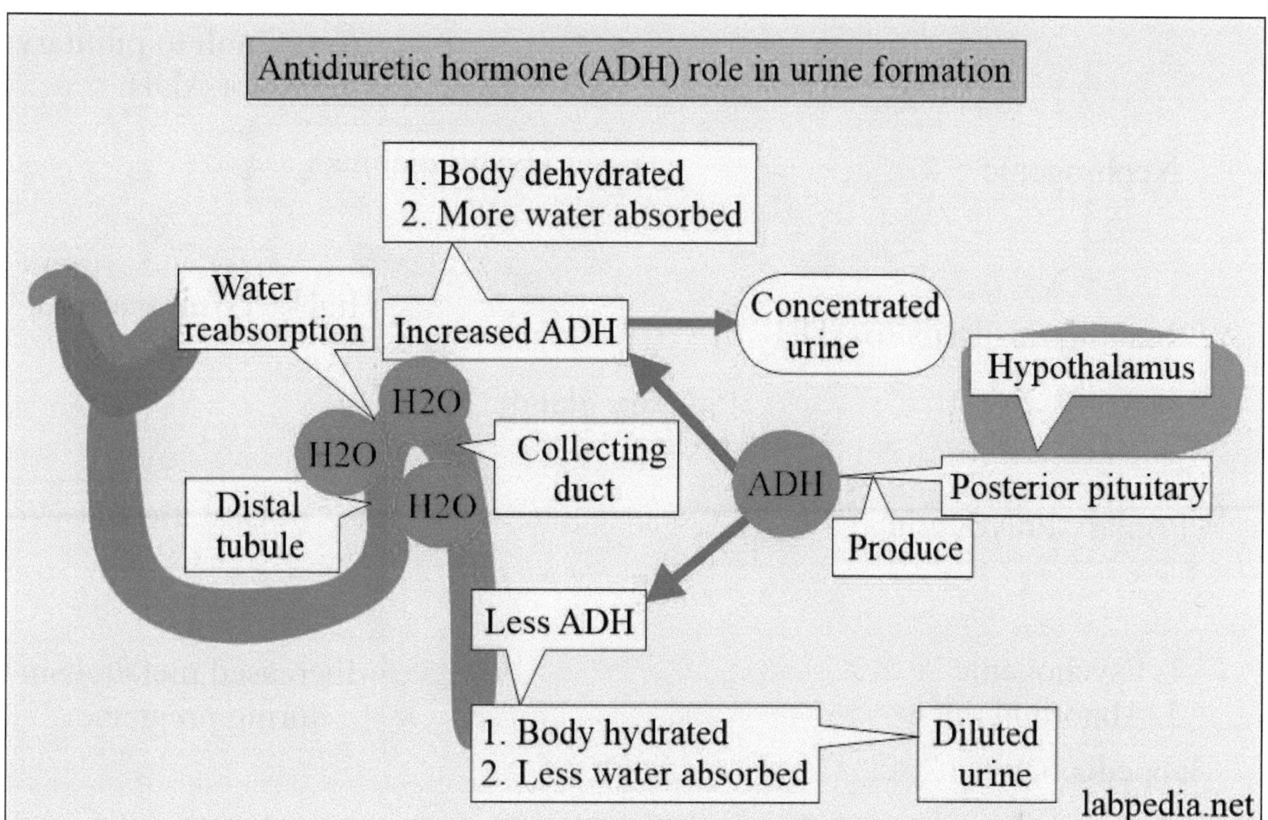

- **Central nervous system**

  Vasopressin released within the brain may have several actions:

  Vasopressin is released into the brain in a circadian rhythm by neurons of the suprachiasmatic nucleus.

  Vasopressin released from posterior pituitary is associated with nausea.

  Recent evidence suggests that vasopressin may have analgesic effects. The analgesia effects of vasopressin were found to be dependent on both stress and sex.

Role of ADH: to maintain normovolemia and the osmolality of plasma by changes in ADH secretion from the posterior pituitary.

Antidiuretic hormone secretion results in:

- Pure water reabsorption from the collecting duct of the nephron via a pathway that involves the V2 receptor and aquaporin 2.
- It increases the urine's concentration

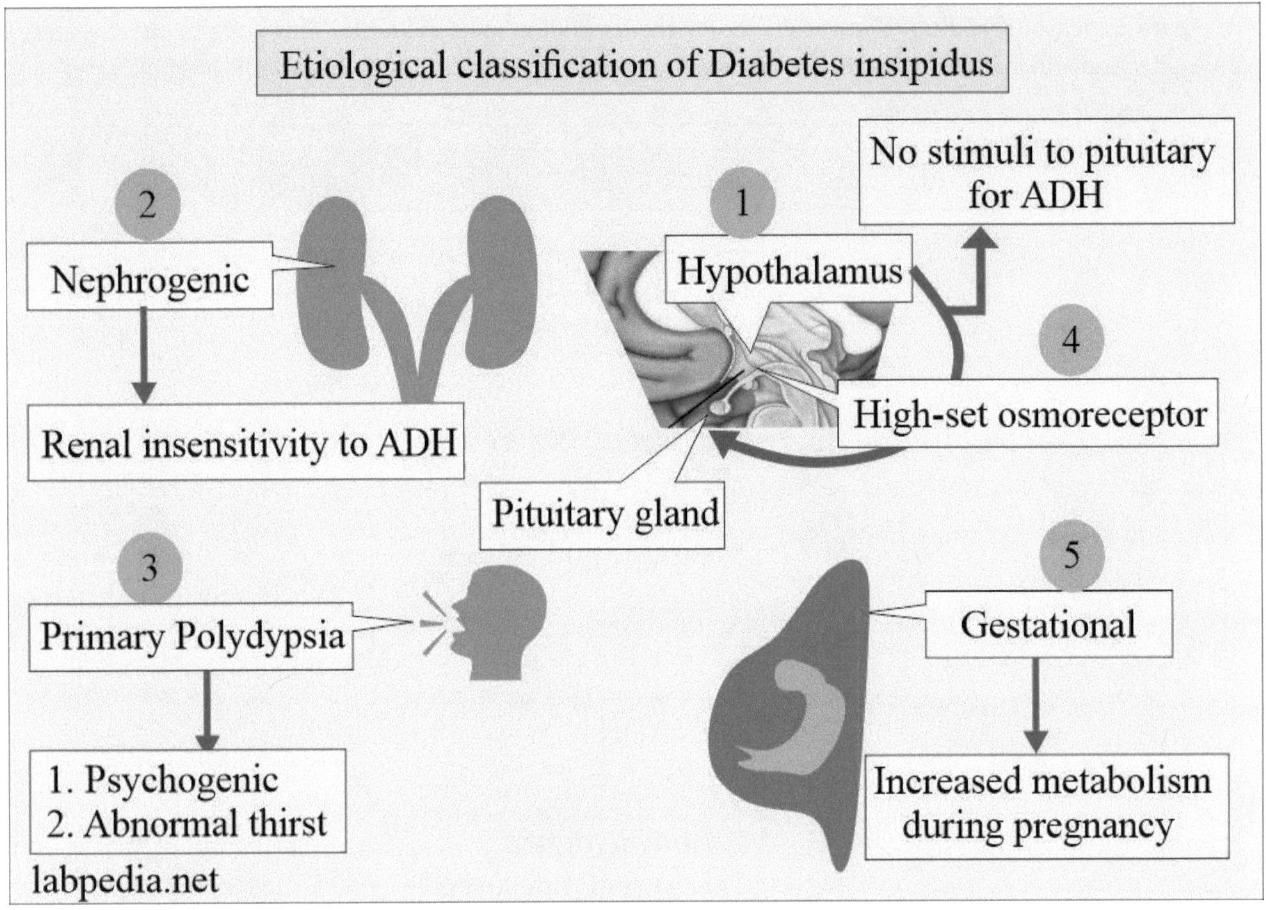

SODIUM IMBALANCE

HYPERNATREMIA

Hypernatremia, also spelled **hypernatraemia**, is a high concentration of sodium in the blood. Early symptoms may include a strong feeling of thirst, weakness, nausea, and loss of appetite. Severe symptoms include confusion, muscle twitching, and bleeding in or around the brain. Normal serum sodium levels are 135–145 mmol/L (135–145 mEq/L). Hypernatremia is generally defined as a serum sodium level of more than 145 mmol/L. Severe symptoms typically only occur when levels are above 160 mmol/L.

Hypernatremia is typically classified by a person's fluid status into low volume, normal volume, and high volume. Low volume hypernatremia can occur from sweating, vomiting, diarrhea, diuretic medication, or kidney disease. Normal volume hypernatremia can be due to fever, extreme thirst, prolonged increased breath rate, diabetes insipidus, and from lithium among other causes. High volume hypernatremia can be due to hyperaldosteronism, excessive administration of intravenous 3% normal saline or sodium bicarbonate, or rarely from eating too much salt. Low blood protein levels can result in a falsely high sodium measurement. The cause can usually be determined by the history of events. Testing the urine can help if the cause is unclear. The underlying mechanism typically involves too little free water in the body. If the onset of hypernatremia was over a few hours, then it can be corrected relatively quickly using intravenousnormal saline and 5% dextrose in water. Otherwise, correction should occur slowly with, for those unable to drink water, half-normal saline. Hypernatremia due to diabetes insipidus as a result of a brain disorder, may be treated with the medication desmopressin. If the diabetes insipidus is due to kidney problems the medication causing the problem may need to be stopped or the underlying electrolyte disturbance corrected. Hypernatremia affects 0.3–1% of people in hospital. It most often occurs in babies, those with impaired mental status, and the elderly. Hypernatremia is associated with an increased risk of death but it is unclear if it is the cause.

Signs and symptoms

The major symptom is thirst. The most important signs result from brain cell shrinkage and include confusion, muscle twitching or spasms. With severe elevations, seizures and comas may occur.

Severe symptoms are usually due to acute elevation of the plasma sodium concentration to above 157 mmol/L (normal blood levels are generally about 135–145 mmol/L for adults and elderly). Values above 180 mmol/L are associated with a high mortality rate, particularly in adults. However, such high levels of sodium rarely occur without severe coexisting medical conditions. Serum sodium concentrations have ranged from 150 to 228 mmol/L in survivors of acute salt overdosage, while levels of 153–255 mmol/L have been observed in fatalities. Vitreous humor is considered to be a better postmortem specimen than postmortem serum for assessing sodium involvement in a death.

Causes

Common causes of hypernatremia include:

Low volume

In those with low volume or hypovolemia:

- Inadequate intake of free water associated with total body sodium depletion. Typically in elderly or otherwise disabled patients who are unable to take in water as their thirst dictates and also are sodium depleted. This is the most common cause of hypernatremia.
- Excessive losses of water from the urinary tract – which may be caused by glycosuria, or other osmotic diuretics (e.g., mannitol) – leads to a combination of sodium and free water losses.
- Water losses associated with extreme sweating.
- Severe watery diarrhea (osmotic diarrhea results in hypotonic (dilute) watery diarrhea resulting in significant loss of free water and a higher concentration of sodium in the blood; this type of water loss can also be seen with viral gastroenteritis).

Normal volume

In those with normal volume or euvolemia:

- Excessive excretion of water from the kidneys caused by diabetes insipidus, which involves either inadequate release of antidiuretic hormone from the pituitary gland, or impaired responsiveness of the kidneys to it.

High volume

In those with high volume or hypervolemia:

- Intake of a hypertonic fluid (a fluid with a higher concentration of solutes than the remainder of the body) with restricted free water intake. This is relatively uncommon, though it can occur after a vigorous resuscitation where a patient receives a large volume of a concentrated sodium bicarbonate solution. Ingesting seawater also causes hypernatremia because seawater is hypertonic and free water is not available. There are several recorded cases of forced ingestion of concentrated salt solution in exorcism rituals leading to death.
- Mineralcorticoid excess due to a disease state such as Conn's syndrome usually does not lead to hypernatremia unless free water intake is restricted.
- Salt poisoning is the most common cause in children. It has also been seen in a number of adults with mental health problems. Too much salt can also occur from drinking seawater or soy sauce.

Diagnosis

Hypernatremia is diagnosed when a basic metabolic panel blood test demonstrates a sodium concentration higher than 145 mmol/L.

Treatment

The cornerstone of treatment is administration of free water to correct the relative water deficit. Water can be replaced orally or intravenously. Water alone cannot be administered intravenously (because of osmolarity issues leading to rupturing of red blood cells in the bloodstream), but rather can be given intravenously in solution with dextrose (sugar) or saline (salt). However, overly rapid correction of hypernatremia is potentially very dangerous. The body (in particular the brain) adapts to the higher sodium concentration. Rapidly lowering the sodium concentration with free water, once this adaptation has occurred, causes water to flow into brain cells and causes them to swell. This can lead to cerebral edema, potentially resulting in seizures, permanent brain damage, or death. Therefore, significant hypernatremia should be treated carefully by a physician or other medical professional with experience in treatment of electrolyte imbalance. Specific treatments such as thiazide diuretics (e.g., chlorthalidone) in congestive heart failure or corticosteroids in nephropathy also can be used.

Keypoints:

Causes

1. Excessive sodium load (excessive normal saline (0.9%) or hypertonic solutions e.g. 3% NaCl - >145 of Na)

2. Hyperaldosteronism; aldosterone promotes water & Na+ retention (rare)

3. Reduced water intake by fasting, nausea and vomiting, or reduced consciousness as in Alzheimer's patient/ elderly (they forget to drink)

4. Increased water loss by sweating (pyrexia, hot environment), respiratory tract loss (increased ventilation, administra:on of dry gases) or burns.

5. Inappropriate urinary water loss by diabetes insipidus (pituitary or nephrogenic) or diabetes mellitus

6. Patients with CHF, cirrhosis, and nephrotic syndrome are prone to this complication

Symptoms Similar to water excess symptoms, includes coma, convulsions and confusion.

Diagnosis It is established when serum sodium >145 mEq/L

Treatment

- Water intake
- Decrease sodium infusion in IVF (e.g. 0.45% NaCl or D5%Water).

HYPONATREMIA

Hyponatremia or **hyponatraemia** is a low concentration of sodium in the blood. It is generally defined as a sodium concentration of less than 135 mmol/L (135 mEq/L), with severe hyponatremia being below 120 mEq/L. Symptoms can be absent, mild or severe. Mild symptoms include a decreased ability to think, headaches, nausea, and poor balance. Severe symptoms include confusion, seizures, and coma; death can ensue.

The causes of hyponatremia are typically classified by a person's body fluid status into low volume, normal volume, or high volume. Low volume hyponatremia can occur from diarrhea, vomiting, diuretics, and sweating. Normal volume hyponatremia is divided into cases with dilute urine and concentrated urine. Cases in which the urine is dilute include adrenal insufficiency, hypothyroidism, and drinking too much water or too much beer. Cases in which the urine is concentrated include syndrome of inappropriate antidiuretic hormone secretion (SIADH). High volume hyponatremia can occur from heart failure, liver failure, and kidney failure. Conditions that can lead to falsely low sodium measurements include high blood protein levels such as in multiple myeloma, high blood fat levels, and high blood sugar.

Treatment is based on the underlying cause. Correcting hyponatremia too quickly can lead to complications. Rapid partial correction with 3% normal saline is only recommended in those with significant symptoms and occasionally those in whom the condition was of rapid onset. Low volume hyponatremia is typically treated with intravenous normal saline. SIADH is typically treated by correcting the underlying cause and with fluid restriction while high volume hyponatremia is typically treated with both fluid restriction and a diet low in salt. Correction should generally be gradual in those in whom the low levels have been present for more than two days.

Hyponatremia is the most common type of electrolyte imbalance, and is often found in older adults. It occurs in about 20% of those admitted to hospital and 10% of people during or after an endurance sporting event. Among those in hospital, hyponatremia is associated with an increased risk of death. The economic costs of hyponatremia are estimated at $2.6 billion per annum in the United States.

Signs and symptoms of hyponatremia include nausea and vomiting, headache, short-term memory loss, confusion, lethargy, fatigue, loss of appetite, irritability, muscle weakness, spasms or cramps, seizures, and decreased consciousness or coma. Lower levels of plasma sodium are associated with more severe symptoms. However, mild hyponatremia (plasma sodium levels at 131–135 mmol/L) may be associated with complications and subtle symptoms (for example, increased falls, altered posture and gait, reduced attention, impaired cognition, and possibly higher rates of death).

Neurological symptoms typically occur with very low levels of plasma sodium (usually <115 mmol/L). When sodium levels in the blood become very low, water enters the brain cells and causes them to swell (cerebral edema). This results in increased pressure in the skull and causes *hyponatremic encephalopathy*. As pressure increases in the skull, herniation of the brain can occur, which is a squeezing of the brain across the internal structures of the skull. This can lead to headache, nausea, vomiting, confusion, seizures, brain stem compression and respiratory arrest, and non-cardiogenic accumulation of fluid in the lungs. This is usually fatal if not immediately treated.

Symptom severity depends on how fast and how severe the drop in blood sodium level is. A gradual drop, even to very low levels, may be tolerated well if it occurs over several days or weeks, because of neuronal adaptation. The presence of underlying neurological disease such as a seizure disorder or non-neurological metabolic abnormalities, also affects the severity of neurologic symptoms.

Chronic hyponatremia can lead to such complications as neurological impairments. These neurological impairments most often affect gait (walking) and attention, and can lead to increased reaction time and falls. Hyponatremia, by interfering with bone metabolism, has been linked with a doubled risk of osteoporosis and an increased risk of bone fracture.

Causes

The specific causes of hyponatremia are generally divided into those with low tonicity (lower than normal concentration of solutes), without low tonicity, and falsely low sodiums. Those with low tonicity are then grouped by whether the person has high fluid volume, normal fluid volume, or low fluid volume. Too little sodium in the diet alone is very rarely the cause of hyponatremia.

High volume

Both sodium and water content increase: Increase in sodium content leads to hypervolemia and water content to hyponatremia.

- Cirrhosis of the liver
- Congestive heart failure
- Nephrotic syndrome in the kidneys
- Excessive drinking of fluids

Normal volume

There is volume expansion in the body, no edema, but hyponatremia occurs.

- SIADH (and its many causes)
- Hypothyroidism
- Not enough ACTH
- Beer potomania
- Normal physiologic change of pregnancy
- Reset osmostat

Low volume

Hypovolemia (extracellular volume loss) is due to total body sodium loss. Hyponatremia is caused by a relatively smaller loss in total body water.

- Any cause of hypovolemia such as prolonged vomiting, decreased oral intake, severe diarrhea
- Diuretic use (due to the diuretic causing a volume depleted state and thence ADH release, and not a direct result of diuretic-induced urine sodium loss)
- Addison's disease and congenital adrenal hyperplasia in which the adrenal glands do not produce enough steroid hormones (combined glucocorticoid and mineralocorticoid deficiency)
- Isolated hyperchlorhidrosis (Carbonic anhydrase XII deficiency), a rare genetic disorder which results in a lifelong tendency to lose excessive amounts of sodium by sweating.
- Pancreatitis
- Prolonged exercise and sweating, combined with drinking water without electrolytes is the cause of exercise-associated hyponatremia (EAH). It is common in marathon runners and participants of other endurance events.
- The use of MDMA (ecstasy) can result in hyponatremia.

Medication

Antipsychotics have been reported to cause hyponatremia in a review of medical articles from 1946 to 2016.

Available evidence suggests that all classes of psychotropics, i.e., antidepressants, antipsychotics, mood stabilizers, and sedative/hypnotics can lead to hyponatremia. Age is a significant factor for drug induced hyponatremia.

Other causes

Miscellaneous causes that are not included under the above classification scheme include the following:

- False or pseudo hyponatremia is caused by a false lab measurement of sodium due to massive increases in blood triglyceride levels or extreme elevation of immunoglobulins as may occur in multiple myeloma.
- Hyponatremia with elevated tonicity can occur with high blood sugar, causing a shift of excess free water into the serum.

Pathophysiology

The causes of and treatments for hyponatremia can only be understood by having a grasp of the size of the body fluid compartments and subcompartments and their regulation; how under normal circumstances the body is able to maintain the sodium concentration within a narrow range (homeostasis of body fluidosmolality); conditions can cause that feedback system to malfunction (pathophysiology); and the consequences of the malfunction of that system on the size and solute concentration of the fluid compartments.

Normal homeostasis

There is a hypothalamic-kidney feedback system which normally maintains the concentration of the serum sodium within a narrow range. This system operates as follows: in some of the cells of the hypothalamus, there are osmoreceptors which respond to an elevated serum sodium in body fluids by signalling the posterior pituitary gland to secrete antidiuretic hormone (ADH) (vasopressin). ADH then enters the bloodstream and signals the kidney to bring back sufficient solute-free water from the fluid in the kidney tubules to dilute the serum sodium back to normal, and this turns off the osmoreceptors in the hypothalamus. Also, thirst is stimulated. Normally, when mild hyponatremia begins to occur, that is, the serum sodium begins to fall below 135 mEq/L, there is no secretion of ADH, and the kidney stops returning water to the body from the kidney tubule. Also, no thirst is experienced. These two act in concert to raise the serum sodium to the normal range.

Hyponatremia

Hyponatremia occurs

1) when the hypothalamic-kidney feedback loop is overwhelmed by increased fluid intake,

2) the feedback loop malfunctions such that ADH is always "turned on",

3) the receptors in the kidney are always "open" regardless of there being no signal from ADH to be open; or

4) there is an increased ADH even though there is no normal stimulus (elevated serum sodium) for ADH to be increased.

Hyponatremia occurs in one of two ways: either the osmoreceptor-aquaporin feedback loop is *overwhelmed*, or it is *interrupted*. If it is interrupted, it is either *related* or *not related* to ADH. If the feedback system is overwhelmed, this is water intoxication with maximally dilute urine and is caused by

1) pathological water drinking (psychogenic polydipsia),

2) beer potomania,

3) overzealous intravenous solute free water infusion, or 4) infantile water intoxication.

"Impairment of urine diluting ability related to ADH" occurs in nine situations: 1) arterial volume depletion

2) hemodynamically mediated,

3) congestive heart failure,

4) cirrhosis,

5) nephrosis,

6) spinal cord disease,

7) Addison's disease,

8) cerebral salt wasting, and

9) syndrome of inappropriate antidiuretic hormone secretion (SIADH).

If the feed-back system is normal, but an *impairment of urine diluting ability unrelated to ADH* occurs, this is:

1) oliguric kidney failure,

2) tubular interstitial kidney disease,

3) diuretics, or

4) nephrogenic syndrome of antidiuresis.

Sodium is the primary positively charged ion outside of the cell and cannot cross from the interstitial space into the cell. This is because charged sodium ions attract around them up to 25 water molecules, thereby creating a large polar structure too large to pass through the cell membrane: "channels" or "pumps" are required. Cell swelling also produces activation of volume-regulated anion channels which is related to the release of taurine and glutamate from astrocytes.

Diagnosis

The history, physical exam, and laboratory testing are required to determine the underlying cause of hyponatremia. A blood test demonstrating a serum sodium less than 135 mmol/L is diagnostic for hyponatremia. The history and physical exam are necessary to help determine if the person is hypovolemic, euvolemic, or hypervolemic, which has important implications in determining the underlying cause. An assessment is also made to determine if the person is experiencing symptoms from their hyponatremia. These include assessments of alertness, concentration, and orientation.

False hyponatremia

False hyponatremia, also known as spurious, pseudo, hypertonic, or artifactual hyponatremia is when the lab tests read low sodium levels but there is no hypotonicity. In hypertonic hyponatremia, resorption of water by molecules such as glucose (hyperglycemia or diabetes) or mannitol (hypertonic infusion) occurs. In isotonic hyponatremia a measurement error due to high blood triglyceride level (most common) or paraproteinemia occurs. It occurs when using techniques that measure the amount of sodium in a specified volume of serum/plasma, or that dilute the sample before analysis.[35]

True hyponatremia

True hyponatremia, also known as hypotonic hyponatremia, is the most common type. It is often simply referred to as "hyponatremia." Hypotonic hyponatremia is categorized in 3 ways based on the person's blood volume status. Each category represents a different underlying reason for the increase in ADH that led to the water retention and thence hyponatremia:

- **High volume hyponatremia**, wherein there is decreased effective circulating volume (less blood flowing in the body) even though total body volume is increased (by the presence of edema or swelling, especially in the ankles). The decreased effective circulating volume stimulates the release of anti-diuretic hormone (ADH), which in turn leads to water retention. Hypervolemic hyponatremia is most commonly the result of congestive heart failure, liver failure, or kidney disease.
- **Normal volume hyponatremia**, wherein the increase in ADH is secondary to either physiologic but excessive ADH release (as occurs with nausea or severe pain) or inappropriate and non-physiologic secretion of ADH, that is, syndrome of inappropriate antidiuretic hormone hypersecretion (SIADH). Often categorized under euvolemic is hyponatremia due to inadequate urine solute (not enough chemicals or electrolytes to produce urine) as occurs in beer potomania or "tea and toast" hyponatremia, hyponatremia due to hypothyroidism or central adrenal insufficiency, and those rare instances of hyponatremia that are truly secondary to excess water intake.
- **Low volume hyponatremia**, wherein ADH secretion is stimulated by or associated with volume depletion (not enough water in the body) due to decreased effective circulating volume.

Acute versus chronic

Chronic hyponatremia is when sodium levels drop gradually over several days or weeks and symptoms and complications are typically moderate. Chronic hyponatremia is often called asymptomatic hyponatremia in clinical settings because it is thought to have no symptoms; however, emerging data suggests that "asymptomatic" hyponatremia is not actually asymptomatic.

Acute hyponatremia is when sodium levels drop rapidly, resulting in potentially dangerous effects, such as rapid brain swelling, which can result in coma and death.

Treatment

The treatment of hyponatremia depends on the underlying cause. How quickly treatment is required depends on a person's symptoms. Fluids are typically the cornerstone of initial management. In those with severe disease an increase in sodium of about 5 mmol/L over one to four hours is recommended. A rapid rise in serum sodium is anticipated in certain groups when the cause of the hyponatremia is addressed thus warranting closer monitoring in order to avoid overly rapid correction of the blood sodium concentration. These groups include persons who have hypovolemic hyponatremia and receive intravenous fluids (thus correcting their hypovolemia), persons with adrenal insufficiency who receive hydrocortisone, persons in whom a medication causing increased ADH release has been stopped, and persons who have hyponatremia due to decreased salt and/or solute intake in their diet who are treated with a higher solute diet. If large volumes of dilute urine are seen, this can be a warning sign that overcorrection is imminent in these individuals.

Sodium deficit = (140 – serum sodium) x total body water

Total body water = kilograms of body weight x 0.6

Fluids

Options include:

- Mild and asymptomatic hyponatremia is treated with adequate solute intake (including salt and protein) and fluid restriction starting at 500 millilitres per day (mL/d) of water with adjustments based on serum sodium levels. Long-term fluid restriction of 1,200–1,800 mL/d may maintain the person in a symptom-free state.
- Moderate and/or symptomatic hyponatremia is treated by raising the serum sodium level by 0.5 to 1 mmol per liter per hour for a total of 8 mmol per liter during the first day with the use of furosemide and replacing sodium and potassium losses with 0.9% saline.
- Severe hyponatremia or severe symptoms (confusion, convulsions, or coma): consider hypertonic saline (3%) 1–2 mL/kg IV in 3–4 h. Hypertonic saline may lead to a rapid dilute diuresis and fall in the serum sodium. It should not be used in those with an expanded extracellular fluid volume.

Electrolyte abnormalities

In persons with hyponatremia due to low blood volume (hypovolemia) from diuretics with simultaneous low blood potassium levels, correction of the low potassium level can assist with correction of hyponatremia.

Medications

American and European guidelines come to different conclusions regarding the use of medications. In the United States they are recommended in those with SIADH, cirrhosis, or heart failure who fail limiting fluid intake. In Europe they are not generally recommended.

There is tentative evidence that vasopressin receptor antagonists (vaptans), such as conivaptan, may be slightly more effective than fluid restriction in those with high volume or normal volume hyponatremia. They should not be used in people with low volume. They may also be used in people with chronic hyponatremia due to SIADH that is insufficiently responsive to fluid restriction and/or sodium tablets.

Demeclocycline, while sometimes used for SIADH, has significant side effects including potential kidney problems and sun sensitivity. In many people it has no benefit while in others it can result in overcorrection and high blood sodium levels.

Daily use of urea by mouth, while not commonly used due to the taste, has tentative evidence in SIADH. However, it is not available in many areas of the world.

Precautions

Raising the serum sodium concentration too rapidly may cause osmotic demyelination syndrome. Rapid correction of sodium levels can also lead to central pontine myelinolysis (CPM). It is recommended not to raise the serum sodium by more than 10 mEq/L/day.

Epidemiology

Hyponatremia is the most commonly seen water–electrolyte imbalance. The disorder is more frequent in females, the elderly, and in people who are hospitalized. The number of cases of hyponatremia depends largely on the population. In hospital it affects about 15–20% of people; however, only 3–5% of people who are hospitalized have a sodium level less than 130 mmol/L. Hyponatremia has been reported in up to 30% of the elderly in nursing homes and is also present in approximately 30% of people who are depressed on selective serotonin reuptake inhibitors.

People who have hyponatremia who require hospitalisation have a longer length of stay (with associated increased costs) and also have a higher likelihood of requiring readmission. This is particularly the case in men and in the elderly

Key points:

Causes

1. Hyperglycemia (it could be Pseudohyponatremia; diabetic)

↪ Corrected Na^+= BS mg/dl x 0.016 + P (Na) (BS = blood sugar)

2. Excessive IV sodium-free fluid administration (hypotonic solutions)

3. Hyponatremia with volume overload “hypervolemic hyponatremia” usually indicates impaired renal ability to excrete sodium.

Treatment

- Administering the calculated sodium needs in isotonic solution
- In severe hyponatremia (Na+ <120 mEq/L) you give a hypertonic

  Solution.

- Serum Na+ administration shouldn’t be given at a rate > 10-12 mEq/

  L/hr (because rapid correction may cause permanent brain damage due to the osmotic demyelination syndrome)

- Before treating hyponatremia, you should check if it’s true hyponatremia or pseudohyponatremia by checking the glucose levels.

↪ The glucose levels should be corrected in case of pseudohyponatremia, no further treatment is needed.

Potassium imbalance

HYPERKALEMIA

Hyperkalemia is an elevated level of potassium (K^+) in the blood. Normal potassium levels are between 3.5 and 5.0 mmol/L (3.5 and 5.0 mEq/L) with levels above 5.5 mmol/L defined as hyperkalemia. Typically hyperkalemia does not cause symptoms. Occasionally when severe it can cause palpitations, muscle pain, muscle weakness, or numbness. Hyperkalemia can cause an abnormal heart rhythm which can result in cardiac arrest and death.

Common causes of hyperkalemia include kidney failure, hypoaldosteronism, and rhabdomyolysis.

A number of medications can also cause high blood potassium including spironolactone, NSAIDs, and angiotensin converting enzyme inhibitors. The severity is divided into mild (5.5–5.9 mmol/L), moderate (6.0–6.4 mmol/L), and severe (>6.5 mmol/L). High levels can be detected on an electrocardiogram (ECG). Pseudohyperkalemia, due to breakdown of cells during or after taking the blood sample, should be ruled out.

Initial treatment in those with ECG changes is salts, such as calcium gluconate or calcium chloride. Other medications used to rapidly reduce blood potassium levels include insulin with dextrose, salbutamol, and sodium bicarbonate.

Medications that might worsen the condition should be stopped and a low potassium diet should be started. Measures to remove potassium from the body include diuretics such as furosemide, potassium-binders such as polystyrene sulfonate and sodium zirconium cyclosilicate, and hemodialysis. Hemodialysis is the most effective method.

Hyperkalemia is rare among those who are otherwise healthy. Among those who are hospitalized, rates are between 1% and 2.5%. It is associated with an increased mortality, whether due to hyperkalaemia itself or as a marker of severe illness, especially in those without chronic kidney disease. The word *hyperkalemia* comes from *hyper-* 'high' + *kalium* 'potassium' + *-emia* 'blood condition'.

Signs and symptoms

The symptoms of an elevated potassium level are generally few and nonspecific. Nonspecific symptoms may include feeling tired, numbness and weakness. Occasionally palpitations and shortness of breath may occur. Hyperventilation may indicate a compensatory response to metabolic acidosis, which is one of the possible causes of hyperkalemia. Often, however, the problem is detected during screening blood tests for a medical disorder, or after hospitalization for complications such as cardiac arrhythmia or sudden cardiac death. High levels of potassium (> 5.5 mmol/L) have been associated with cardiovascular events.

Causes

Ineffective elimination

Decreased kidney function is a major cause of hyperkalemia. This is especially pronounced in acute kidney injury where the glomerular filtration rate and tubular flow are markedly decreased, characterized by reduced urine output. This can lead to a dramatically elevated potassium in conditions of increased cell breakdown as the potassium is released from the cells and cannot be eliminated in the kidney. In chronic kidney disease, hyperkalemia occurs as a result of reduced aldosterone responsiveness and reduced sodium and water delivery in distal tubules.

Medications that interfere with urinary excretion by inhibiting the renin–angiotensin system is one of the most common causes of hyperkalemia. Examples of medications that can cause hyperkalemia include ACE inhibitors, angiotensin receptor blockers, non-selective beta blockers, and calcineurin inhibitor immunosuppressants such as ciclosporin and tacrolimus. For potassium-sparing diuretics, such as amiloride and triamterene; both the drugs block epithelial sodium channels in the collecting tubules, thereby preventing potassium excretion into urine. Spironolactone acts by competitively inhibiting the action of aldosterone.NSAIDs such as ibuprofen, naproxen, or celecoxib inhibit prostaglandin synthesis, leading to reduced production of renin and aldosterone, causing potassium retention. The antibiotic trimethoprim and the antiparasitic medicationpentamidine inhibits potassium excretion, which is similar to mechanism of action by amiloride and triamterene.

Mineralocorticoid (aldosterone) deficiency or resistance can also cause hyperkalemia. Primary adrenal insufficiency are: Addison's disease and congenital adrenal hyperplasia (CAH) (including enzyme deficiencies such as 21α hydroxylase, 17α hydroxylase, 11β hydroxylase, or 3β dehydrogenase).

- Type IV renal tubular acidosis (aldosterone resistance of the kidney's tubules)
- Gordon's syndrome (pseudohypoaldosteronism type II) ("familial hypertension with hyperkalemia"), a rare genetic disorder caused by defective modulators of salt transporters, including the thiazide-sensitive Na-Cl cotransporter.

Excessive release from cells

Metabolic acidosis can cause hyperkalemia as the elevated hydrogen ions in the cells can displace potassium, causing the potassium ions to leave the cell and enter the bloodstream. However, in respiratory acidosis or organic acidosis such as lactic acidosis, the effect on serum potassium are much less significant although the mechanisms are not completely understood.

Insulin deficiency can cause hyperkalemia as the hormoneinsulin increases the uptake of potassium into the cells. Hyperglycemia can also contribute to hyperkalemia by causing hyperosmolality in extracellular fluid, increasing water diffusion out of the cells and causes potassium to move alongside water out of the cells also. The co-existence of insulin deficiency, hyperglycemia, and hyperosmolality is often seen in those affected by diabetic ketoacidosis.

Apart from diabetic ketoacidosis, there are other causes that reduce insulin levels such as the use of the medication octreotide, and fasting which can also cause hyperkalemia. Increased tissue breakdown such as rhabdomyolysis, burns, or any cause of rapid tissue necrosis, including tumor lysis syndrome can cause the release of intracellular potassium into blood, causing hyperkalemia.

Beta2-adrenergic agonists act on beta-2 receptors to drive potassium into the cells. Therefore, beta blockers can raise potassium levels by blocking beta-2 receptors. However, the rise in potassium levels is not marked unless there are other co-morbidities present. Examples of drugs that can raise the serum potassium are non-selective beta-blockers such as propranolol and labetalol. Beta-1 selective blockers such as metoprolol do not increase serum potassium levels.

Exercise can cause a release of potassium into bloodstream by increasing the number of potassium channels in the cell membrane. The degree of potassium elevation varies with the degree of exercise, which range from 0.3 meq/L in light exercise to 2 meq/L in heavy exercise, with or without accompanying ECG changes or lactic acidosis. However, peak potassium levels can be reduced by prior physical conditioning and potassium levels are usually reversed several minutes after exercise. High levels of adrenaline and noradrenaline have a protective effect on the cardiac electrophysiology because they bind to beta 2 adrenergic receptors, which, when activated, extracellularly decrease potassium concentration.

Hyperkalemic periodic paralysis is an autosomal dominant clinical condition where there is a mutation in gene located at 17q23 that regulates the production of protein SCN4A. SCN4A is an important component of sodium channels in skeletal muscles. During exercise, sodium channels would open to allow influx of sodium into the muscle cells for depolarization to occur. But in hyperkalemic periodic paralysis, sodium channels are slow to close after exercise, causing excessive influx of sodium and displacement of potassium out of the cells.

Rare causes of hyperkalemia are discussed as follows. Acute digitalis overdose such as digoxin toxicity may cause hyperkalemia through the inhibition of sodium-potassium-ATPase pump. Massive blood transfusion can cause hyperkalemia in infants due to leakage of potassium out of the red blood cells during storage. Giving succinylcholine to people with conditions such as burns, trauma, infection, prolonged immobilisation can cause hyperkalemia due to widespread activation of acetylcholine receptors rather than a specific group of muscles. Arginine hydrochloride is used to treat refractory metabolic alkalosis. The arginine ions can enter cells and displace potassium out of the cells, causing hyperkalemia. Calcineurin inhibitors such as cyclosporine, tacrolimus, diazoxide, and minoxidil can cause hyperkalemia. Box jellyfish venom can also cause hyperkalemia.

Excessive intake

Excessive intake of potassium is not a primary cause of hyperkalemia because the human body usually can adapt to the rise in the potassium levels by increasing the excretion of potassium into urine through aldosterone hormone secretion and increasing the number of potassium secreting channels in kidney tubules. Acute hyperkalemia in infants is also rare even though their body volume is small, with accidental ingestion of potassium salts or potassium medications. Hyperkalemia usually develops when there are other co-morbidities such as hypoaldosteronism and chronic kidney disease.

Pseudohyperkalemia

Pseudohyperkalemia occurs when the measured potassium level is falsely elevated. This condition is usually suspected when the patient is clinically well without any ECG changes. Mechanical trauma during blood drawing can cause potassium leakage out of the red blood cells due to haemolysis of the blood sample. Repeated fist clenching during the blood draw can cause a transient rise in potassium levels. Prolonged length of blood storage can also increase serum potassium levels. Hyperkalemia may become apparent when a person's platelet concentration is more than 500,000/microL in a clotted blood sample (serum blood sample). Potassium leaks out of platelets after clotting has occurred. A high white cell count (greater than 120,000/microL) in people with chronic lymphocytic leukemia increases the fragility of red blood cells, thus causing pseudohyperkalemia during blood processing. This problem can be avoided by processing serum samples, because clot formation protects the cells from haemolysis during processing. A familial form of pseudohyperkalemia, a benign condition characterised by increased serum potassium in whole blood stored at cold temperatures, also exists. This is due to increased potassium permeability in red blood cells.

Mechanism

Potassium is the most abundant intracellularcation and about 98% of the body's potassium is found inside cells, with the remainder in the extracellular fluid including the blood. Membrane potential is maintained principally by the concentration gradient and membrane permeability to potassium with some contribution from the Na+/K+ pump. The potassium gradient is critically important for many physiological processes, including maintenance of cellular membrane potential, homeostasis of cell volume, and transmission of action potentials in nerve cells.

Potassium is eliminated from the body through the gastrointestinal tract, kidney and sweat glands. In the kidneys, elimination of potassium is passive (through the glomeruli), and reabsorption is active in the proximal tubule and the ascending limb of the loop of Henle. There is active excretion of potassium in the distal tubule and the collecting duct; both are controlled by aldosterone. In sweat glands potassium elimination is quite similar to the kidney, its excretion is also controlled by aldosterone.

Regulation of serum potassium is a function of intake, appropriate distribution between intracellular and extracellular compartments, and effective bodily excretion. In healthy individuals, homeostasis is maintained when cellular uptake and kidney excretion naturally counterbalance a patient's dietary intake of potassium. When kidney function becomes compromised, the ability of the body to effectively regulate serum potassium via the kidney declines. To compensate for this deficit in function, the colon increases its potassium secretion as part of an adaptive response. However, serum potassium remains elevated as the colonic compensating mechanism reaches its limits.

Elevated potassium

Hyperkalemia develops when there is excess production (oral intake, tissue breakdown) or ineffective elimination of potassium. Ineffective elimination can be hormonal (in aldosterone deficiency) or due to causes in the kidney that impair excretion.

Increased extracellular potassium levels result in depolarization of the membrane potentials of cells due to the increase in the equilibrium potential of potassium. This depolarization opens some voltage-gated sodium channels, but also increases the inactivation at the same time. Since depolarization due to concentration change is slow, it never generates an action potential by itself; instead, it results in accommodation. Above a certain level of potassium the depolarization inactivates sodium channels, opens potassium channels, thus the cells become refractory. This leads to the impairment of neuromuscular, cardiac, and gastrointestinal organ systems. Of most concern is the impairment of cardiac conduction, which can cause ventricular fibrillation and/or abnormally slow heart rhythms.

Diagnosis

To gather enough information for diagnosis, the measurement of potassium must be repeated, as the elevation can be due to hemolysis in the first sample. The normal serum level of potassium is 3.5 to 5 mmol/L. Generally, blood tests for kidney function (creatinine, blood urea nitrogen), glucose and occasionally creatine kinase and cortisol are performed. Calculating the trans-tubular potassium gradient can sometimes help in distinguishing the cause of the hyperkalemia.

Also, electrocardiography (ECG) may be performed to determine if there is a significant risk of abnormal heart rhythms. Physicians taking a medical history may focus on kidney disease and medication use (e.g. potassium-sparing diuretics), both of which are known causes of hyperkalemia.

Definitions

Normal serum potassium levels are generally considered to be between 3.5 and 5.3 mmol/L.

Levels above 5.5 mmol/L generally indicate hyperkalemia, and those below 3.5 mmol/L indicate **hypokalemia.**

ECG findings

With mild to moderate hyperkalemia, there is prolongation of the PR interval and development of peaked T waves. Severe hyperkalemia results in a widening of the QRS complex, and the ECG complex can evolve to a sinusoidal shape. There appears to be a direct effect of elevated potassium on some of the potassium channels that increases their activity and speeds membrane repolarisation. Also, (as noted above), hyperkalemia causes an overall membrane depolarization that inactivates many sodium channels. The faster repolarisation of the cardiac action potential causes the tenting of the T waves, and the inactivation of sodium channels causes a sluggish conduction of the electrical wave around the heart, which leads to smaller P waves and widening of the QRS complex. Some of potassium currents are sensitive to extracellular potassium levels, for reasons that are not well understood. As the extracellular potassium levels increase, potassium conductance is increased so that more potassium leaves the myocyte in any given time period. To summarize, classic ECG changes associated with hyperkalemia are seen in the following progression: peaked T wave, shortened QT interval, lengthened PR interval, increased QRS duration, and eventually absence of the P wave with the QRS complex becoming a sine wave. Bradycardia, junctional rhythms and QRS widening are particularly associated with increased risk of adverse outcomes.

The serum potassium concentration at which electrocardiographic changes develop is somewhat variable. Although the factors influencing the effect of serum potassium levels on cardiac electrophysiology are not entirely understood, the concentrations of other electrolytes, as well as levels of catecholamines, play a major role.

ECG findings are not a reliable finding in hyperkalemia. In a retrospective review, blinded cardiologists documented peaked T-waves in only 3 of 90 ECGs with hyperkalemia. Sensitivity of peaked-Ts for hyperkalemia ranged from 0.18 to 0.52 depending on the criteria for peak-T waves.

Prevention

Preventing recurrence of hyperkalemia typically involves reduction of dietary potassium, removal of an offending medication, and/or the addition of a diuretic (such as furosemide or hydrochlorothiazide). Sodium polystyrene sulfonate and sorbitol (combined as Kayexalate) are occasionally used on an ongoing basis to maintain lower serum levels of potassium though the safety of long-term use of sodium polystyrene sulfonate for this purpose is not well understood.

High dietary sources include vegetables such as avocados, tomatoes and potatoes, fruits such as bananas, oranges and nuts.

Treatment

Emergency lowering of potassium levels is needed when new arrhythmias occur at any level of potassium in the blood, or when potassium levels exceed 6.5 mmol/L. Several agents are used to temporarily lower K^+ levels. The choice depends on the degree and cause of the hyperkalemia, and other aspects of the person's condition.

Myocardial excitability

Calcium (calcium chloride or calcium gluconate) increases threshold potential through a mechanism that is still unclear, thus restoring normal gradient between threshold potential and resting membrane potential, which is elevated abnormally in hyperkalemia. A standard ampule of 10% calcium chloride is 10 mL and contains 6.8 mmol of calcium. A standard ampule of 10% calcium gluconate is also 10 mL but has only 2.26 mmol of calcium. Clinical practice guidelines recommend giving 6.8 mmol for typical EKG findings of hyperkalemia. This is 10 mL of 10% calcium chloride or 30 mL of 10% calcium gluconate. Though calcium chloride is more concentrated, it is caustic to the veins and should only be given through a central line. Onset of action is less than one to three minutes and lasts about 30–60 minutes. The goal of treatment is to normalise the EKG and doses can be repeated if the EKG does not improve within a few minutes.

Some textbooks suggest that calcium should not be given in digoxin toxicity as it has been linked to cardiovascular collapse in humans and increased digoxin toxicity in animal models. Recent literature questions the validity of this concern.

Temporary measures

Several medical treatments shift potassium ions from the bloodstream into the cellular compartment, thereby reducing the risk of complications. The effect of these measures tends to be short-lived, but may temporise the problem until potassium can be removed from the body.

- Insulin (e.g. intravenous injection of 10 units of regular insulin along with 50 mL of 50% dextrose to prevent the blood sugar from dropping too low) leads to a shift of potassium ions into cells, secondary to increased activity of the sodium-potassium ATPase. Its effects last a few hours, so it sometimes must be repeated while other measures are taken to suppress potassium levels more permanently. The insulin is usually given with an appropriate amount of glucose to help prevent hypoglycemia following the insulin administration, though hypoglycaemia remains common especially in the context of acute or chronic renal impairment and capillary blood glucose measurements should be taken regularly after administration to identify this.
- Salbutamol (albuterol), a β_2-selective catecholamine, is administered by nebuliser (e.g. 10–20 mg). This medication also lowers blood levels of K^+ by promoting its movement into cells, and will work within 30 minutes. It is recommended to use 20 mg for maximum potassium lowering effect, but to use lower doses if the patient is tachycardic or has ischaemic heart disease. Note that 12-40% of patients do not respond to salbutamol therapy for reasons unknown, especially if on beta-blockers, so it should not be used as monotherapy
- Sodium bicarbonate may be used with the above measures if it is believed the person has metabolic acidosis, though time to effectiveness is longer and its use is controversial.

Elimination

Severe cases require hemodialysis, which are the most rapid methods of removing potassium from the body. These are typically used if the underlying cause cannot be corrected swiftly while temporising measures are instituted or there is no response to these measures.

Loop diuretics (furosemide, bumetanide, torasemide) and thiazide diuretics (e.g., chlortalidone, hydrochlorothiazide, or chlorothiazide) can increase kidney potassium excretion in people with intact kidney function.

Potassium can bind to a number of agents in the gastrointestinal tract. Sodium polystyrene sulfonate with sorbitol (Kayexalate) has been approved for this use and can be given by mouth or rectally. However, high quality evidence to demonstrate the effectiveness of sodium polystyrene are lacking, and use of sodium polystyrene sulfonate, particularly with high sorbitol content, is uncommonly but convincingly associated with colonicnecrosis. There are no systematic studies (>6 months) looking at the long-term safety of this medication.

Patiromer is taken by mouth and works by binding free potassium ions in the gastrointestinal tract and releasing calcium ions for exchange, thus lowering the amount of potassium available for absorption into the bloodstream and increasing the amount lost via the feces. The net effect is a reduction of potassium levels in the blood serum.

Sodium zirconium cyclosilicate is a medication that binds potassium in the gastrointestinal tract in exchange for sodium and hydrogen ions. Onset of effects occurs in one to six hours. It is taken by mouth.

Key points:

Causes

- Increase K+ infusion in IVF
- Tissue injury, surgery, Rhabdomyolysis
- Metabolic acidosis (causes a shiv of potassium from intracellular space into extracellular space)

- Renal failure (excretion)
- Blood transfusion (RBCs contain high concentra:ons of K+)
- Hemodialysis

Signs & Symptoms Arrhythmia
Diagnosis Increase serum K+ > 6 mEq/L and ECG changes (bradycardia and peaked T wave)

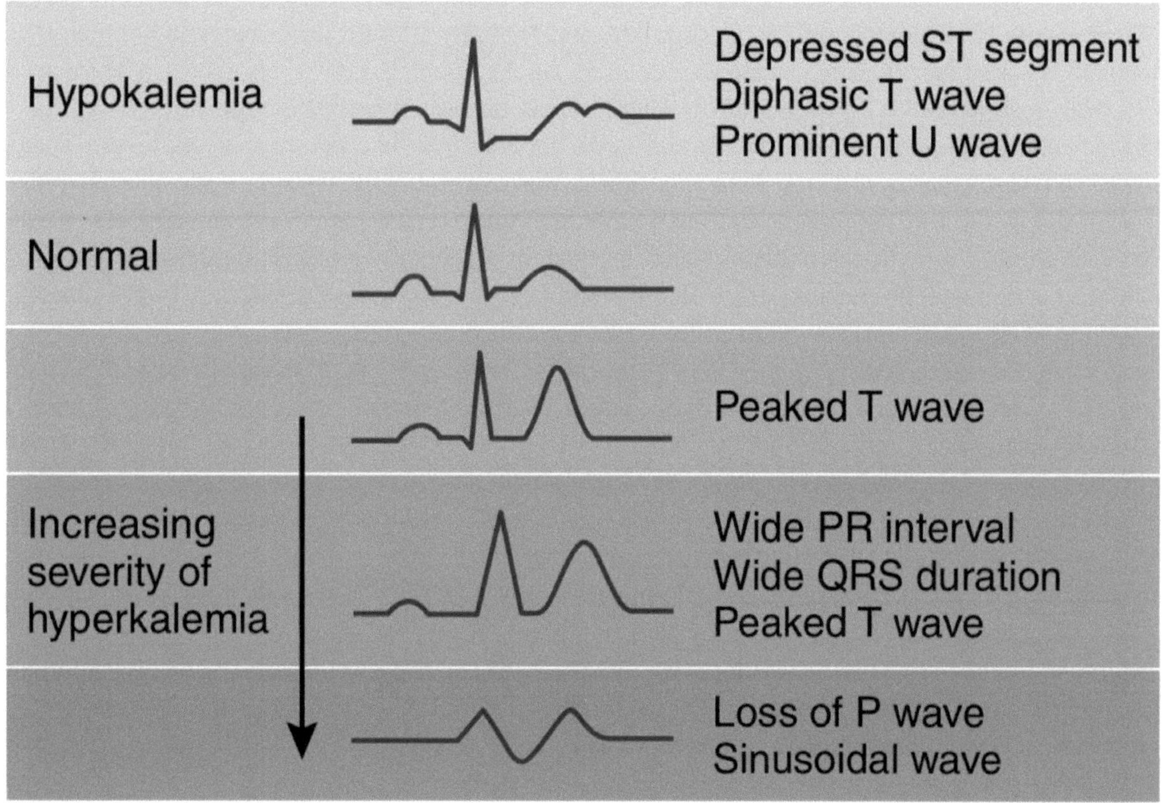

Typical ECG changes associated with hyperkalemia. It is important to note that ECG changes may not correlate closely with serum potassium concentration or be useful in predicting outcomes. As such, a normal ECG should not necessarily be regarded as reassuring if elevated potassium concentration has been definitively observed. Such patients may still experience sudden hyperkalemic cardiac arrest episodes. Reproduced with permission [48].

Fig. 18

Treatment

- Insulin: 10 IU (shivs K+ back into intracellular compartment) + glucose: 1ampule of Dextrose 50% (prevent hypoglycemia from insulin) – over 15 minutes
- Calcium oxalate enemas (can also be given orally)
- Lasix 20-40 mg IV
- Dialysis (if needed)

HYPOKALEMIA

Hypokalemia is a low level of potassium (K^+) in the blood serum. Mild low potassium does not typically cause symptoms. Symptoms may include feeling tired, leg cramps, weakness, and constipation. Low potassium also increases the risk of an abnormal heart rhythm, which is often too slow and can cause cardiac arrest.

Causes of hypokalemia include vomiting, diarrhea, medications like furosemide and steroids, dialysis, diabetesinsipidus, hyperaldosteronism, hypomagnesemia, and not enough intake in the diet. Normal potassium levels in humans are between 3.5 and 5.0 mmol/L (3.5 and 5.0 mEq/L) with levels below 3.5 mmol/L defined as hypokalemia. It is classified as severe when levels are less than 2.5 mmol/L. Low levels may also be suspected based on an electrocardiogram (ECG). Hyperkalemia is a high level of potassium in the blood serum.

The speed at which potassium should be replaced depends on whether or not there are symptoms or abnormalities on an electrocardiogram. Potassium levels that are only slightly below the normal range can be managed with changes in the diet. Lower levels of potassium require replacement with supplements either taken by mouth or given intravenously. If given intravenously, potassium is generally replaced at rates of less than 20 mmol/hour. Solutions containing high concentrations of potassium (>40 mmol/L) should generally be given using a central venous catheter. Magnesium replacement may also be required.

Hypokalemia is one of the most common water–electrolyte imbalances. It affects about 20% of people admitted to hospital. The word *hypokalemia* comes from *hypo-* 'under' + *kalium* 'potassium' + *-emia* 'blood condition'.

Signs and symptoms

Mild hypokalemia is often without symptoms, although it may cause elevation of blood pressure, and can provoke the development of an abnormal heart rhythm. Severe hypokalemia, with serum potassium concentrations of 2.5–3 meq/L (Nl: 3.5–5.0 meq/L), may cause muscle weakness, myalgia, tremor, and muscle cramps (owing to disturbed function of skeletal muscle), and constipation (from disturbed function of smooth muscle). With more severe hypokalemia, flaccid paralysis and hyporeflexia may result. Reports exist of rhabdomyolysis occurring with profound hypokalemia with serum potassium levels less than 2 meq/L. Respiratory depression from severe impairment of skeletal muscle function is found in some people. Psychological symptoms associated with severe hypokalemia can include delirium, hallucinations, depression, or psychosis.

Causes

Hypokalemia can result from one or more of these medical conditions:

Inadequate potassium intake

Not eating a diet with enough potassium-containing foods or fasting can cause the gradual onset of hypokalemia. This is a rare cause and may occur in those with anorexia nervosa or those on a ketogenic diet.

Gastrointestinal or skin loss

A more common cause is excessive loss of potassium, often associated with heavy fluid losses that flush potassium out of the body. Typically, this is a consequence of diarrhea, excessive perspiration, or losses associated with muscle-crush injury, or surgical procedures. Vomiting can also cause hypokalemia, although not much potassium is lost from the vomitus. Rather, heavy urinary losses of K^+ in the setting of post-emetic bicarbonaturia force urinary potassium excretion. (See discussion of alkalosis below.) Other gastrointestinal causes include pancreatic fistulae and the presence of adenoma.

Urinary loss

- Certain medications can cause excess potassium loss in the urine. Blood pressure medications such as loop diuretics (e.g. furosemide) and thiazide diuretics (e.g. hydrochlorothiazide) commonly cause hypokalemia. Other medications such as the antifungal amphotericin B or the cancer drug cisplatin can also cause long-term hypokalemia. Diuretic abuse among athletes and people with eating disorders may present with hypokalemia due to urinary potassium loss.

- A special case of potassium loss occurs with diabetic ketoacidosis. Hypokalemia is observed with low total body potassium and a low intracellular concentration of potassium. In addition to urinary losses from polyuria and volume contraction, also an obligate loss of potassium from kidney tubules occurs as a cationic partner to the negatively charged ketone, β-hydroxybutyrate.
- A low level of magnesium in the blood can also cause hypokalemia. Magnesium is required for adequate processing of potassium. This may become evident when hypokalemia persists despite potassium supplementation. Other electrolyte abnormalities may also be present.

- An increase in the pH of the blood (alkalosis) can cause temporary hypokalemia by causing a shift of potassium out of the plasma and interstitial fluids into the urine via a number of interrelated mechanisms.
1) Type B intercalated cells in the collecting duct reabsorb H^+ and secrete HCO_3, while in type A intercalated cells protons are secreted via both H^+-K^+ATPases and H^+ ATP-ases on the apical/luminal surface of the cell. By definition, the H^+-K^+ATPase reabsorbs one potassium ion into the cell for every proton it secretes into the lumen of the collecting duct of a nephron. In addition, when H^+ is expelled from the cell (by H^+ATP-ase), cations—in this case potassium—are taken up by the cell in order to maintain electroneutrality (but not through direct exchange as with the H^+-K^+ATPase). In order to correct the pH during alkalosis, these cells will use these mechanisms to reabsorb great amounts of H^+, which will concomitantly increase their intracellular concentrations of potassium. This concentration gradient drives potassium to be secreted across the apical surface of the cell into the tubular lumen through potassium channels (this facilitated diffusion occurs in both Type B intercalated cells and Principal cells in the collecting duct).
2) Metabolic alkalosis is often present in states of volume depletion, such as vomiting, so potassium is also lost via aldosterone-mediated mechanisms.
3) During metabolic alkalosis, the acute rise of plasma HCO_3^- concentration (caused by vomiting, for example) will exceed the capacity of the renal proximal tubule to reabsorb this anion, and potassium will be excreted as an obligate cation partner to the bicarbonate.
- Disease states that lead to abnormally high aldosterone levels can cause hypertension and excessive urinary losses of potassium. These include renal artery stenosis and tumors (generally nonmalignant) of the adrenal glands, e.g., Conn's syndrome (primary hyperaldosteronism). Cushing's syndrome can also lead to hypokalemia due to excess cortisol binding the Na^+/K^+ pump and acting like aldosterone. Hypertension and hypokalemia can also be seen with a deficiency of the 11-beta-hydroxysteroid dehydrogenase type 2 enzyme which allows cortisols to stimulate aldosterone receptors. This deficiency—known as apparent mineralocorticoid excess syndrome—can either be congenital or caused by consumption of glycyrrhizin, which is contained in extract of licorice, sometimes found in herbal supplements, candies, and chewing tobacco.
- Rare hereditary defects of renal salt transporters, such as Bartter syndrome or Gitelman syndrome, can cause hypokalemia, in a manner similar to that of diuretics. As opposed to disease states of primary excesses of aldosterone, blood pressure is either normal or low in Bartter's or Gitelman's.

Distribution away from extracellular fluid

- In addition to alkalosis, other factors can cause transient shifting of potassium into cells, presumably by stimulation of the Na^+/K^+ pump. These hormones and medications include insulin, epinephrine, and other beta agonists (e.g. salbutamol or salmeterol), and xanthines (e.g. theophylline). Stimulants (amphetamines, methylphenidate, cocaine) can also cause hypokalemia by stimulating beta-2 receptors.
- Rare hereditary defects of muscular ion channels and transporters that cause hypokalemic periodic paralysis can precipitate occasional attacks of severe hypokalemia and muscle weakness. These defects cause a heightened

sensitivity to the normal changes in potassium produced by catecholamines and/or insulin and/or thyroid hormone, which lead to movement of potassium from the extracellular fluid into the muscle cells.

Others

- A handful of published reports describe individuals with severe hypokalemia related to chronic extreme consumption (4–10 L/day) of colas. The hypokalemia is thought to be from the combination of the diuretic effect of caffeine[21] and copious fluid intake, although it may also be related to diarrhea caused by heavy fructose ingestion.

Pseudohypokalemia

- Pseudohypokalemia is a decrease in the amount of potassium that occurs due to excessive uptake of potassium by metabolically active cells in a blood sample after it has been drawn. It is a laboratory artifact that may occur when blood samples remain in warm conditions for several hours before processing.

Pathophysiology

About 98% of the body's potassium is found inside cells, with the remainder in the extracellular fluid including the blood. This concentration gradient is maintained principally by the Na^+/K^+ pump.

Potassium is essential for many body functions, including muscle and nerve activity. The electrochemical gradient of potassium between the intracellular and extracellular space is essential for nerve function; in particular, potassium is needed to repolarize the cell membrane to a resting state after an action potential has passed. Lower potassium levels in the extracellular space cause hyperpolarization of the resting membrane potential. This hyperpolarization is caused by the effect of the altered potassium gradient on resting membrane potential as defined by the Goldman equation. As a result, a greater-than-normal stimulus is required for depolarization of the membrane to initiate an action potential.

In the heart, hypokalemia causes arrhythmias because of less-than-complete recovery from sodium-channel inactivation, making the triggering of an action potential less likely. In addition, the reduced extracellular potassium (paradoxically) inhibits the activity of the I_{Kr} potassium current and delays ventricular repolarization. This delayed repolarization may promote reentrant arrhythmias.

Diagnosis

Blood

Normal potassium levels are between 3.5 and 5.0 mmol/L with levels below 3.5 mmol/L (less than 3.5 mEq/L) defined as hypokalemia.

Electrocardiogram

Hypokalemia leads to characteristic ECG changes (PR prolongation, ST-segment and T-wave depression, U-wave formation).

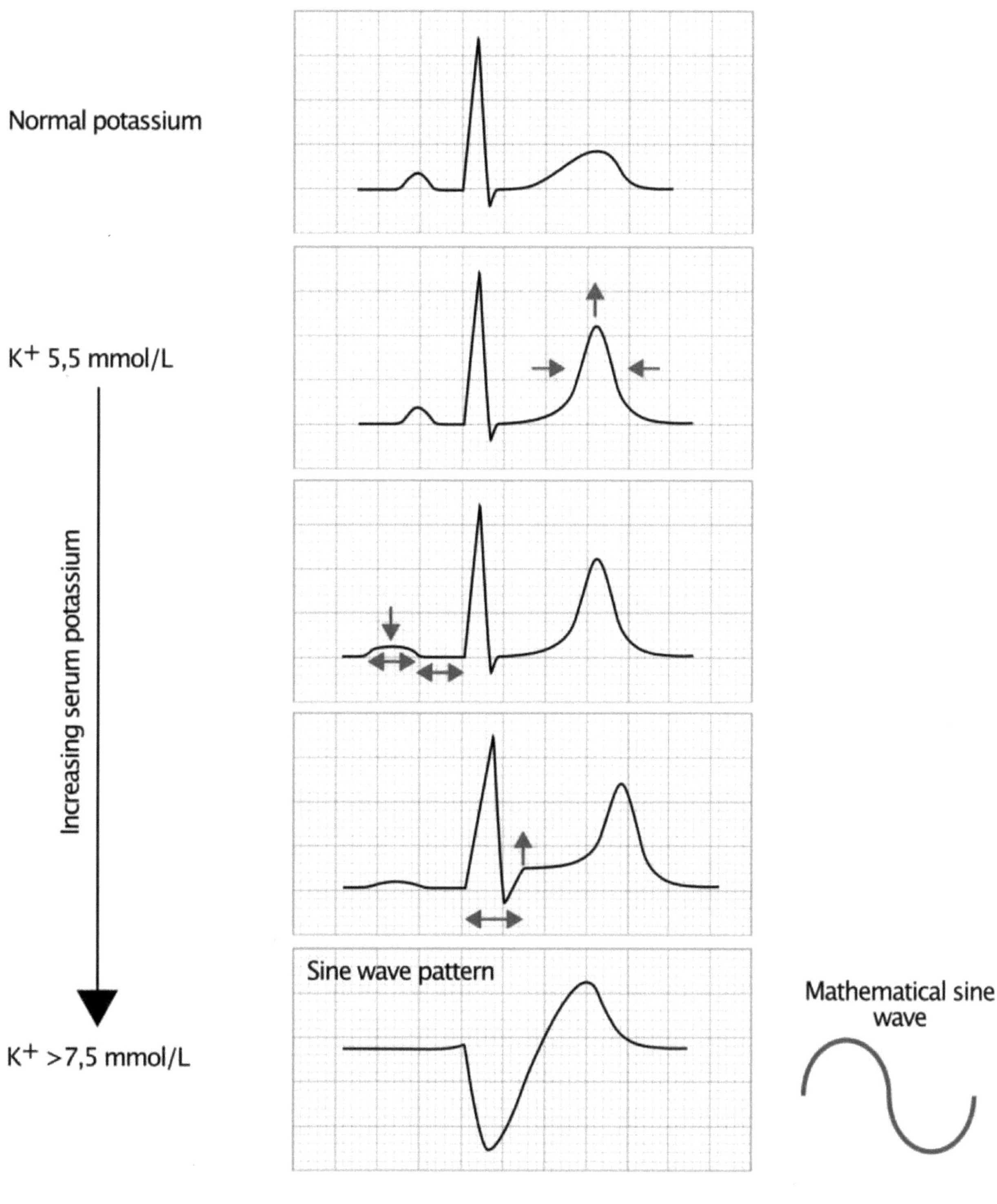

Fig. 17

The earliest electrocardiographic (ECG) findings, associated with hypokalemia, are decreased T wave height. Then, ST depressions and T inversions appear as serum potassium levels reduce further. Due to prolonged repolarization of ventricular Purkinje fibers, prominent U waves occur (usually seen at V2 and V3 leads), frequently superimposed upon T waves, therefore producing the appearance of prolonged QT intervals, when serum potassium levels fall below 3 mEq/L.

Amount

The amount of potassium deficit can be calculated using the following formula:

$K_{deficit}$ (in mmol) = ($K_{normal\ lower\ limit} - K_{measured}$) × body weight (kg) × 0.4

Meanwhile, the daily body requirement of potassium is calculated by multiplying 1 mmol to body weight in kilograms. Adding potassium deficit and daily potassium requirement would give the total amount of potassium need to be corrected in mmol. Dividing mmol by 13.4 will give the potassium in grams.

Treatment

Treatment includes addressing the cause, such as improving the diet, treating diarrhea, or stopping an offending medication. People without a significant source of potassium loss and who show no symptoms of hypokalemia may not require treatment. Acutely, repletion with 10 mEq of potassium is typically expected to raise serum potassium by 0.1 mEq/L immediately after administration. However, for those with chronic hypokalemia, repletion takes time due to tissue redistribution. For example, correction by 1 mEq/L can take more than 1000 mEq of potassium over many days.

Oral potassium supplementation

Mild hypokalemia (>3.0 mEq/L) may be treated by eating potassium-containing foods or by taking potassium chloride supplements in a tablet or syrup form (by mouth supplements). Foods rich in potassium include dried fruits (particularly dried figs), nuts, bran cereals and wheat germ, lima beans, molasses, leafy green vegetables, broccoli, winter squash, beets, carrots, cauliflower, potatoes, avocados, tomatoes, coconut water, citrus fruits (particularly oranges), cantaloupe, kiwis, mangoes, bananas, and red meats.

Eating potassium-rich foods may not be sufficient for correcting low potassium; potassium supplements may be recommended. Potassium contained in foods is almost entirely coupled with phosphate and is thus ineffective in correcting hypokalemia associated with hypochloremia that may occur due to vomiting, diuretic therapy, or nasogastric drainage. Additionally, replacing potassium solely through diet may be costly and result in weight gain due to potentially large amounts of food needed. An effort should also be made to limit dietary sodium intake due to an inverse relationship with serum potassium. Increasing magnesium intake may also be beneficial for similar physiological reasons.

Potassium chloride supplements by mouth have the advantage of containing precise quantities of potassium, but the disadvantages of a taste which may be unpleasant, and the potential for side-effects including nausea and abdominal discomfort. Potassium bicarbonate is preferred when correcting hypokalemia associated with metabolic acidosis.

Intravenous potassium replacement

Severe hypokalemia (<3.0 mEq/L) may require intravenous supplementation. Typically, a saline solution is used, with 20–40 meq/L KCl per liter over 3–4 hours. Giving IV potassium at faster rates (20–25 meq/hr) may inadvertently expose the heart to a sudden increase in potassium, potentially causing dangerous abnormal heart rhythms such as heart block or asystole. Faster infusion rates are therefore generally only performed in locations in which the heart rhythm can be continuously monitored such as a critical care unit. When replacing potassium intravenously, particularly when higher concentrations of potassium are used, infusion by a central line is encouraged to avoid the occurrence of a burning sensation at the site of infusion, or the rare occurrence of damage to the vein. When peripheral infusions are necessary, the burning can be reduced by diluting the potassium in larger amounts of fluid, or adding a small dose of lidocaine to the intravenous fluid, although adding lidocaine may increase the likelihood of medical errors. Even in severe hypokalemia, oral supplementation is preferred given its safety profile. Sustained-release formulations should be avoided in acute settings.

Potassium-sparing diuretics

Hypokalemia which is recurrent or resistant to treatment may be amenable to a potassium-sparing diuretic, such as amiloride, triamterene, spironolactone, or eplerenone. Concomitant hypomagnesemia will inhibit potassium replacement, as magnesium is a cofactor for potassium uptake.

Key points:

Causes

- The most common surgical abnormality
- Inadequate replacement (e.g. during surgery)
- Diure:cs (e.g. Lasix)
- Metabolic alkalosis (shifts K+ to intracellular compartment)
- Hyperaldosteronism (promotes K+ excretion in kidneys)
- Gastrointes:nal tract losses: (Vomi:ng, Gastric aspira:on/drainage, Fistulae, Diarrhea , Ileus (disruption of the normal propulsive gastrointes:nal track that causes obstruc:on which prevents bowel contents, such as stool, fluid and gas, from moving through the intestine, which becomes distended), Intestinal obstruction, Potassium-secreting villous adenomas
- Urinary loss
- Renal tubular disorders (e.g. Bartner syndrome, renal tubular acidosis, amphotericin-induced tubular damage)

Signs & Symptoms
Weakness and fa:gue (most common), muscle cramps and pain (severe cases), altered level of consciousness, arrhythmias
Diagnosis Occurs when serum K+<3 mEq/L.
Treatment

- K+ replacement (KCl solu:on) infusion or orally.
- Should not be administered at rate greater than 10-20 mmol/hr

CALCIUM DISTURBANCES

Hypercalcemia

Hypercalcemia, also spelled hypercalcaemia, is a high calcium (Ca^{2+}) level in the blood serum. The normal range is 2.1–2.6 mmol/L (8.8–10.7 mg/dL, 4.3–5.2 mEq/L), with levels greater than 2.6 mmol/L defined as hypercalcemia. Those with a mild increase that has developed slowly typically have no symptoms. In those with greater levels or rapid onset, symptoms may include abdominal pain, bone pain, confusion, depression, weakness, kidney stones or an abnormal heart rhythm including cardiac arrest.

Most outpatient cases are due to primary hyperparathyroidism and inpatient cases due to cancer. Other causes of hypercalcemia include sarcoidosis, tuberculosis, Paget disease, multiple endocrine neoplasia (MEN), vitamin D toxicity, familial hypocalciuric hypercalcaemia and certain medications such as lithium and hydrochlorothiazide. Diagnosis should generally include either a corrected calcium or ionized calcium level and be confirmed after a week. Specific changes, such as a shortened QT interval and prolonged PR interval, may be seen on an electrocardiogram (ECG).

Treatment may include intravenous fluids, furosemide, calcitonin, intravenous bisphosphonate, in addition to treating the underlying cause. The evidence for furosemide use, however, is poor. In those with very high levels, hospitalization may be required. Haemodialysis may be used in those who do not respond to other treatments. In those with vitamin D toxicity, steroids may be useful. Hypercalcemia is relatively common. Primary hyperparathyroidism occurs in 1–7 per 1,000 people, and hypercalcaemia occurs in about 2.7% of those with cancer.

Signs and symptoms

Mnemonic for symptoms	
Stones	Kidney or biliary
Bones	Bone pain
Groans	Abdominal discomfort
Moans	Complaints of non-specific symptoms
Thrones	Constipation and excessive urination volume
Muscle tone	Muscle weakness, decreased reflexes
Psychiatric overtones	Depression, anxiety, cognitive dysfunction

Table 11

The neuromuscular symptoms of hypercalcaemia are caused by a negative bathmotropic effect due to the increased interaction of calcium with sodium channels. Since calcium blocks sodium channels and inhibits depolarization of nerve and muscle fibers, increased calcium raises the threshold for depolarization. This results in diminished deep tendon reflexes (hyporeflexia), and skeletal muscle weakness.

Other symptoms include cardiac arrhythmias (especially in those taking digoxin), fatigue, nausea, vomiting (emesis), loss of appetite, abdominal pain, & paralytic ileus. If kidney impairment occurs as a result, manifestations can include increased urination, urination at night, and increased thirst. Psychiatric manifestation can include emotional instability, confusion, delirium, psychosis, and stupor. Calcium deposits known as limbus sign may be visible in the eyes.

Symptoms are more common at high calcium blood values (12.0 mg/dL or 3 mmol/L). Severe hypercalcaemia (above 15–16 mg/dL or 3.75–4 mmol/L) is considered a medical emergency: at these levels, coma and cardiac arrest can result. The high levels of calcium ions decrease the neuron membrane permeability to sodium ions, thus decreasing excitability, which leads to hypotonicity of smooth and striated muscle. This explains the fatigue, muscle weakness, low tone and sluggish reflexes in muscle groups. The sluggish nerves also explain drowsiness, confusion, hallucinations, stupor or coma. In the gut this causes constipation. Hypocalcaemia causes the opposite by the same mechanism.

Hypercalcaemic crisis

A hypercalcaemic crisis is an emergency situation with a severe hypercalcaemia, generally above approximately 14 mg/dL (or 3.5 mmol/L).

The main symptoms of a hypercalcaemic crisis are oliguria or anuria, as well as somnolence or coma. After recognition, primary hyperparathyroidism should be proved or excluded.

In extreme cases of primary hyperparathyroidism, removal of the parathyroid gland after surgical neck exploration is the only way to avoid death. The diagnostic program should be performed within hours, in parallel with measures to lower serum calcium. Treatment of choice for acutely lowering calcium is extensive hydration and calcitonin, as well as bisphosphonates (which have effect on calcium levels after one or two days).

Causes

Primary hyperparathyroidism and malignancy account for about 90% of cases of hypercalcaemia.

Causes of hypercalcemia can be divided into those that are PTH dependent or PTH independent.

Parathyroid function

- Primary hyperparathyroidism
    - Solitary parathyroid adenoma
    - Primary parathyroid hyperplasia
    - Parathyroid carcinoma
    - Multiple endocrine neoplasia (MEN1 & MEN2A)
    - Familial isolated hyperparathyroidism
- Lithium use
- Familial hypocalciuric hypercalcemia/familial benign hypercalcemia.

- Solid tumour with metastasis (e.g. breast cancer or classically squamous cell carcinoma, which can be PTHrP-mediated)
- Solid tumour with humoral mediation of hypercalcaemia (e.g. lung cancer, most commonly non-small cell lung cancer or kidney cancer, phaeochromocytoma)
- Haematologiccancers (multiple myeloma, lymphoma, leukaemia)
- Ovarian small cell carcinoma of the hypercalcemic type

Vitamin-D disorders

- Hypervitaminosis D (vitamin D intoxication)
- Elevated $1,25(OH)_2D$ (see calcitriol under Vitamin D) levels (e.g. sarcoidosis and other granulomatous diseases such as tuberculosis, berylliosis, histoplasmosis, Crohn's disease, and granulomatosis with polyangiitis)
- Idiopathic hypercalcaemia of infancy
- Rebound hypercalcaemia after rhabdomyolysis

High bone-turnover

- Hyperthyroidism
- Multiple myeloma
- Prolonged immobilization
- Paget's disease
- Thiazide use
- Vitamin A intoxication

Kidney failure

- Tertiary hyperparathyroidism
- Aluminium intoxication
- Milk-alkali syndrome

Others

- Acromegaly
- Adrenal insufficiency
- Zollinger–Ellison syndrome
- Williams Syndrome

Diagnosis

Diagnosis should generally include either a calculation of corrected calcium or direct measurement of ionized calcium level and be confirmed after a week. This is because either high or low serum albumin levels does not show the true levels of ionised calcium. There is, however, controversy around the usefulness of corrected calcium as it may be no better than total calcium.

Once calcium is confirmed to be elevated, a detailed history taken from the subject, including review of medications, any vitamin supplementations, herbal preparations, and previous calcium values. Chronic elevation of calcium with absent or mild symptoms often points to primary hyperparathyroidism or Familial hypocalciuric hypercalcemia. For those who has underlying malignancy, the cancers may be sufficiently severe to show up in history and examination to point towards the diagnosis with little laboratory investigations.

If detailed history and examination does not narrow down the differential diagnoses, further laboratory investigations are performed. Intact PTH (iPTH, biologically active parathyroid hormone molecules) is measured with immunoradiometric or immunochemoluminescent assay. Elevated (or high-normal) iPTH with high urine calcium/creatinine ratio (more than 0.03) is suggestive of primary hyperparathyroidism, usually accompanied by low serum phosphate. High iPTH with low urine calcium/creatinine ratio is suggestive of familial hypocalciuric hypercalcemia. Low iPTH should be followed up with Parathyroid hormone-related protein (PTHrP) measurements (though not available in all labs). Elevated PTHrP is suggestive of malignancy. Normal PTHrP is suggestive of multiple myeloma, vitamin A excess, milk-alkali syndrome, thyrotoxicosis, and immobilisation. Elevated Calcitriol is suggestive of lymphoma, sarcoidosis, granulomatous disorders, and excessive calcitriol intake. Elevated calcifediol is suggestive of vitamin D or excessive calcifediol intake.

The normal range is 2.1–2.6 mmol/L (8.8–10.7 mg/dL, 4.3–5.2 mEq/L), with levels greater than 2.6 mmol/L defined as hypercalcaemia. Moderate hypercalcaemia is a level of 2.88–3.5 mmol/L (11.5–14 mg/dL) while severe hypercalcaemia is > 3.5 mmol/L (>14 mg/dL).

ECG

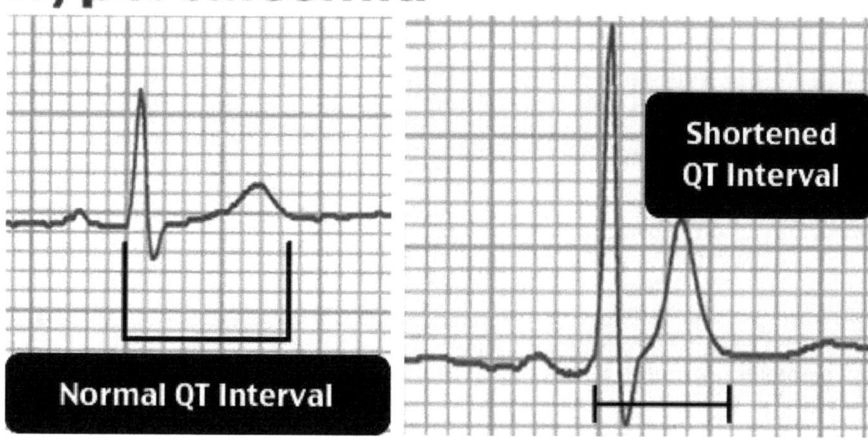

Fig. 19

An Osborn wave, an abnormal EKG tracing that can be associated with hypercalcemia.

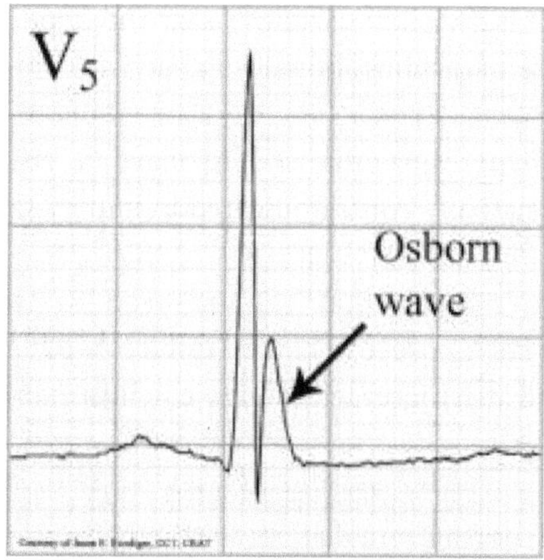

Fig. 20

Abnormal heart rhythms can also result, and ECG findings of a short QT intervalsuggest hypercalcaemia. Significant hypercalcaemia can cause ECG changes mimicking an acute myocardial infarction. Hypercalcaemia has also been known to cause an ECG finding mimicking hypothermia, known as an Osborn wave.

Treatments

The goal of therapy is to treat the hypercalcaemia first and subsequently effort is directed to treat the underlying cause.

Fluids and diuretics

Initial therapy:

- hydration, increasing salt intake, and forced diuresis.
  - hydration is needed because many patients are dehydrated due to vomiting or kidney defects in concentrating urine.

- increased salt intake also can increase body fluid volume as well as increasing urine sodium excretion, which further increases urinary calcium excretion.
- after rehydration, a loop diuretic such as furosemide can be given to permit continued large volume intravenous salt and water replacement while minimizing the risk of blood volume overload and pulmonary oedema. In addition, loop diuretics tend to depress calcium reabsorption by the kidney thereby helping to lower blood calcium levels
- can usually decrease serum calcium by 1–3 mg/dL within 24 hours
- caution must be taken to prevent potassium or magnesium depletion

Bisphosphonates and calcitonin
Additional therapy:

- bisphosphonates are pyrophosphate analogues with high affinity for bone, especially areas of high bone-turnover.
    - they are taken up by osteoclasts and inhibit osteoclastic bone resorption
    - current available drugs include (in order of potency): (1st gen) etidronate, (2nd gen) tiludronate, IV pamidronate, alendronate (3rd gen) zoledronate and risedronate
    - all people with cancer-associated hypercalcaemia should receive treatment with bisphosphonates since the 'first line' therapy (above) cannot be continued indefinitely nor is it without risk. Further, even if the 'first line' therapy has been effective, it is a virtual certainty that the hypercalcaemia will recur in the person with hypercalcaemia of malignancy. Use of bisphosphonates in such circumstances, then, becomes both therapeutic and preventative
    - people in kidney failure and hypercalcaemia should have a risk-benefit analysis before being given bisphosphonates, since they are relatively contraindicated in kidney failure.

- Denosumab is a bone anti-resorptive agent that can be used to treat hypercalcemia in patients with a contraindication to bisphosphonates such as severe kidney failure or allergy.
- Calcitonin blocks bone resorption and also increases urinary calcium excretion by inhibiting calcium reabsorption by the kidney
    - Usually used in life-threatening hypercalcaemia along with rehydration, diuresis, and bisphosphonates
    - Helps prevent recurrence of hypercalcaemia
    - Dose is 4 international units per kilogram via subcutaneous or intramuscular route every 12 hours, usually not continued indefinitely due to quick onset of decreased response to calcitonin

Other therapies

- rarely used, or used in special circumstances
    - plicamycin inhibits bone resorption (rarely used)
    - gallium nitrate inhibits bone resorption and changes structure of bone crystals (rarely used)
    - glucocorticoids increase urinary calcium excretion and decrease intestinal calcium absorption
        - no effect on calcium level in normal or primary hyperparathyroidism
        - effective in hypercalcaemia due to osteolytic malignancies (multiple myeloma, leukaemia, Hodgkin's lymphoma, carcinoma of the breast) due to antitumour properties
        - also effective in hypervitaminosis D and sarcoidosis

- dialysis usually used in severe hypercalcaemia complicated by kidney failure. Supplemental phosphate should be monitored and added if necessary
- phosphate therapy can correct the hypophosphataemia in the face of hypercalcaemia and lower serum calcium

Other animals

Research has led to a better understanding of hypercalcemia in non-human animals. Often the causes of hypercalcemia have a correlation to the environment in which the organisms live. Hypercalcemia in house pets is typically due to disease, but other cases can be due to accidental ingestion of plants or chemicals in the home. Outdoor animals commonly develop hypercalcemia through vitamin D toxicity from wild plants within their environments.

Household pets

Household pets such as dogs and cats are found to develop hypercalcemia. It is less common in cats, and many feline cases are idiopathic. In dogs, lymphosarcoma, Addison's disease, primary hyperparathyroidism, and chronic kidney failure are the main causes of hypercalcemia, but there are also environmental causes usually unique to indoor pets. Ingestion of small amounts of calcipotriene found in psoriasis cream can be fatal to a pet.Calcipotriene causes a rapid rise in calcium ion levels. Calcium ion levels can remain high for weeks if untreated and lead to an array of medical issues. There are also cases of hypercalcemia reported due to dogs ingesting rodenticides containing a chemical similar to calcipotriene found in psoriasis cream. Additionally, ingestion of household plants is a cause of hypercalcemia. Plants such as *Cestrum diurnum*, and *Solanum malacoxylon* contain ergocalciferol or cholecalciferol which cause the onset of hypercalcemia. Consuming small amounts of these plants can be fatal to pets. Observable symptoms may develop such as polydipsia, polyuria, extreme fatigue, or constipation.

Trisetum flavescens (yellow oat grass)

In certain outdoor environments, animals such as horses, pigs, cattle, and sheep experience hypercalcemia commonly. In southern Brazil and Mattewara India, approximately 17 percent of sheep are affected, with 60 percent of these cases being fatal. Many cases are also documented in Argentina, Papua New Guinea, Jamaica, Hawaii, and Bavaria. These cases of hypercalcemeia are usually caused by ingesting *Trisetum flavescens* before it has dried out. Once *Trisetum flavescens* is dried out, the toxicity of it is diminished. Other plants causing hypercalcemia are *Cestrum diurnum*, *Nierembergia veitchii*, *Solanum esuriale*, *Solanum torvum*, and *Solanum malacoxylon*. These plants contain calcitriol or similar substances that cause rises in calcium ion levels. Hypercalcemia is most common in grazing lands at altitudes above 1500 meters where growth of plants like *Trisetum flavescens* is favorable. Even if small amounts are ingested over long periods of time, the prolonged high levels of calcium ions have large negative effects on the animals. The issues these animals experience are muscle weakness, and calcification of blood vessels, heart valves, liver, kidneys, and other soft tissues, which eventually can lead to death.

Key points:

Causes hyperparathyroidism and malignancy.

Symptoms confusion, weakness, lethargy, anorexia, vomiting, epigastric abdominal pain (due to pancreatitis), and polyuria (nephrogenic diabetes insipidus)

Diagnosis by measuring the **free** Ca++ >10mg/dl

Treatment includes normal saline infusion

↪ If Ca >14mg/dl with ECG changes: additional diuretics, calcitonin, and mithramycin (antineoplastic antibiotic that has been discontinued) might be necessary.

HYPOCALCEMIA

Hypocalcemia is a medical condition characterized by low calcium levels in the blood serum. The normal range of blood calcium is typically between 2.1–2.6 mmol/L (8.8–10.7 mg/dL, 4.3–5.2 mEq/L) while levels less than 2.1 mmol/L are defined as hypocalcemic. Mildly low levels that develop slowly often have no symptoms. Otherwise symptoms may include numbness, muscle spasms, seizures, confusion, or cardiac arrest.

The most common cause for hypocalcemia is iatrogenichypoparathyroidism. Other causes include other forms of hypoparathyroidism, vitamin D deficiency, kidney failure, pancreatitis, calcium channel blocker overdose, rhabdomyolysis, tumor lysis syndrome, and medications such as bisphosphonates or denosumab. Diagnosis should generally be confirmed with a corrected calcium or ionized calcium level. Specific changes may be seen on an electrocardiogram (ECG).

Initial treatment for severe disease is with intravenous calcium chloride and possibly magnesium sulfate. Other treatments may include vitamin D, magnesium, and calcium supplements. If due to hypoparathyroidism, hydrochlorothiazide, phosphate binders, and a low salt diet may also be recommended. About 18% of people who are being treated in hospital have hypocalcemia.

Signs and symptoms

Purpura

The neuromuscular symptoms of hypocalcemia are caused by a positive bathmotropic effect (i.e. increased responsiveness) due to the decreased interaction of calcium with sodium channels. Since calcium blocks sodium channels and inhibits depolarization of nerve and muscle fibers, reduced calcium lowers the threshold for depolarization. The symptoms can be recalled by the mnemonic "CATs go numb" - convulsions, arrhythmias, tetany, and numbness in the hands and feet and around the mouth.

- Petechiae which appear as on-off spots, then later become confluent, and appear as purpura (larger bruised areas, usually in dependent regions of the body).
- Oral, perioral and acral paresthesias, tingling or 'pins and needles' sensation in and around the mouth and lips, and in the extremities of the hands and feet. This is often the earliest symptom of hypocalcaemia.
- Carpopedal and generalized tetany (unrelieved and strong contractions of the hands, and in the large muscles of the rest of the body) are seen.
- Latent tetany
    - Trousseau sign of latent tetany (eliciting carpal spasm by inflating the blood pressure cuff and maintaining the cuff pressure above systolic)
    - Chvostek's sign (tapping of the inferior portion of the cheekbone will produce facial spasms)[8]
- Tendon reflexes are hyperactive
- Life-threatening complications
    - Cardiac arrhythmias
- Effects on cardiac output
    - Negative chronotropic effect, or a decrease in heart rate.
    - Negative inotropic effect, or a decrease in contractility
- ECG changes include the following:
    - Intermittent QT prolongation, or intermittent prolongation of the QTc (corrected QT interval) on the ECG (electrocardiogram) is noted. The implications of intermittent QTc prolongation predisposes to life-threatening cardiac electrical instability (and this is therefore a more critical condition than constant QTc prolongation). This type of electrical instability puts the person at high risk of torsades de pointes, a specific type of ventricular tachycardia which appears on an EKG (or ECG) as something which looks a bit like a sine wave with a regularly increasing and decreasing amplitude. (Torsades de pointes can cause death, unless the person can be medically or electrically cardioverted and returned to a normal cardiac rhythm.)

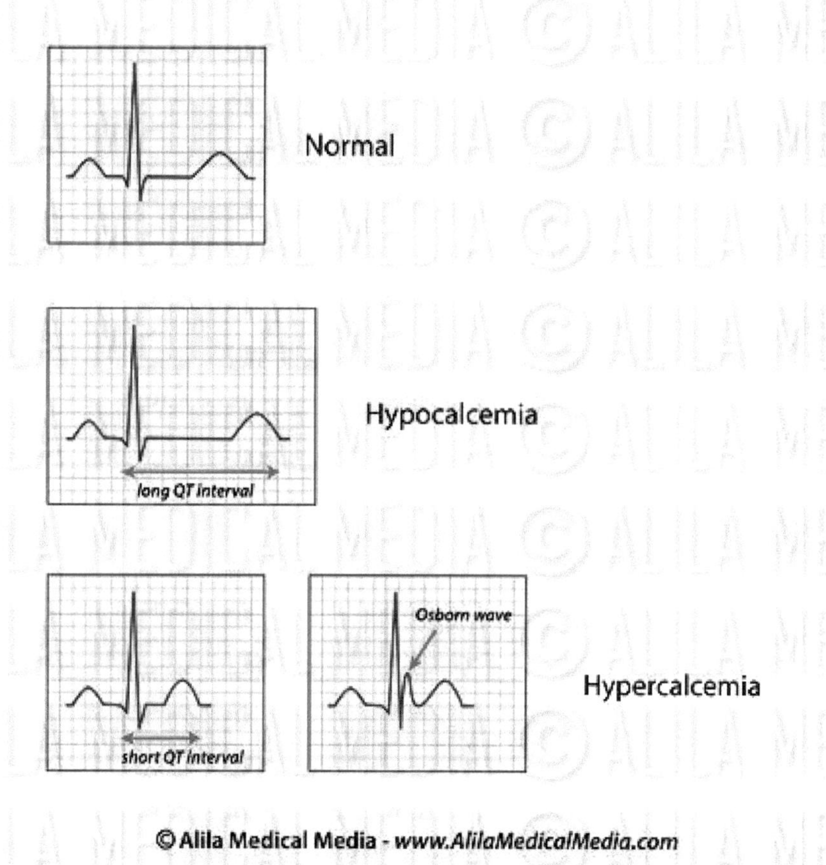

Fig. 21

Causes

Hypoparathyroidism is a common cause of hypocalcemia. Calcium is tightly regulated by the parathyroid hormone (PTH). In response to low calcium levels, PTH levels rise, and conversely if there are high calcium levels then PTH secretion declines. However, in the setting of absent, decreased, or ineffective PTH hormone, the body loses this regulatory function, and hypocalcemia ensues. Hypoparathyroidism is commonly due to surgical destruction of the parathyroid glands. Hypoparathyroidism may also be due to autoimmune problem. Some causes of hypocalcaemia are as follows:

- Hyperphosphatemia
- Vitamin D deficiency
- Chronic liver disease
- Edetate disodium
- Magnesium deficiency
- Prolonged use of medications/laxatives (magnesium)
- Osteomalacia
- Chronic kidney failure
- Ineffective active vitamin D
- Hypoparathyroidism/genetic
- After surgery hypoparathyroidism
- Hungry bone syndrome

- Tumour lysis syndrome
- Acute kidney injury
- Rhabdomyolysis (initial stage)
- As a complication of pancreatitis
- Alkalosis
- Massive red blood cell transfusion due to excess citrate in the blood
- As blood plasma hydrogen ion concentration decreases, caused by respiratory or metabolic alkalosis, the concentration of freely ionized calcium, the biologically active component of blood calcium, decreases. Because a portion of both hydrogen ions and calcium are bound to serum albumin, when blood becomes alkalotic, the bound hydrogen ions dissociate from albumin, freeing up the albumin to bind with more calcium and thereby decreasing the freely ionized portion of total serum calcium. For every 0.1 increase in pH, ionized calcium decreases by about 0.05 mmol/L. This hypocalcaemia related to alkalosis is partially responsible for the cerebral vasoconstriction that causes the lightheadedness, fainting, and paraesthesia often seen with hyperventilation.
- Neonatal hypocalcemia
- Gain of function mutations of the calcium-sensing receptor
- Foscarnet use
- Loop diuretic use
- Crohn disease
- High level of lactic acid in the blood
- Pseudohypoparathyroidism
- Trauma

Mechanism

Physiologically, blood calcium is tightly regulated within a narrow range for proper cellular processes. Calcium in the blood exists in three primary states: bound to proteins (mainly albumin), bound to anions such as phosphate and citrate, and as free (unbound) ionized calcium. Only the unbound ionized calcium is physiologically active. Normal blood calcium level is between 8.5 and 10.5 mg/dL (2.12 to 2.62 mmol/L) and that of unbound calcium is 4.65 to 5.25 mg/dL (1.16 to 1.31 mmol/L).

Diagnosis

Because a significant portion of calcium is bound to albumin, any alteration in the level of albumin will affect the measured level of calcium. A corrected calcium level based on the albumin level is: Corrected calcium (mg/dL) = measured total Ca (mg/dL) + 0.8 * (4.0 - serum albumin [g/dL]). Since calcium is also bound to small anions, it may be more useful to correct total calcium for both albumin and the anion gap.

Management

Management of this condition includes:

- Intravenouscalcium gluconate 10% can be administered, or if the hypocalcaemia is severe, calcium chloride is given instead. This is only appropriate if the hypocalcemia is acute and has occurred over a relatively short time frame. But if the hypocalcemia has been severe and chronic, then this regimen can be fatal, because there is a degree of acclimatization that occurs. The neuromuscular excitability, cardiac electrical instability, and associated symptoms are then not cured or relieved by prompt administration of corrective doses of calcium, but rather exacerbated. Such rapid administration of calcium would result in effective over correction – symptoms of hypercalcemia would follow.
- However, in either circumstance, maintenance doses of both calcium and vitamin-D (often as 1,25-$(OH)_2$-D_3, i.e; calcitriol) are often necessary to prevent further decline

Key points:

Causes

- from low parathyroid hormone aver thyroid or parathyroid surgeries.
- low vitamin D.
- Pseudohypocalcemia (low albumin and hyperventilation).
- Other less common causes include: pancreatitis, necrotizing fascitis, high output G.I. fistula, and massive blood transfusion.

Symptoms

- Numbness and tingling sensation circumorally or at the fingers' tips.
- Tetany and seizures may occur at a very low calcium level.

Signs Tremor, hyperreflexia, carpopedal spasms and positive Chvostek sign.
Diagnosis serum Ca < 8.5 mg/dl (2.1 mmol/L)
Treatment

- Should start by treating the cause.
- Calcium supplementation with calcium gluconate or calcium carbonate i.v. or orally.
- Vitamin D supplementation especially in chronic cases.

MAGNESIUM IMBALANCE
Hypermagnesemia
Hypermagnesemia is an electrolyte disorder in which there is a high level of magnesium in the blood. Symptoms include weakness, confusion, decreased breathing rate, and decreased reflexes. Complications may include low blood pressure and cardiac arrest.

It is typically caused by kidney failure or is treatment-induced such as from antacids that contain magnesium. Less common causes include tumor lysis syndrome, seizures, and prolonged ischemia. Diagnosis is based on a blood level of magnesium greater than 1.1 mmol/L (2.6 mg/dL). It is severe if levels are greater than 2.9 mmol/L (7mg/dL). Specific electrocardiogram (ECG) changes may be present.

Treatment involves stopping the magnesium a person is getting. Treatment when levels are very high include calcium chloride, intravenous normal saline with furosemide, and hemodialysis. Hypermagnesemia is uncommon.[3] Rates among hospitalized patients in renal failure may be as high as 10%.

Signs and symptoms

Symptoms include weakness, confusion, decreased breathing rate, and decreased reflexes.[1][3] As well as nausea, low blood pressure, low blood calcium,[7]abnormal heart rhythms and asystole, dizziness, and sleepiness.

Abnormal heart rhythms and asystole are possible complications of hypermagnesemia related to the heart.[8] Magnesium acts as a physiologic calcium blocker, which results in abnormalities of the electrical conduction system of the heart.

Consequences related to serum concentration:

- 4.0 mEq/L – Decreased reflexes
- >5.0 mEq/L – Prolonged atrioventricular conduction
- >10.0 mEq/L – Complete heart block
- >13.0 mEq/L – Cardiac arrest

The therapeutic range for the prevention of the pre-eclamptic uterine contractions is: 4.0–7.0 mEq/L. As per Lu and Nightingale, serum magnesium concentrations associated with maternal toxicity (also neonate depression, hypotonia and low Apgar scores) are:

- 7.0–10.0 mEq/L – Loss of patellar reflex
- 10.0-13.0 mEq/L – Respiratory depression
- 15.0-25.0 mEq/L – Altered atrioventricular conduction and (further) complete heart block
- >25.0 mEq/L – Cardiac arrest

Complications

Severe hypermagnesemia (levels greater than 12 mg/dL) can lead to cardiovascular complications (hypotension and arrhythmias) and neurological disorder (confusion and lethargy). Higher values of serum magnesium (exceeding 15 mg/dL) can induce cardiac arrest and coma.

Causes

Magnesium status depends on three organs: uptake in the intestine, storage in the bone, and excretion in the kidneys. Hypermagnesemia is therefore often due to problems in these organs, mostly the intestine or kidney.[11]

Predisposing conditions

- Hemolysis, magnesium concentration in red blood cells is approximately three times greater than in serum, therefore hemolysis can increase plasma magnesium. Hypermagnesemia is expected only in massive hemolysis.
- Chronic kidney disease, excretion of magnesium becomes impaired when creatinine clearance falls below 30 ml/min. However, hypermagnesemia is not a prominent feature of chronic kidney disease unless magnesium intake is increased.
- Magnesium toxicity from emergency pre-eclampsia treatment during labor and delivery.
- Other conditions that can predispose to mild hypermagnesemia are diabetic ketoacidosis, adrenal insufficiency, hypothyroidism, hyperparathyroidism, and lithiumintoxication.

Diagnosis

Hypermagnesemia is diagnosed by measuring the concentration of magnesium in the blood. Concentrations of magnesium greater than 1.1 mmol/L are considered diagnostic.

Treatment

People with normal kidney function (glomerular filtration rate (GFR) over 60 ml/min) and mild asymptomatic hypermagnesemia require no treatment except for the removal of all sources of exogenous magnesium. One must consider that the half-time of elimination of magnesium is approximately 28 hours.

In more severe cases, close monitoring of the ECG, blood pressure, and neuromuscular function and early treatment are necessary:

Intravenous calcium gluconate or calcium chloride since the actions of magnesium in neuromuscular and cardiac function become antagonized by calcium.

Severe clinical conditions require increasing renal magnesium excretion through:

Intravenous loop diuretics (e.g., furosemide), or hemodialysis, when kidney function is impaired, or the patient is symptomatic from severe hypermagnesemia. This approach usually removes magnesium efficiently (up to 50% reduction after a 3- to 4-hour treatment). Dialysis can, however, increase the excretion of calcium by developing hypocalcemia, thus possibly worsening the symptoms and signs of hypermagnesemia.

The use of diuretics must be associated with infusions of saline solutions to avoid further electrolyte disturbances (e.g., hypokalemia) and metabolic alkalosis. The clinician must perform serial measurements of calcium and magnesium. In association with electrolytic correction, it is often necessary to support cardiorespiratory activity. As a consequence, the treatment of this electrolyte disorder can frequently require intensive care unit (ICU) admission.

Particular clinical conditions require a specific approach. For instance, during the management of eclampsia, the magnesium infusion is stopped if urine output drops to less than 80 mL (in 4 hours), deep tendon reflexes are absent, or the respiratory rate is below 12 breaths/minute. A 10% calcium gluconate or chloride solution can serve as an antidote.

Prognosis

The prognosis of hypermagnesemia depends on magnesium values and on the clinical condition that induced hypermagnesemia. Values that are not excessively high (mild hypermagnesemia) and in the absence of triggering and aggravating conditions (e.g., chronic kidney disease) are benign conditions. On the contrary, high values (severe hypermagnesemia) expose the patient to high risks and high mortality.

Epidemiology

Hypermagnesemia is an uncommon electrolyte disorder. It occurs in approximately 10 to 15% of hospitalized patients with renal failure. Furthermore, epidemiological data suggest that there is a significant prevalence of high levels of serum magnesium in selected healthy populations. For instance the overall prevalence of hypermagnesemia was 3.0%, especially in males in Iran. High magnesium concentrations were typical in people with cardiovascular disease, and 2.3 mg/dL or higher values wcrc associated with worse hospital mortality.

Key points:

Causes

- Mostly occurs in association with renal failure, when Mg+ excretion is impaired.
- The use of antacids containing Mg^{+} may aggravate hypermagnesaemia.

Hypermagnesemia and hypophosphatemia are all conditions of renal failure.

Treatment Treatment includes rehydration and renal dialysis.

HYPOMAGNESEMIA

HYPOMAGNESEMIA

Magnesium deficiency is an electrolyte disturbance in which there is a low level of magnesium in the body. It can result in multiple symptoms. Symptoms include tremor, poor coordination, muscle spasms, loss of appetite, personality changes, and nystagmus. Complications may include seizures or cardiac arrest such as from torsade de pointes. Those with low magnesium often have low potassium.

Causes include low dietary intake, alcoholism, diarrhea, increased urinary loss, poor absorption from the intestines, and diabetes mellitus. A number of medications may also cause low magnesium, including proton pump inhibitors (PPIs) and furosemide. The diagnosis is typically based on finding low blood magnesium levels (hypomagnesemia). Normal magnesium levels are between 0.6 and 1.1 mmol/L (1.46–2.68 mg/dL) with levels less than 0.6 mmol/L (1.46 mg/dL) defining hypomagnesemia. Specific electrocardiogram (ECG) changes may be seen.

Treatment is with magnesium either by mouth or intravenously. For those with severe symptoms, intravenous magnesium sulfate may be used. Associated low potassium or low calcium should also be treated. The condition is relatively common among people in hospitals.

Signs and symptoms

Deficiency of magnesium can cause tiredness, generalized weakness, muscle cramps, abnormal heart rhythms, increased irritability of the nervous system with tremors, paresthesias, palpitations, low potassium levels in the blood, hypoparathyroidism which might result in low calcium levels in the blood, chondrocalcinosis, spasticity and tetany, migraines, epileptic seizures, basal ganglia calcifications and in extreme and prolonged cases coma, intellectual disability or death. Magnesium plays an important role in carbohydrate metabolism and its deficiency may worsen insulin resistance, a condition that often precedes diabetes, or may be a consequence of insulin resistance.

People being treated on an intensive care unit (ICU) who have a low magnesium level may have a higher risk of requiring mechanical ventilation, and death.

Causes

Magnesium deficiency may result from gastrointestinal or kidney causes. Gastrointestinal causes include low dietary intake of magnesium, reduced gastrointestinal absorption or increased gastrointestinal loss due to rapid gastrointestinal transits. Kidney causes involve increased excretion of magnesium. Poor dietary intake of magnesium has become an increasingly important factor – many people consume diets high in refined foods such as white bread and polished rice which have been stripped of magnesium-rich plant fiber.

Magnesium deficiency is not uncommon in hospitalized patients. Up to 12% of all people admitted to hospital, and as high as 60–65% of people in an intensive care unit, have hypomagnesemia.

About 57% of the US population does not meet the US RDA for dietary intake of magnesium. The kidneys are very efficient at maintaining body levels; however, if the diet is deficient, or certain medications such as diuretics or proton pump inhibitors are used, or in chronic alcoholism, levels may drop.

Low levels of magnesium in blood may be due to not enough magnesium in the diet, the intestines not absorbing enough magnesium, or the kidneys excreting too much magnesium. Deficiencies may be due to the following conditions:

Medications

- Loop and thiazide diuretic use (the most common cause of hypomagnesemia)
- Antibiotics (i.e. aminoglycoside, amphotericin, pentamidine, gentamicin, tobramycin, viomycin) block resorption in the loop of Henle. 30% of patients using these antibiotics have hypomagnesemia.
- Long term, high dosage use of proton-pump inhibitors such as omeprazole
- Other drugs
    - Digitalis, displaces magnesium into the cell. Digitalis causes an increased intracellular concentration of sodium, which in turn increases intracellular calcium by passively increasing the action of the sodium-calcium exchanger in the sarcolemma. The increased intracellular calcium gives a positive inotropic effect.
    - Adrenergics, displace magnesium into the cell
    - Cisplatin, stimulates kidney excretion
    - Ciclosporin, stimulates kidney excretion
    - Mycophenolate mofetil

Genetics

- Gitelman-like diseases, which include the syndromes caused by genetic mutations in *SLC12A3*, *CLNCKB*,*BSND*, *KCNJ10*, *FXYD2*, *HNF1B* or *PCBD1*. In these diseases, the hypomagnesemia is accompanied by other defects in electrolyte handling such as hypocalciuria and hypokalemia. The genes involved in this group of diseases all encode proteins that are involved in reabsorbing electrolytes (including magnesium) in the distal convoluted tubule of the kidney.
- Hypercalciuric hypomagnesemic syndromes, which encompass the syndromes caused by mutations in *CLDN16*, *CLDN19*, *CASR* or *CLCNKB*. In these diseases, reabsorption of divalent cations (such as magnesium and calcium) in the thick ascending limb of Henle's loop of the kidney is impaired. This results in loss of magnesium and calcium in the urine.
- Mitochondriopathies, especially mutations in the mitochondrial tRNAs *MT-TI* or *MT-TF*. Mutations in *SARS2*, or mitochondrial DNA deletions as seen with Kearns-Sayre syndrome, can also cause hypomagnesemia.
- Other genetic causes of hypomagnesemia, such as mutations in *TRPM6*, *CNNM2*, *EGF*, *EGFR*, *KCNA1* or *FAM111A*. Many of the proteins encoded by these genes play a role in the transcellular absorption of magnesium in the distal convoluted tubule.

Metabolic abnormalities

- Insufficient selenium, vitamin D or sunlight exposure, or vitamin B6.
- Gastrointestinal causes: the distal digestive tract secretes high levels of magnesium. Therefore, secretory diarrhea can cause hypomagnesemia. Thus, Crohn's disease, ulcerative colitis, Whipple's disease and celiac sprue can all cause hypomagnesemia.
- Postobstructive diuresis, diuretic phase of acute tubular necrosis (ATN) and kidney transplant.

Other

- Chronic alcoholism: Alcohol intake leads to enhanced diuresis of electrolytes. Chronic consumption leads to the depletion of body stores of magnesium.
- Acute myocardial infarction: within the first 48 hours after a heart attack, 80% of patients have hypomagnesemia. This could be the result of an intracellular shift because of an increase in catecholamines.
- Malabsorption
- Acute pancreatitis
- Fluoride poisoning
- Massive transfusion (MT) is a lifesaving treatment of hemorrhagic shock, but can be associated with significant complications.

Pathophysiology

Magnesium is a co-factor in over 300 functions in the body regulating many kinds of biochemical reactions. It is involved in protein synthesis, muscle and nerve functioning, bone development, energy production, the maintenance of normal heart rhythm, and the regulation of glucose and blood pressure, among other important roles. Low magnesium intake over time can increase the risk of illnesses, including high blood pressure and heart disease, diabetes mellitus type 2, osteoporosis, and migraines.

There is a direct effect on sodium (Na), potassium (K), and calcium (Ca) channels. Magnesium has several effects:

Potassium

Potassium channel efflux is inhibited by magnesium. Thus hypomagnesemia results in an increased excretion of potassium in kidney, resulting in a hypokalaemia. This condition is believed to occur secondary to the decreased normal physiologic magnesium inhibition of the ROMK channels in the apical tubular membrane.

In this light, hypomagnesemia is frequently the cause of hypokalaemic patients failing to respond to potassium supplementation. Thus, clinicians should ensure that both magnesium and potassium is replaced when deficient. Patients with diabetic ketoacidosis should have their magnesium levels monitored to ensure that the serum loss of potassium, which is driven intracellularly by insulin administration, is not exacerbated by additional urinary losses.

Calcium

Release of calcium from the sarcoplasmic reticulum is inhibited by magnesium. Thus hypomagnesemia results in an increased intracellular calcium level. This inhibits the release of parathyroid hormone, which can result in hypoparathyroidism and hypocalcemia. Furthermore, it makes skeletal and muscle receptors less sensitive to parathyroid hormone.

Arrhythmia

Magnesium is needed for the adequate function of the Na^+/K^+-ATPase pumps in cardiac myocytes, the muscles cells of the heart. A lack of magnesium inhibits reuptake of potassium, causing a decrease in intracellular potassium. This decrease in intracellular potassium results in a tachycardia.

Pre-eclampsia

Magnesium has an indirect antithrombotic effect upon platelets and endothelial function. Magnesium increases prostaglandins, decreases thromboxane, and decreases angiotensin II, microvascular leakage, and vasospasm through its function similar to calcium channel blockers. Convulsions are the result of cerebral vasospasm. The vasodilatatory effect of magnesium seems to be the major mechanism.

Asthma

Magnesium exerts a bronchodilatatory effect, probably by antagonizing calcium-mediated bronchoconstriction.

Neurological effects

- reducing electrical excitation
- modulating release of acetylcholine

- antagonising *N*-methyl-D-aspartate (NMDA) glutamate receptors, an excitatory neurotransmitter of the central nervous system and thus providing neuroprotection from excitoxicity.

Diabetes mellitus

Magnesium deficiency is frequently observed in people with type 2 diabetes mellitus, with an estimated prevalence ranging between 11.0 and 47.7%. Magnesium deficiency is strongly associated with high glucose and insulin resistance, which indicate that it is common in poorly controlled diabetes. Patients with type 2 diabetes and a magnesium deficiency have a higher risk of heart failure, atrial fibrillation and microvascular complications. Oral magnesium supplements has been demonstrated to improve insulin sensitivity and lipid profile. A 2016 meta-analysis not restricted to diabetic subjects found that increasing dietary magnesium intake, while associated with a reduced risk of stroke, heart failure, diabetes, and all-cause mortality, was not clearly associated with lower risk of coronary heart disease (CHD) or total cardiovascular disease (CVD).

A 2021 study on blood from 4,400 diabetic patients over 6 to 11 years reported that "People with higher levels of magnesium in the blood were found to have a significantly lower risk of cardiovascular disease", and also of diabetic foot and diabetic retinopathy. The researchers, however, stated that "we have [not] demonstrated that magnesium supplements work. Further research is needed."

Homeostasis

Magnesium is abundant in nature. It can be found in green vegetables, chlorophyll (chloroplasts), cocoa derivatives, nuts, wheat, seafood, and meat. It is absorbed primarily in the duodenum of the small intestine. The rectum and sigmoid colon can absorb magnesium. Forty percent of dietary magnesium is absorbed. Hypomagnesemia stimulates and hypermagnesemia inhibits this absorption.

The body contains 21–28 grams of magnesium (0.864–1.152 mol). Of this, 53% is located in bone, 19% in non-muscular tissue, and 1% in extracellular fluid. For this reason, blood levels of magnesium are not an adequate means of establishing the total amount of available magnesium.

The majority of serum magnesium is bound to chelators, including proteins and citrate. Roughly 33% is bound to proteins, and 5–10% is not bound. This "free" magnesium is essential in regulating intracellular magnesium. Normal plasma Mg is 1.7–2.3 mg/dL (0.69–0.94 mmol/L).

The kidneys regulate the serum magnesium. About 2400 mg of magnesium passes through the kidneys daily, of which 5% (120 mg) is excreted through urine. The loop of Henle is the major site for magnesium homeostasis, and 60% is reabsorbed.

Magnesium homeostasis comprises three systems: kidney, small intestine, and bone. In the acute phase of magnesium deficiency there is an increase in absorption in the distal small intestine and tubular resorption in the kidneys. When this condition persists, serum magnesium drops and is corrected with magnesium from bone tissue. The level of intracellular magnesium is controlled through the reservoir in bone tissue.

Diagnosis

Magnesium deficiency or depletion is a low *total body* level of magnesium; it is not easy to measure directly. Typically the diagnosis is based on finding hypomagnesemia, a low *blood* magnesium level, which often reflects low body magnesium; however, magnesium deficiency can be present without hypomagnesemia, and vice versa. A plasma magnesium concentration of less than 0.6 mmol/L (1.46 mg/dL) is considered to be hypomagnesemia; severe disease generally has a level of less than 0.50 mmol/L (1.25 mg/dL).

Electrocardiogram

The electrocardiogram (ECG) change may show a tachycardia with a prolonged QT interval.[43] Other changes may include prolonged PR interval, ST segment depression, flipped T waves, and long QRS duration.

ECG Changes

- **(K) Hypokalemia:**
  - ST depression
  - Flat/inverted T wave
  - U wave
- **(K) Hyperkalemia:**
  - Flat P wave
  - Prolonged PR interval
  - QRS widening
  - Tall, peaked T wave
- **(Ca) Hypocalcemia**
  - Prolonged ST segment
  - Prolonged QT interval
- **(Ca) Hypercalcemia**
  - Shortened ST segment
  - Widened T wave
- **(Mg) Hypomagnesemia**
  - Tall T wave
  - ST depression
- **(Mg) Hypermagnesemia**
  - Prolonged PR interval
  - QRS widening

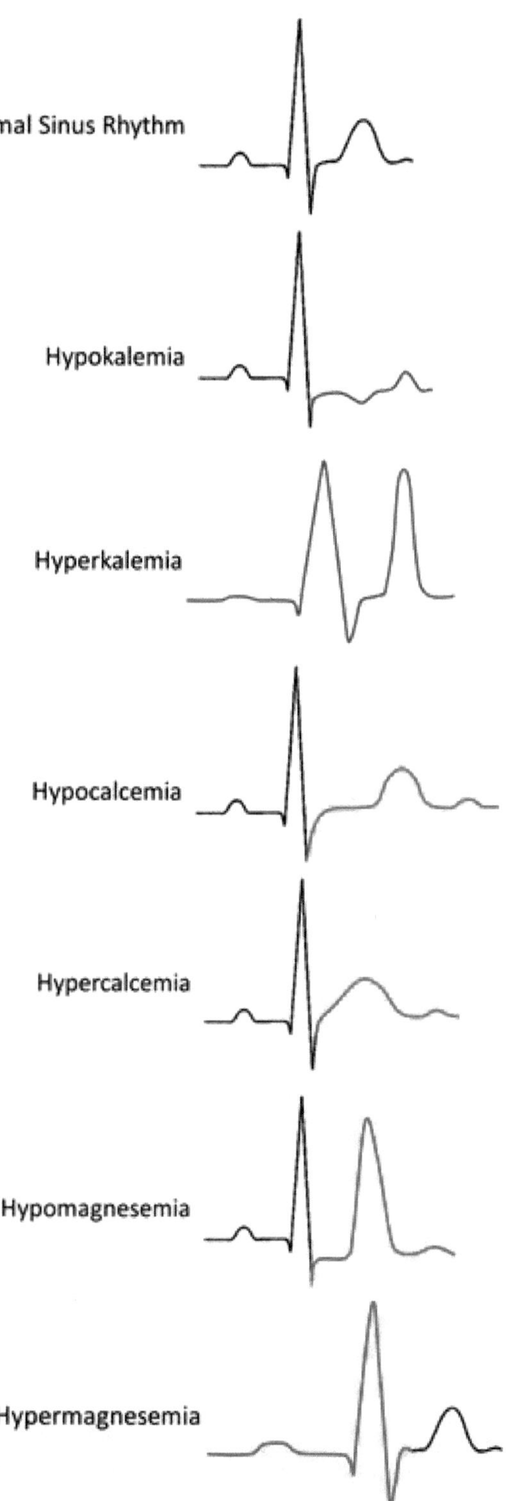

Fig. 22

Treatments

Magnesium (medical use)

Treatment of magnesium deficiency depends on the degree of deficiency and the clinical effects. Replacement by mouth is appropriate for people with mild symptoms, while intravenous replacement is recommended for people with severe effects.

Numerous oral magnesium preparations are available. In two trials of magnesium oxide, one of the most common forms in magnesium dietary supplements because of its high magnesium content per weight, was found to be less bioavailable than magnesium citrate, chloride, lactate or aspartate. Amino-acid chelate was also less bioavailable.

Intravenous magnesium sulfate ($MgSO_4$) can be given in response to heart arrhythmias to correct for hypokalemia, preventing pre-eclampsia, and has been suggested as having a potential use in asthma.

Key points

Causes

- Magnesium is important for neuromuscular activities. (cannot correct K^+ nor Ca^{2+})
- It happens from inadequate replacement in depleted surgical patients with major GI fistula and those on TPN.

Symptoms Usually there are no symptoms but when you want to correct Ca or K levels they don't get corrected.

Treatment

When Mg decreases the Ca and K will decrease as well even though they were in their normal levels.

But when correcting the magnesium everything will go back to normal

The majority of magnesium is intracellular with only <1% in the extracellular space.

HYPERPHOSPHATEMIA

PHOSPHATE IMBALANCE

Hyperphosphatemia

Causes Mostly associated with renal failure and hypocalcaemia due to hypoparathyroidism, which reduces renal phosphate excretion.

HYPOPHOSPHATEMIA

Hypophosphatemia

Causes

- Inadequate intestinal absorption.
- Increased renal excretion,
- Hyperparathyroidism
- Massive liver resection
- Inadequate replacement aver recovery from significant starvation and catabolism.

Symptoms Muscle weakness and inadequate tissue oxygenation due to reduced 2,3- bisphosphoglycerate levels.

Treatment Early recognition and replacement will improve these symptoms.

Mg and phosphate abnormalities occur with chronic diseases, before replacing them check the renal system, caused all the time by renal failure

➲ **Prescribing fluids:**

- 2 basic types. Crystalloids are simple solutions of small solutes, whilst colloids are suspensions of macromolecules, or in the case of blood, cells.
- most commonly used crystalloids are saline and dextrose

↳ The standard saline solu:on is 0.9% saline, oven referred to as " normal saline" being slightly hypertonic, and hypernatraemic.

↳ Dextrose is usually given as 5% dextrose, which means that it contains 5 grams of glucose per 100 ml of water. This solution is roughly isotonic to serum, but them glucose is rapidly utilised, leaving behind pure water.

- Multiple colloid prepara:ons are available, but the essen:al ones are either:

↪ natural, such as blood, human albumin or plasma.

↪ or synthetic, where the macromolecule is manufactured. Common synthe:c colloids are haemaccel and gelofusine, in which hydrolysed gelatin is suspended in saline.

➲ The rules of fluid replacement:

- Replace blood with blood
- Replace plasma with colloid
- Resuscitate with colloid
- Replace ECF deple:on with saline
- Rehydrate with dextrose

➲ Colloids

Giving 2 litres of blood, will expand their intravascular compartment.
None of this fluid will escape across the blood vessel walls (in the short term at least) and the other compartments are unaffected.
This is the right treatment for blood loss.

Giving 2L colloid into the vascular space results in animmediate expansion of the intravascular compartment by 2litres, as does blood.

- Colloid does not escape from the vascular space, but does increase oncotic pressure markedly causing water to be drawn into the vascular space from the interstitial and intracellular reservoirs. Giving colloid therefore not only expands the vascular space itself, but does so by moving water from other spaces.

Crystalloids

Saline, does not remain within the vascular space, will diffuse into the interstitial space. The sodium it carries will not enter the intracellular space. Saline will therefore cause immediate expansion of the intravascular volume, followed by equilibration between the vascular and interstitial spaces, the osmolality of which are equal, but are now slightly greater than that of the intracellular space, due to the increased sodium load water movement from the intracellular space in order to equalise osmolality throughout all three compartments.

5% Dextrose is isotonic to plasma. Giving 2 litres of 5% dextrose will cause the immediate expansion of the vascular compartment, but, as its glucose content is rapidly metabolised, the remaining water will distribute itself between all compartments and very little will remain within the blood space.

For this simple reason, dextrose is not a fluid of resuscitation.

CHAPTER ELEVEN

ACID–BASE PHYSIOLOGY

Acid–base homeostasis is the homeostatic regulation of the pH of the body's extracellular fluid (ECF). The proper balance between the acids and bases (i.e. the pH) in the ECF is crucial for the normal physiology of the body—and for cellular metabolism. The pH of the intracellular fluid and the extracellular fluid need to be maintained at a constant level.

The three dimensional structures of many extracellular proteins, such as the plasma proteins and membrane proteins of the body's cells, are very sensitive to the extracellular pH. Stringent mechanisms therefore exist to maintain the pH within very narrow limits. Outside the acceptable range of pH, proteins are denatured (i.e. their 3D structure is disrupted), causing enzymes and ion channels (among others) to malfunction.

An acid–base imbalance is known as acidemia when the pH is acidic, or alkalemia when the pH is alkaline.

Lines of defense

In humans and many other animals, acid–base homeostasis is maintained by multiple mechanisms involved in three lines of defense:

Chemical: The first lines of defense are immediate, consisting of the various chemical buffers which minimize pH changes that would otherwise occur in their absence. These buffers include the bicarbonate buffer system, the phosphate buffer system, and the protein buffer system.

Respiratory component: The second line of defense is rapid consisting of the control the carbonic acid (H2CO3) concentration in the ECF by changing the rate and depth of breathing by hyperventilation or hypoventilation. This blows off or retains carbon dioxide (and thus carbonic acid) in the blood plasma as required.

Metabolic component: The third line of defense is slow, best measured by the base excess, and mostly depends on the renal system which can add or remove bicarbonate ions (HCO–
3) to or from the ECF. Bicarbonate ions are derived from metabolic carbon dioxide which is enzymatically converted to carbonic acid in the renal tubular cells. There, carbonic acid spontaneously dissociates into hydrogen ions and bicarbonate ions.When the pH in the ECF falls, hydrogen ions are excreted into urine, while bicarbonate ions are secreted into blood plasma, causing the plasma pH to rise. The converse happens if the pH in the ECF tends to rise: bicarbonate ions are then excreted into the urine and hydrogen ions into the blood plasma.

The second and third lines of defense operate by making changes to the buffers, each of which consists of two components: a weak acid and its conjugate base. It is the ratio concentration of the weak acid to its conjugate base that determines the pH of the solution. Thus, by manipulating firstly the concentration of the weak acid, and secondly that of its conjugate base, the pH of the extracellular fluid (ECF) can be adjusted very accurately to the correct value. The bicarbonate buffer, consisting of a mixture of carbonic acid (H2CO3) and a bicarbonate (HCO3-) salt in solution, is the most abundant buffer in the extracellular fluid, and it is also the buffer whose acid-to-base ratio can be changed very easily and rapidly.

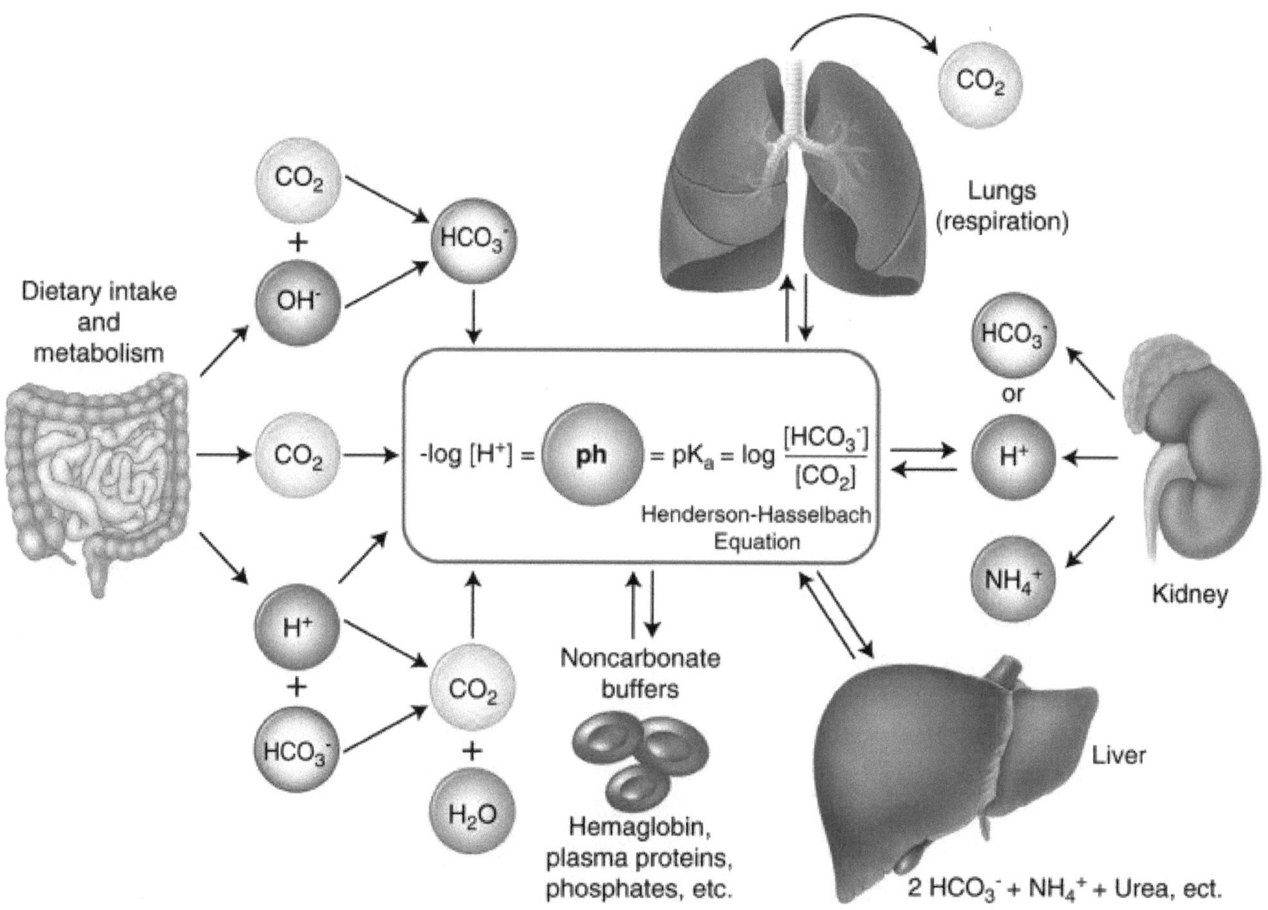

Fig. 23

Acid–base balance

The pH of the extracellular fluid, including the blood plasma, is normally tightly regulated between 7.32 and 7.42 by the chemical buffers, the respiratory system, and the renal system. The normal pH in the fetus differs from that in the adult. In the fetus, the pH in the umbilical vein pH is normally 7.25 to 7.45 and that in the umbilical artery is normally 7.18 to 7.38.

Aqueous buffer solutions will react with strong acids or strong bases by absorbing excess H+ ions, or OH− ions, replacing the strong acids and bases with weak acids and weak bases. This has the effect of damping the effect of pH changes, or reducing the pH change that would otherwise have occurred. But buffers cannot correct abnormal pH levels in a solution, be that solution in a test tube or in the extracellular fluid. Buffers typically consist of a pair of compounds in solution, one of which is a weak acid and the other a weak base.[13] The most abundant buffer in the ECF consists of a solution of carbonic acid (H2CO3), and the bicarbonate (HCO−3) salt of, usually, sodium (Na+). Thus, when there is an excess of OH−ions in the solution carbonic acid partially neutralizes them by forming H2O and bicarbonate (HCO−3) ions. Similarly an excess of H+ ions is partially neutralized by the bicarbonate component of the buffer solution to form carbonic acid (H2CO3), which, because it is a weak acid, remains largely in the undissociated form, releasing far fewer H+ ions into the solution than the original strong acid would have done.

The pH of a buffer solution depends solely on the ratio of the molar concentrations of the weak acid to the weak base. The higher the concentration of the weak acid in the solution (compared to the weak base) the lower the resulting pH of the solution. Similarly, if the weak base predominates the higher the resulting pH.

This principle is exploited to regulate the pH of the extracellular fluids (rather than just buffering the pH). For the carbonic acid-bicarbonate buffer, a molar ratio of weak acid to weak base of 1:20 produces a pH of 7.4; and vice versa—when the pH of the extracellular fluids is 7.4 then the ratio of carbonic acid to bicarbonate ions in that fluid is 1:20.

Henderson–Hasselbalch equation

The Henderson–Hasselbalch equation, when applied to the carbonic acid-bicarbonate buffer system in the extracellular fluids, states that:

pH=pka H2CO3+log10 ([HCO3−][H2CO3]),

where:

pH is the negative logarithm (or cologarithm) of molar concentration of hydrogen ions in the extracellular fluid.

pKa H2CO3 is the cologarithm of the acid dissociation constant of carbonic acid. It is equal to 6.1.

[HCO−3] is the molar concentration of bicarbonate in the blood plasma.

[H2CO3] is the molar concentration of carbonic acid in the extracellular fluid.

However, since the carbonic acid concentration is directly proportional to the partial pressure of carbon dioxide (pCO2) in the extracellular fluid, the equation can be rewritten as follows:

pH=6.1+log10 ([HCO3−]0.0307×pCO2),

where:

pH is the negative logarithm of molar concentration of hydrogen ions in the extracellular fluid.

[HCO−3] is the molar concentration of bicarbonate in the plasma.

PCO2 is the partial pressure of carbon dioxide in the blood plasma.

The pH of the extracellular fluids can thus be controlled by the regulation of pCO2 and the other metabolic acids.

Homeostatic mechanisms

Homeostatic control can change the PCO2 and hence the pH of the arterial plasma within a few seconds. The partial pressure of carbon dioxide in the arterial blood is monitored by the central chemoreceptors of the medulla oblongata. These chemoreceptors are sensitive to the levels of carbon dioxide and pH in the cerebrospinal fluid.

The central chemoreceptors send their information to the respiratory centers in the medulla oblongata and pons of the brainstem. The respiratory centres then determine the average rate of ventilation of the alveoli of the lungs, to keep the PCO2 in the arterial blood constant. The respiratory center does so via motor neurons which activate the muscles of respiration (in particular, the diaphragm). A rise in the PCO2 in the arterial blood plasma above 5.3 kPa (40 mmHg) reflexly causes an increase in the rate and depth of breathing. Normal breathing is resumed when the partial pressure of carbon dioxide has returned to 5.3 kPa. The converse happens if the partial pressure of carbon dioxide falls below the normal range. Breathing may be temporally halted, or slowed down to allow carbon dioxide to accumulate once more in the lungs and arterial blood.

The sensor for the plasma HCO−3 concentration is not known for certain. It is very probable that the renal tubular cells of the distal convoluted tubules are themselves sensitive to the pH of the plasma. The metabolism of these cells produces CO2, which is rapidly converted to H+ and HCO−
3 through the action of carbonic anhydrase. When the extracellular fluids tend towards acidity, the renal tubular cells secrete the H+ ions into the tubular fluid from where they exit the body via the urine. The HCO−3 ions are simultaneously secreted into the blood plasma, thus raising the bicarbonate ion concentration in the plasma, lowering the carbonic acid/bicarbonate ion ratio, and consequently raising the pH of the plasma. The converse happens when the plasma pH rises above normal: bicarbonate ions are excreted into the urine, and hydrogen ions into the plasma. These combine with the bicarbonate ions in the plasma to form carbonic acid (H+ + HCO−3 ⇌ H2CO3), thus raising the carbonic acid:bicarbonate ratio in the extracellular fluids, and returning its pH to normal.

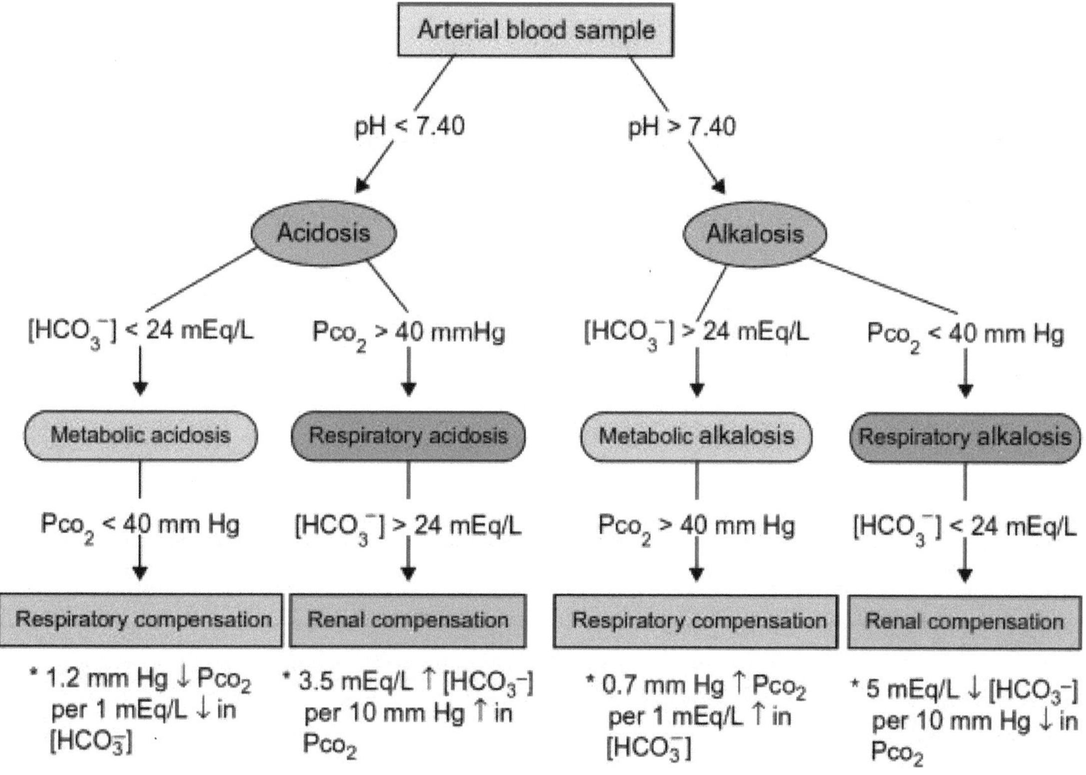

Fig. 24

In general, metabolism produces more waste acids than bases. Urine produced is generally acidic and is partially neutralized by the ammonia (NH3) that is excreted into the urine when glutamate and glutamine (carriers of excess, no longer needed, amino groups) are deaminated by the distal renal tubular epithelial cells. Thus some of the "acid content" of the urine resides in the resulting ammonium ion (NH4+) content of the urine, though this has no effect on pH homeostasis of the extracellular fluids.

Imbalance

An acid-base diagram for human plasma, showing the effects on the plasma pH when PCO2 in mmHg or Standard Base Excess (SBE) occur in excess or are deficient in the plasma

Acid–base imbalance occurs when a significant insult causes the blood pH to shift out of the normal range (7.32 to 7.42). An abnormally low pH in the extracellular fluid is called an acidemia and an abnormally high pH is called an alkalemia.

Acidemia and alkalemia unambiguously refer to the actual change in the pH of the extracellular fluid (ECF). Two other similar sounding terms are acidosis and alkalosis. They refer to the customary effect of a component, respiratory or metabolic. Acidosis would cause an acidemia on its own (i.e. if left "uncompensated" by an alkalosis). Similarly, an alkalosis would cause an alkalemia on its own. In medical terminology, the terms acidosis and alkalosis should always be qualified by an adjective to indicate the etiology of the disturbance: respiratory (indicating a change in the partial pressure of carbon dioxide), or metabolic (indicating a change in the Base Excess of the ECF). There are therefore four different acid-base problems: metabolic acidosis, respiratory acidosis, metabolic alkalosis, and respiratory alkalosis. One or a combination of these conditions may occur simultaneously. For instance, a metabolic acidosis (as in uncontrolled diabetes mellitus) is almost always partially compensated by a respiratory alkalosis (hyperventilation). Similarly, a respiratory acidosis can be completely or partially corrected by a metabolic alkalosis.

Acid–base homeostasis is the homeostatic regulation of the pH of the body's extracellular fluid (ECF). The proper balance between the acids and bases (i.e. the pH) in the ECF is crucial for the normal physiology of the body—and for cellular metabolism. The pH of the intracellular fluid and the extracellular fluid need to be maintained at a constant level..

Acid–base physiology deals with the maintenance of normal hydrogen ion concentration (abbreviated as [H+]) in body fluids. The normal [H+] in the extracellular fluid is about 40 nmol/L or 40 nEq/L (range 38–42 nmol/L), which is precisely regulated by an interplay between body buffers, lungs, and kidneys. Since many functions of the cell are dependent on the optimum [H+], it is extremely important to maintain [H+] in blood ~ 40 nmol/L. Any deviation from this [H+] results either in acidemia ([H+] >40 nmol/L) or alkalemia ([H+] <40 nmol/L). This chapter provides an overview of the role of buffers, lungs, and kidneys in regulating [H+] in body fluids. The [H+] in blood is so low that it is not measured routinely.

Thus, pH is defined as the negative logarithm of the [H+]. An inverse relationship exists between pH and [H+]. In other words, as the pH increases, the [H+] decreases and vice versa. Cells cannot function at a pH below 6.8 and above 7.8.

The normal arterial pH ranges from 7.38 to 7.42, which translates to a [H+] of 38–42 nmol/L.

Blood pH is under constant threat by endogenous acid and base loads. If not removed, these loads can cause severe disturbances in blood pH and thus impair cellular function. However, three important regulatory systems prevent changes in pH and thus maintain blood pH in the normal range. These protective systems, as previously stated, are buffers, lungs, and kidneys.

Production of Endogenous Acids and Bases

An acid is a proton donor, whereas a base is a proton acceptor. Under physiological conditions, the diet is a major contributor to endogenous acid and base production.

Endogenous Acids

The oxidation of dietary carbohydrates, fats, and amino acids yields CO_2. About 15,000 mmol of CO_2 are produced by cellular metabolism daily. This CO_2 combines with water in the blood to form carbonic acid (H_2CO_3):

This reaction is catalyzed by carbonic anhydrase (CA), an enzyme present in tissues and red blood cells but absent in plasma. When H_2CO_3 dissociates into CO_2 and H_2O (a process called dehydration), the CO_2 is eliminated by the lungs. For this reason, H_2CO_3 is called a *volatile acid*.

In addition to volatile acid, the body also generates *nonvolatile (fixed) acids* from cellular metabolism. These nonvolatile acids are produced from sulfur-containing amino acids (i.e., cysteine and methionine) and phosphoproteins. The acids produced are sulfuric acid and phosphoric acid, respectively. Other sources of endogenous nonvolatile acids include glucose, which yields lactic and pyruvic acids; triglycerides, which yield acetoacetic and β-hydroxybutyric acids; and nucleoproteins, which yield uric acid. Hydrochloric acid is also formed from the metabolism of cationic amino acids (i.e., lysine, arginine, and histidine). Sulfuric acid accounts for 50% of all acids produced. A typical North American diet produces 1 mmol/kg/day of endogenous nonvolatile acid.

Under certain conditions, acids are produced from sources other than the diet. For example, starvation produces ketoacids, which can accumulate in the blood. Similarly, strenuous exercise generates lactic acid. Drugs such as corticosteroids cause endogenous acid production by enhancing catabolism of muscle proteins.

Endogenous Bases

Endogenous base (HCO_3^-) is generated from anionic amino acids (glutamate and aspartate) in the diet. Also, citrate or lactate generated during metabolism of carbohydrate yields HCO_3^-. Vegetarian diets contain high amounts of anionic amino acids and small amounts of sulfur- and phosphate-containing proteins. Therefore, these diets generate more bases than acids. In general, the production of acid exceeds that of base in a person ingesting a typical North American diet.

Maintenance of Normal pH

Buffers

All acids that are produced must be removed from the body in order to maintain normal blood pH. Although the kidneys eliminate most of these acids, it takes hours to days to complete the process. Buffers (both cellular and extracellular) are the first line of defense against wide fluctuations in pH.

The most important buffer in blood is bicarbonate/carbon dioxide ($HCO3^-/CO2$).

Other buffer systems are disodium phosphate/monosodium phosphate ($Na2HPO_4^{2-}$/ NaH2PO4–) and plasma proteins. In addition, erythrocytes contain the important hemoglobin (Hb) system, reduced Hb (HHb–), and oxyhemoglobin ($HbO2^{2-}$). Bones also participate in buffering.

It should be noted from the Henderson–Hasselbalch equation that the pH of a

solution is determined by the pKa and the ratio of [HCO3–] to pCO2 and not by their absolute values. Thus, because the kidneys regulate the [HCO3–] and the lungs pCO2, the kidneys and lungs determine the pH of extracellular fluids.

Phosphate buffers are effective in regulating intracellular pH more efficiently than extracellular pH. Their increased effectiveness intracellularly is due to their higher concentrations inside the cell. Also, the pKa of this system is 6.8, which is close to the intracellular pH.

Plasma proteins contain several ionizable groups in their amino acids that buffer either acids or bases. For example, the imidazole groups of histidine and the N-terminal amino groups have pKa that are close to extracellular pH and thus function as effective buffers. In blood, Hb is an important protein buffer because of its abundance in red blood cells.

Extracellular buffering to an acid load is complete within 30 min. Subsequent buffering occurs intracellularly and takes several hours to complete. Most of this intracellular buffering occurs in the bone. The bone becomes an important source of buffering acid load acutely by an uptake of H+ in exchange for Na+, K+, and bone minerals. These bone minerals rescue the HCO3 –/CO2 system in severe acidosis.

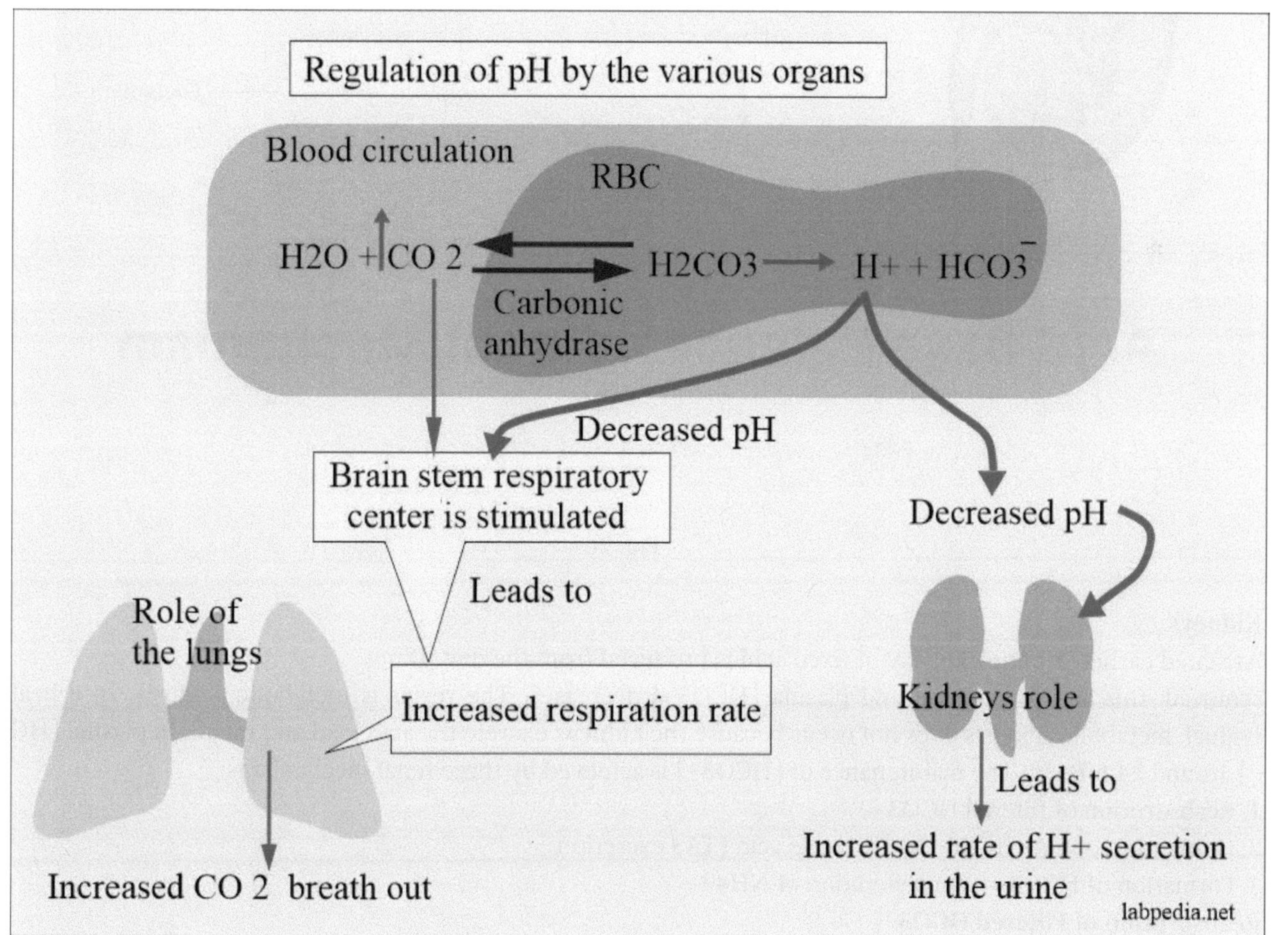

Fig. 25

Lungs

After buffers, the lungs are the second line of defense against pH disturbance. In a normal individual, pCO2 is maintained around 40 mmHg. This pCO2 is achieved by expelling the CO2 that is produced by cellular metabolism through the lungs. Any disturbance in the elimination of CO2 may cause a change in blood pH. Thus, alveolar ventilation maintains normal pCO2 to prevent an acute change in pH. Alveolar ventilation is controlled by chemoreceptors located centrally in the medulla and peripherally in the carotid body and aortic arch. Blood [H+] and pCO2 are important regulators of alveolar ventilation. The chemoreceptors sense the changes in [H+] or pCO2 and alter alveolar ventilatory rate. For example, an increase in [H+], i.e., a

decrease in pH, stimulates ventilatory rate and decreases pCO2. These responses, in turn, raise pH (see Eq. 26.4). Conversely, a decrease in [H+] or an increase in pH depresses alveolar ventilation and causes retention of pCO2 so that the pH is returned to near normal. An increase in pCO2 stimulates ventilatory rate, whereas a decrease depresses the ventilatory rate. The respiratory response to changes in [H+] takes several hours to complete.

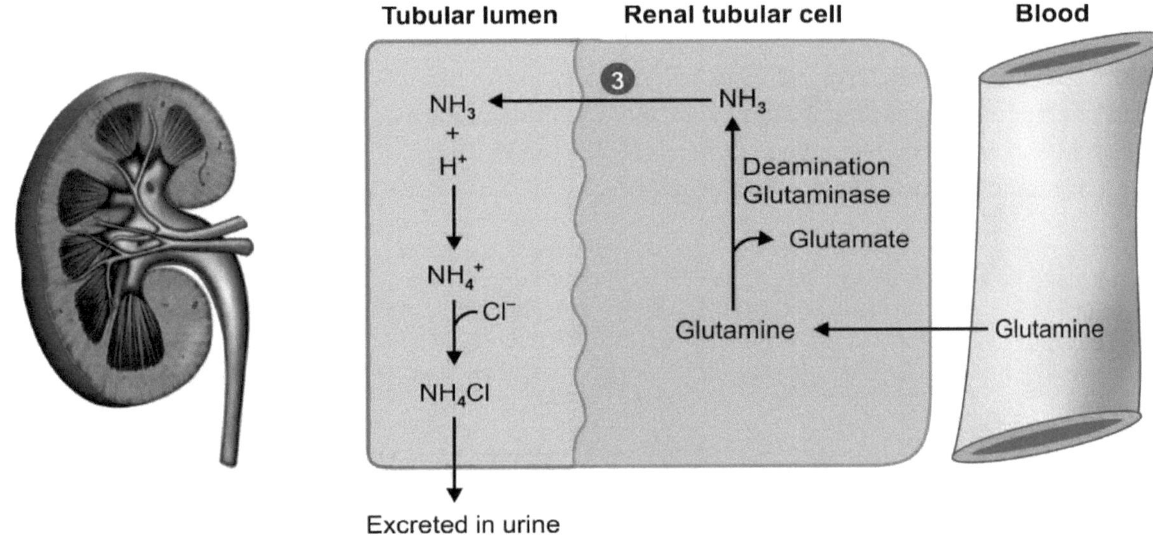

Fig. 26

Kidneys

As stated earlier, 1 mmol/kg/day of fixed acid is produced from the diet. If not

removed, this acid is retained and plasma [HCO3−] decreases. The result is metabolic acidosis. In a healthy individual, metabolic acidosis does not occur because the kidneys excrete the acid load and maintain plasma [HCO3 −] around 24 mEq/L. The maintenance of [HCO3−] is achieved by three renal mechanisms:

1. Reabsorption of filtered HCO3−
2. Generation of new HCO3− by titratable acid (TA) excretion
3. Formation of HCO3− from generation of NH4+

Reabsorption of Filtered HCO3−

HCO3− is freely filtered at the glomerulus. The daily filtered load (plasma concentration× glomerular filtration rate) of HCO3− is 4,320 mEq (24 mEq/L × 180 L/day= 4,320 mEq/day). Almost all of this HCO3− is reabsorbed by the tubular segmentsof the nephron, and urinary excretion is negligible (< 3 mEq). HCO_3^- reabsorption by various segments of the nephron can be summarized as follows:

- Proximal tubule, 80%
- Loop of Henle, 10%
- Distal tubule, 6%
- Collecting duct, 4%

Proximal Tubule

As stated earlier, the proximal tubule has a high capacity for HCO_3^- reabsorption.

This reabsorption occurs because of H^+ secretion into the tubular lumen via the Na/H exchanger (Fig. 26.1). Another transporter, called H-ATPase, is also responsible for transport of some protons into the lumen (see Fig. 26.1). The H^+ combines with the filtered HCO_3^- to form H_2CO_3. The apical membrane is rich in carbonic anhydrase IV, which splits H_2CO_3 into H_2O and CO_2. The CO_2 diffuses into the cell where it is hydrated to form H_2CO_3 in the presence of carbonic anhydrase II. H_2CO_3 is dehydrated to form H^+ and HCO_3^-. H^+ are subsequently secreted into the lumen via the Na/H exchanger and H-ATPase to start the cycle again.

HCO_3^- exit across the basolateral membrane occurs via an Na/HCO3 symporter, in which 2–3 HCO_3^- ions are transported for each Na^+ ion. Another mechanism occurs through the Cl/HCO3 antiporter, in which one HCO_3^- is exchanged for one Cl^-. Both the energy and electrochemical gradient for H^+ secretion and HCO_3^- exit are provided by the Na/K-ATPase pump located in the basolateral membrane.

Loop of Henle

Most HCO_3^- reabsorption occurs in the thick ascending Henle's loop. The mechanisms for H^+ secretion into the lumen and HCO_3^- exit across the basolateral membrane appear to be similar to those described for the proximal tubule.

Distal Tubule

For the purpose of understanding HCO_3^- reabsorption, it is helpful to divide the distal tubule into three distinct segments: (1) distal convoluted tubule, (2)connecting tubule, and (3) cortical collecting duct. Very little is known about H^+ secretion and HCO_3^- reabsorption by the distal convoluted tubule. This tubule consists of only one cell type, which contains H-ATPase in its apical membrane.

The other two segments of the distal tubule consist of principal cells and intercalated cells. The latter cells are responsible for acid–base transport. The intercalated cells in the cortical collecting duct are of three types: Type A, Type B, and Type C cells. Type A intercalated cells contain H-ATPase and K/H exchanger in the apical membrane. H^+ that is formed inside the cell from dehydration of H_2CO_3 is secreted into the lumen by these transporters (Fig. 26.2). HCO_3^- exit is facilitated by the Cl/HCO3 exchanger.

In contrast, Type B intercalated cells secrete HCO_3^- into the lumen.

These cells possess pendrin, a Cl/HCO3 exchanger, in the apical membrane and H-ATPase in the basolateral membrane. HCO_3^- secretion is stimulated by alkali loading and inhibited by depletion of luminal Cl^-.

Type C (formerly non-A, non-B) cells express H-ATPase and pendrin (Cl/HCO3 exchanger) in the apical membrane. These cells also participate in HCO_3^- handling.

Collecting Duct

The collecting duct includes the cortical portion and outer and inner medullary portions.

The cellular mechanisms of HCO_3^- reabsorption in the cortical collecting duct have been discussed in the previous paragraph. The intercalated cells of the outer medullary and inner medullary collecting duct reabsorb HCO_3^- and secrete protons similar to the Type A cell mechanisms (see Fig. 26.2). The cells of outer medullary and inner medullary collecting duct do not secrete HCO_3^- into the lumen.

Regulation of HCO_3^- Reabsorption

A number of factors influence HCO3– reabsorption both in the proximal tubule and distal segments of the nephron.

Since the Na/H antiporter is the major mechanism for H+ secretion, any factor

that enhances or inhibits this antiporter stimulates or decreases HCO3–reabsorption.

Aldosterone plays an important role in HCO3– reabsorption and H+ secretion by the intercalated (Type A) cell. It also stimulates Na+ reabsorption by the principal cell. As a result of this Na+ reabsorption, the lumen becomes electrically negative, which promotes H+ secretion. Aldosterone seems to have little effect on HCO3– reabsorption in the proximal tubule.

Generation of New HCO3– by Titratable Acid Excretion

Generally, one HCO3– ion is reclaimed for each H+ that is secreted into the lumen.

This mechanism alone does not replenish the HCO3– lost in buffering the daily acid load. Additional HCO3– has to be generated. How does the new HCO3– form The answer is as follows: whenever an H+ is secreted into the tubule, it combines with the filtered HCO3– or with two important urinary buffers, namely, HPO^{4}_{2-} and NH_3.

CHAPTER TWELVE

ACID BASE DISORDERS

↪ **Metabolic acidosis:**

Metabolic acidosis is a serious electrolyte disorder characterized by an imbalance in the body's acid-base balance. Metabolic acidosis has three main root causes: increased acid production, loss of bicarbonate, and a reduced ability of the kidneys to excrete excess acids. Metabolic acidosis can lead to acidemia, which is defined as arterial blood pH that is lower than 7.35. Acidemia and acidosis are not mutually exclusive – pH and hydrogen ion concentrations also depend on the coexistence of other acid-base disorders; therefore, pH levels in people with metabolic acidosis can range from low to high.

Acute metabolic acidosis, lasting from minutes to several days, often occurs during serious illnesses or hospitalizations, and is generally caused when the body produces an excess amount of organic acids (ketoacids in ketoacidosis, or lactic acid in lactic acidosis). A state of chronic metabolic acidosis, lasting several weeks to years, can be the result of impaired kidney function (chronic kidney disease) and/or bicarbonate wasting. The adverse effects of acute versus chronic metabolic acidosis also differ, with acute metabolic acidosis impacting the cardiovascular system in hospital settings, and chronic metabolic acidosis affecting muscles, bones, kidney and cardiovascular health.

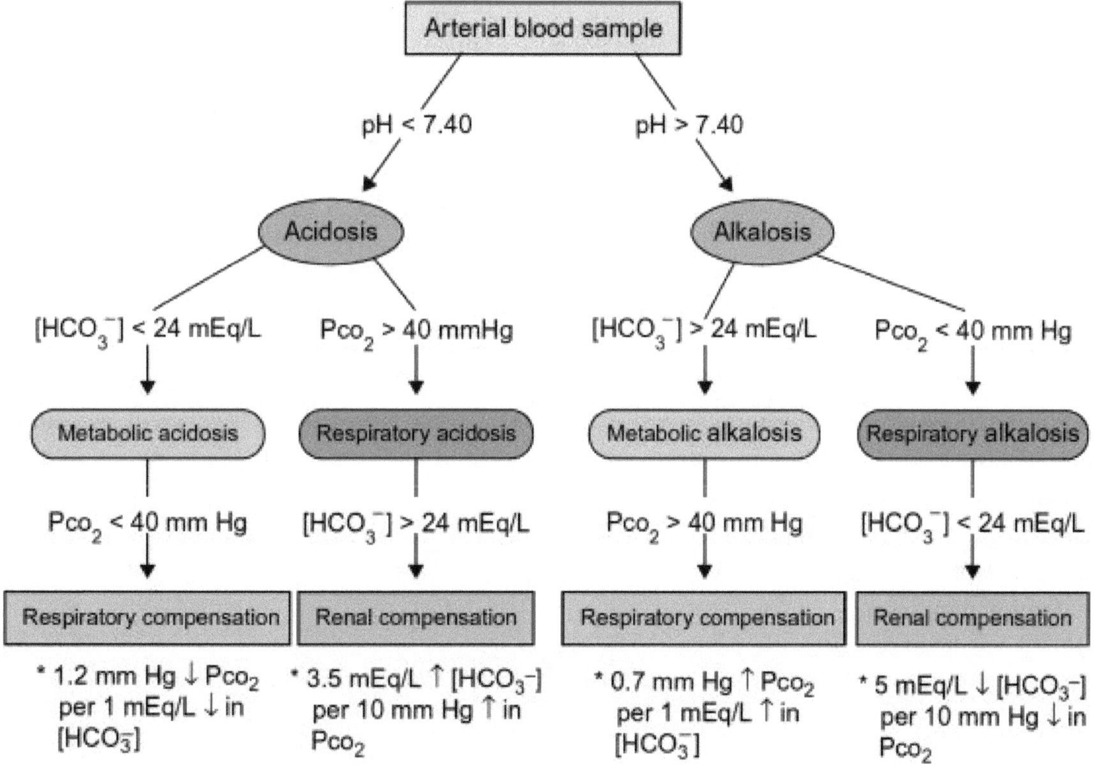

Fig. 27

Signs and symptoms

Acute metabolic acidosis

Symptoms are not specific, and diagnosis can be difficult unless patients present with clear indications for arterial blood gas sampling. Symptoms may include palpitations, headache, altered mental status such as severe anxiety due to hypoxia, decreased visual acuity, nausea, vomiting, abdominal pain, altered appetite and weight gain, muscle weakness, bone pain, and joint pain. People with acute metabolic acidosis may exhibit deep, rapid breathing called Kussmaul respirations which is classically associated with diabetic ketoacidosis. Rapid deep breaths increase the amount of carbon dioxide exhaled, thus lowering the serum carbon dioxide levels, resulting in some degree of compensation. Overcompensation via respiratory alkalosis to form an alkalemia does not occur.

Extreme acidemia can also lead to neurological and cardiac complications:

- Neurological: lethargy, stupor, coma, seizures
- Cardiac: Abnormal heart rhythms (e.g., ventricular tachycardia) and decreased response to epinephrine, both leading to low blood pressure

Physical examination can occasionally reveal signs of the disease, but is often otherwise normal. Cranial nerve abnormalities are reported in ethylene glycol poisoning, and retinaledema can be a sign of methanol intoxication.

Chronic metabolic acidosis

Chronic metabolic acidosis has non-specific clinical symptoms but can be readily diagnosed by testing serum bicarbonate levels in patients with Chronic Kidney Disease (CKD) as part of a comprehensive metabolic panel. Patients with CKD Stages G3-G5 should be routinely screened for metabolic acidosis.

Diagnostic approach and causes

Metabolic acidosis is defined as a reduced serum pH, and an abnormal serum bicarbonate concentration of <22 mEq/L, below the normal range of 22 to 29 mEq/L. However, if a patient has other coexisting acid-base disorders, the pH level may be low, normal or high in the setting of metabolic acidosis. In the absence of chronic respiratory alkalosis, metabolic acidosis can be clinically diagnosed by measuring serum bicarbonate levels in the blood, which is generally a standard component of blood panels. Imperatively, when weighing a metabolic acidosis diagnosis, the change in serum bicarbonate levels over time should be considered; if baseline bicarbonate results are unknown, a single set of values may be misinterpreted.

Causes

Generally, metabolic acidosis occurs when the body produces too much acid (e.g., lactic acidosis, see below section), there is a loss of bicarbonate from the blood, or when the kidneys are not removing enough acid from the body.

Chronic metabolic acidosis is most often caused by a decreased capacity of the kidneys to excrete excess acids through renal ammoniagenesis. The typical Western diet generates 75-100 mEq of acid daily, and individuals with normal kidney function increase the production of ammonia to get rid of this dietary acid. As kidney function declines, the tubules lose the ability to excrete excess acid, and this results in buffering of acid using serum bicarbonate, as well as bone and muscle stores.

There are many causes of acute metabolic acidosis, and thus it is helpful to group them by the presence or absence of a normal anion gap.

Increased anion gap

Main article: High anion gap metabolic acidosis

Causes of increased anion gap include:

- Lactic acidosis
- Ketoacidosis (e.g., Diabetic, alcoholic, or starvation)
- Chronic kidney failure

- Transient 5-oxoprolinemia due to long-term ingestion of high-doses of acetaminophen (often seen with sepsis, liver failure, kidney failure, or malnutrition)[18]
- Intoxication:
    - Salicylates, methanol, ethylene glycol
    - Organic acids, paraldehyde, ethanol, formaldehyde
    - Carbon monoxide, cyanide, ibuprofen, metformin
- Propylene glycol (metabolized to L and D-lactate and is often found in infusions for certain intravenous medications used in the intensive care unit)
- Massive rhabdomyolysis
- Isoniazid, iron, phenelzine, tranylcypromine, valproic acid, verapamil
- Topiramate
- Sulfates

Normal anion gap

Main article: Normal anion gap acidosis

Causes of normal anion gap include

- Inorganic acid addition
    - Infusion/ingestion of HCl, NH_4Cl
- Gastrointestinal base loss
    - Diarrhea
    - Small bowel fistula/drainage
    - Surgical diversion of urine into gut loops
- Renal base loss/acid retention:
    - Proximal renal tubular acidosis
    - Distal renal tubular acidosis
- Hyperalimentation
- Addison disease
- Acetazolamide
- Spironolactone
- Saline infusion

To distinguish between the main types of metabolic acidosis, a clinical tool called the anion gap is considered very useful. It is calculated by subtracting the sum of the chloride and bicarbonate levels from the sum of the sodium and potassium levels. As sodium is the main extracellular cation, and chloride and bicarbonate are the main anions, the result should reflect the remaining anions. Normally, this concentration is about 8–16 mmol/L (12±4). An elevated anion gap (i.e. > 16 mmol/L) can indicate particular types of metabolic acidosis, such as types caused by certain poisons, lactate acidosis, and ketoacidosis. It is important to note that the anion gap can be spuriously normal in sampling errors of the sodium level, e.g. in extreme hypertriglyceridemia. The anion gap can also be increased due to relatively low levels of cations other than sodium and potassium (e.g. calcium or magnesium).

As a differential diagnosis is made, other tests may be necessary, including toxicological screening and imaging of the kidneys, along with testing of electrolytes (including chloride), glucose, kidney function, and a full blood count. Urinalysis can reveal acidity (salicylate poisoning) or alkalinity (renal tubular acidosis type I). In addition, it can show ketones in ketoacidosis. It is also important to differentiate between acidosis-induced hyperventilation and asthma; otherwise, treatment could lead to inappropriate bronchodilation.

	Primary change	Compensation	Effect on pH
Metabolic acidosis	↓ HCO_3^-	↓ Pco_2	↓ pH
Metabolic alkalosis	↑ HCO_3^-	↑ Pco_2	↑ pH
Respiratory acidosis	↑ Pco_2	↑ HCO_3^-	↓ pH
Respiratory alkalosis	↓ Pco_2	↓ HCO_3^-	↑ pH

Fig. 28

Pathophysiology

Compensatory mechanisms

Metabolic acidosis is characterized by a low concentration of bicarbonate (HCO^-_3), which can happen with increased generation of acids (such as ketoacids or lactic acid), excess loss of HCO^-_3 by the kidneys or gastrointestinal tract, or an inability to generate sufficient HCO^-_3. Thus demonstrating the importance of maintaining balance between acids and bases in the body for maintaining optimal functioning of organs, tissues and cells.

The body regulates the acidity of the blood by four buffering mechanisms.

- Bicarbonate buffering system
- Intracellular buffering by absorption of hydrogen atoms by various molecules, including proteins, phosphates and carbonate in bone.
- Respiratory compensation. Hyperventilation will cause more carbon dioxide to be removed from the body and thereby increases pH.
- Kidney compensation =6.1+1.3 =7.4

Acute Metabolic Acidosis

Acute Metabolic Acidosis most often occurs during hospitalizations, and acute critical illnesses. It is often associated with poor prognosis, with a mortality rate as high as 57% if the pH remains untreated at 7.20. At lower pH levels, acute metabolic acidosis can lead to impaired circulation and end organ function.

Bicarbonate therapy is generally administered In patients with severe acute acidemia (pH < 7.11), or with less severe acidemia (pH 7.1-7.2) who have severe acute kidney injury. Bicarbonate therapy is not recommended for people with less severe acidosis (pH ≥ 7.1), unless severe acute kidney injury is present. In the BICAR-ICU trial, bicarbonate therapy for maintaining a pH >7.3 had no overall effect on the composite outcome of all-cause mortality and the presence of at least one organ failure at day 7. However, amongst the sub-group of patients with severe acute kidney injury, bicarbonate therapy significantly decreased the primary composite outcome, and 28-day mortality, along with the need for dialysis.

Chronic Metabolic Acidosis

Chronic metabolic acidosis commonly occurs in people with Chronic Kidney Disease with an eGFR of less than 45 ml/min/1.73m^2, most often with mild to moderate severity; however, metabolic acidosis can manifest earlier on in the course of Chronic Kidney Disease. Multiple animal and human studies have shown that metabolic acidosis in Chronic Kidney Disease, given its chronic nature, has a profound adverse impact on cellular function, overall contributing to high morbidities in patients.

The most adverse consequences of chronic metabolic acidosis in people with Chronic Kidney Disease and in particular, for those who have end-stage renal disease (ESRD), are detrimental changes to the bones and muscles. Acid buffering leads to loss of bone density, resulting in an increased risk of bone fractures, renal osteodystrophy, and bone disease; as well, increased protein catabolism leads to muscle wasting. Furthermore, metabolic acidosis in Chronic Kidney Disease is also associated with a reduction in eGFR; it is both a complication of Chronic Kidney Disease, as well as an underlying cause of Chronic Kidney Disease progression.

Treatment

Treatment of metabolic acidosis depends on the underlying cause, and should target reversing the main process. When considering course of treatment, it is important to distinguish between acute versus chronic forms.

For people with Chronic Kidney Disease, treating metabolic acidosis slows the progression of chronic kidney disease. Dietary interventions for treatment of chronic metabolic acidosis include base-inducing fruits and vegetables that assist with reducing the urine net acid excretion, and increase TCO2. Recent research has also suggested that dietary protein restriction, through ketoanalogue-supplemented vegetarian very low protein diets are also a nutritionally safe option for correction of metabolic acidosis in people with Chronic Kidney Disease.

Currently, the most commonly used treatment for chronic metabolic acidosis is oral bicarbonate. The NKF/ KDOQI guidelines recommend starting treatment when serum bicarbonate levels are <22 mEq/L, in order to maintain levels ≥ 22 mEq/L. Studies investigating the effects of oral alkali therapy demonstrated improvements in serum bicarbonate levels, resulting in a slower decline in kidney function, and reduction in proteinuria – leading to a reduction in the risk of progressing to kidney failure. However, side effects of oral alkali therapy include gastrointestinal intolerance, worsening edema, and worsening hypertension. Furthermore, large doses of oral alkali are required to treat chronic metabolic acidosis, and the pill burden can limit adherence.

Veverimer (TRC 101) is a promising investigational drug designed to treat metabolic acidosis by binding with the acid in the gastrointestinal tract and removing it from the body through excretion in the feces, in turn decreasing the amount of acid in the body, and increasing the level of bicarbonate in the blood. Results from a Phase 3, double-blind placebo-controlled 12-week clinical trial in people with CKD and metabolic acidosis demonstrated that Veverimer effectively and safely corrected metabolic acidosis in the short-term, and a blinded, placebo-controlled, 40-week extension of the trial assessing long-term safety, demonstrated sustained improvements in physical function and a combined endpoint of death, dialysis, or 50% decline in eGFR.

High Anion Gap Metabolic Acidosis

In the previous chapter, we presented various causes of high anion gap (AG) metabolic acidosis. For discussion purpose, these causes can be conveniently divided into the following categories:

1. *Acidosis due to kidney injury*

Acute kidney injury

Chronic kidney disease (CKD) stages 4–5

2. *Acidosis due to accumulation of organic acids*

l-Lactic acidosis

d-Lactic acidosis

Diabetic ketoacidosis

Alcoholic ketoacidosis

Starvation ketoacidosis

3. *Acidosis due to toxins*

Methanol

Ethylene glycol
Propylene glycol
Isopropyl alcohol
Salicylates
5-Oxoproline (pyroglutamic acid)
Paraldehyde

All of the above acidoses except for acidosis due to CKD stages 4 and 5 are acute in nature, whereas acidosis of CKD is chronic in nature. Acute metabolic acidosis develops in hours to days, moderate to severe in nature, and improves with appropriate therapy. Except for acute hemodynamic instability (see "Clinical Manifestations"), survivors do not experience any long-term complications. On the other hand, patients with chronic metabolic acidosis experience bone disease, muscle weakness, progression of kidney disease, and electrolyte abnormalities. Alkali therapy improves many of these complications.

Clinical Manifestations of Metabolic Acidosis

Metabolic acidosis affects almost all organ systems; however, following are the most important clinical manifestations:

Cardiovascular

Increased heart rate and contractility at pH <7.2
Decreased contractility at pH <7.1
Decreased cardiac responsiveness to catecholamines
Decreased renal and hepatic blood flow
Decreased fibrillation threshold
Increased peripheral vasodilation and hypotension

Neurologic

Increased sympathetic stimulation
Altered mental status
Increased cerebral blood flow
Decreased cerebral metabolism

Respiratory

Increased minute ventilation
Dyspnea
Decreased diaphragmatic contractility

Other

Inhibition of anaerobic metabolism
Increased protein catabolism
Increased metabolic rate
Impaired phagocytosis
Decreased ATP production
Impaired skeletal growth
Bone pain

Let us briefly review each of these high AG metabolic acidoses.

Acidosis Due to Kidney Injury

Acute Kidney Injury (AKI)

- AKI other than prerenal azotemia usually causes high AG metabolic acidosis.
- Positive H+ balance due to decreased excretion of H+ and accumulation of sulfate and phosphate account for high AG metabolic acidosis.

Treatment

If serum [HCO3−] is <10 mEq/L, administration of NaHCO3 improves blood pH. Patients not in congestive heart failure (CHF) will tolerate NaHCO3 well.

Otherwise renal replacement therapy improves acidosis.

Chronic Kidney Disease Stages 4–5

• High AG metabolic acidosis develops only if GFR is < 15 mL/min.

• Serum [HCO_3^-] does not fall <16 mEq/L in patients with GFR < 10 mL/min because of bone buffering.

• Possible causes of high AG acidosis include:

1. Decreased NH_4^+ excretion and production by the failing kidney (GFR < 10 mL/min) with positive H^+ balance.
2. Decreased synthesis of NH_4^+ by hyperkalemia.
3. Decreased conservation of HCO_3^- by the failing kidney.
4. Titratable acid (phosphate) excretion may be normal or slightly decreased.
5. Increased production of anions (sulfate, phosphate).
6. Increased catabolism in some malnourished patients generating sulfate and phosphate.
7. Relative hypoaldosteronisms due to diabetes, hypertension, interstitial disease, or drugs, such as ACE-Is, angiotensin receptor blockers, K^+-sparing diuretics, and NSAIDs, may aggravate high AG acidosis by lowering GFR even further.

Treatment Includes protein restriction, $NaHCO_3$, sodium citrate, calcium carbonate, or renal replacement therapy, if indicated.

• In CKD patients, serum [HCO_3^-] should be maintained ≥ 22 mEq/L.

Acidosis Due to Accumulation of Organic Acids

L-Lactic Acidosis

Production

• Lactic acidosis occurs whenever production of lactate exceeds its utilization.

• Lactic acid is formed from pyruvate in the process of glycolysis. The reaction is catalyzed by lactate dehydrogenase (LDH) in the presence of NADH. NADH/

NAD^+ ratio determines the conversions between pyruvate and lactate. The normal lactate-to-pyruvate ratio is 10:1.

Pyruvate + NADH + H^+ Lactate + NAD^+LDH

From the above reaction, excess lactate production can be expected by the following pathophysiologic processes:

1. Increased pyruvate production caused by intravenous (IV) glucose or epinephrine infusion and metabolic or respiratory alkalosis
2. An increase in NADH/NAD^+ ratio due to hypoxic conditions
3. Combination of above two processes

Causes

• Lactic acidosis is divided into two types: type A and type B acidosis.

• Type A acidosis results from generalized or regional tissue hypoxia.

• Type B acidosis results from biochemical abnormalities due to systemic diseases or toxins.

• Note that both type A and type B conditions can be superimposed on one another rather commonly in any patient (metformin use in CHF patient).

Lactic Acidosis Due to Hereditary or Acquired Enzymatic Defects

• Lactic acidosis can occur due to a variety of inherited defects in enzymes involved in glycogen storage diseases, gluconeogenesis, citric acid cycle (pyruvate oxidation), and electron transport (complex I deficiency; complex I, III, and IV deficiency; and complex I and IV deficiency). These are inborn errors associated with "primary" lactic acidosis.

• Disorders associated with "secondary" lactic acidosis include organic acidurias (propionic acidemia, methylmalonic acidemia, etc.), defects in fatty acid oxidation, and urea cycle enzymes.

Diabetic Ketoacidosis (DKA)

• DKA is caused by insulin deficiency and relative glucagon excess.

• DKA presents with a triad of hyperglycemia (glucose >300 mg/dL), ketones in blood and urine, and high AG metabolic acidosis.

• The accumulated ketoacids are acetoacetate and β-hydroxybutyrate (BHB).

• Insulin deficiency promotes lipolysis and fatty acid release, whereas glucagon stimulates the hepatic production of ketoacids from fatty acids.

Diagnosis Diagnosis of DKA is made by high AG metabolic acidosis with documentation of ketones in blood and urine. Volume depletion and many electrolyte abnormalities are commonly associated with DKA.

• The dipstick that is used to detect ketones contains nitroprusside, which reacts strongly (2–4+) with acetoacetate and poorly with BHB (1+). If initial dipstick reaction is 1+ and then 4+ during treatment of DKA, it suggests that severe acidosis initially is due to BHB, and patient's acidosis is improving.

• Use NaHCO3, as previously discussed.

• Follow changes in AG, and adjust the requirement for NaHCO3 administration.

• Changes in AG also indicate the potential HCO3
– regeneration from ketoacids.

• As AG improves, the HCO3
– space or deficit decreases.

Treatment Insulin administration and correction of fluids and electrolytes improve high AG acidosis.

• Note that hyperchloremic metabolic acidosis does develop during treatment of DKA in some patients because the regeneration of HCO3
– from ketones is
decreased due to loss of excess ketones in the urine prior to hospitalization.

Alcoholic Ketoacidosis

• Develops following alcohol abstinence as a result of nausea, vomiting, abdominal pain, and possibly starvation.

• Most common in women and diabetics following binge.

• Alcohol withdrawal also precipitates ketoacidosis due to catecholamine release.

• Pathogenesis includes ethanol itself, starvation, insulin deficiency, excess glucagon and catecholamines, and vomiting.

• Ethanol inhibits gluconeogenesis and stimulates lipolysis. It is metabolized to acetaldehyde (catalyzed by alcohol dehydrogenase) and then to acetic acid (catalyzed by aldehyde dehydrogenase). These reactions involve conversion of NAD+ to NADH, which enhances the production of lactate from pyruvate and BHB from acetoacetate.

• Starvation depletes hepatic glycogen store. Excess glucagon stimulates lipolysis and production of ketoacids from fatty acids.

• Ketoacids are also formed from acetic acid.

• Hypoglycemia is present in some patients.

Treatment Includes fluid replacement with D5W and normal saline, thiamine, and correction of electrolytes.

• Note that hyperchloremic metabolic acidosis develops during the recovery phase of alcoholic ketoacidosis.

Starvation Ketoacidosis

• Starvation ketoacidosis is mild and self-limited.

• Relative decrease in insulin secretion and an increase in glucagon secretion cause ketoacid formation.

• Unlike DKA, the presence of insulin prevents progression of full-blown ketoacidosis.

• Also, insulin secretion is stimulated by ketones and fatty acids during prolonged fasting, thereby minimizing even further the formation of ketoacids.

• Intense ketonuria with a weak serum reaction to nitroprusside test is usually observed in starvation ketosis.

Treatment Resumption of food intake corrects ketoacidosis

METABOLIC ALKALOSIS

Metabolic alkalosis is a metabolic condition in which the pH of tissue is elevated beyond the normal range (7.35–7.45). This is the result of decreased hydrogen ion concentration, leading to increased bicarbonate, or alternatively a direct result of increased bicarbonate concentrations. The condition typically cannot last long if the kidneys are functioning properly.

Signs and symptoms

Mild cases of metabolic alkalosis often cause no symptoms. Typical manifestations of moderate to severe metabolic alkalosis include abnormal sensations, neuromuscular irritability, tetany, abnormal heart rhythms (usually due to accompanying electrolyte abnormalities such as low levels of potassium in the blood), coma, seizures, and temporary waxing and waning confusion.

Causes

The causes of metabolic alkalosis can be divided into two categories, depending upon urine chloride levels.

Chloride-responsive (Urine chloride < 25 mEq/L)

- **Loss of hydrogen ions** – Most often occurs via two mechanisms, either vomiting or via the kidney.
  - Vomiting results in the loss of hydrochloric acid (hydrogen and chloride ions) with the stomach contents. In the hospital setting this can commonly occur from nasogastric suction tubes.
  - Severe vomiting also causes loss of potassium (hypokalemia) and sodium (hyponatremia). The kidneys compensate for these losses by retaining sodium in the collecting ducts at the expense of hydrogen ions (sparing sodium/potassium pumps to prevent further loss of potassium), leading to metabolic alkalosis.
- Congenital chloride diarrhea – rare for being a diarrhea that causes alkalosis instead of acidosis.
- Contraction alkalosis – This results from a loss of water in the extracellular space, such as from dehydration. Decreased extracellular volume triggers the renin-angiotensin-aldosterone system, and aldosterone subsequently stimulates reabsorption of sodium (and thus water) within the nephron of the kidney. However, a second action of aldosterone is to stimulate renal excretion of hydrogen ions (while retaining bicarbonate), and it is this loss of hydrogen ions that raises the pH of the blood.
  - **Diuretic therapy** – loop diuretics and thiazides can both initially cause increase in chloride, but once stores are depleted, urine excretion will be below < 25 mEq/L. The loss of fluid from sodium excretion causes a contraction alkalosis. Diuretic abuse among athletes and people with eating disorders may present with metabolic alkalosis.
- **Posthypercapnia** – Hypoventilation (decreased respiratory rate) causes hypercapnia (increased levels of CO_2), which results in respiratory acidosis. Renal compensation with excess bicarbonate retention occurs to lessen the effect of the acidosis. Once carbon dioxide levels return to base line, the higher bicarbonate levels reveal

themselves putting the patient into metabolic alkalosis.

- Cystic fibrosis – excessive loss of sodium chloride in the sweat leads to contraction of the extracellular volume in the same way as contraction alkalosis, as well chloride depletion.
- **Alkalotic agents** – Alkalotic agents, such as bicarbonate (administrated in cases of peptic ulcer or hyperacidity) or antacids, administered in excess can lead to an alkalosis.

Chloride-indeterminate alkalosis

- Milk alkali syndrome
- Blood product administration since this contains sodium citrate which is then metabolized into sodium bicarbonate. Typically, this is seen with large volume transfusions such as more than 8 units.
- Decreases in albumin and phosphate will cause metabolic alkalosis.

Chloride-resistant (Urine chloride > 40 mEq/L)

- **Retention of bicarbonate** – Retention of bicarbonate would lead to alkalosis.
- **Shift of hydrogen ions into intracellular space** – Seen in hypokalemia. Due to a low extracellular potassium concentration, potassium shifts out of the cells. In order to maintain electrical neutrality, hydrogen shifts into the cells, raising blood pH.
- **Hyperaldosteronism** – Loss of hydrogen ions in the urine occurs when excess aldosterone (Conn's syndrome) increases the activity of a sodium-hydrogen exchange protein in the kidney. This increases the retention of sodium ions whilst pumping hydrogen ions into the renal tubule. Excess sodium increases extracellular volume and the loss of hydrogen ions creates a metabolic alkalosis. Later, the kidney responds through the aldosterone escape to excrete sodium and chloride in urine.
- **Excess glycyrrhizin consumption**
- Low levels of magnesium in the blood
- Severely high levels of calcium in the blood
- **Bartter syndrome** and **Gitelman syndrome** – syndromes with presentations analogous to taking diuretics characterized with normotensive patients
- **Liddle syndrome** – a gain of function mutation in the genes encoding the epithelial sodium channel (ENaC) which is characterized by hypertension and hypoaldosteronism.
- **11β-hydroxylase deficiency** and **17α-hydroxylase deficiency** – both characterized by hypertension
- Aminoglycoside toxicity can induce a hypokalemic metabolic alkalosis via activating the calcium sensing receptor in the thick ascending limb of the nephron, inactivating the NKCC2 cotransporter, creating a Bartter's syndrome like effect.

Compensation

Compensation for metabolic alkalosis occurs mainly in the lungs, which retain carbon dioxide (CO_2) through slower breathing, or hypoventilation (respiratory compensation). CO_2 is then consumed toward the formation of the carbonic acid intermediate, thus decreasing pH. Respiratory compensation, though, is incomplete. The decrease in [H+] suppresses the peripheral chemoreceptors, which are sensitive to pH. But, because respiration slows, there is an increase in pCO_2 which would cause an offset of the depression because of the action of the central chemoreceptors which are sensitive to the partial pressure of CO_2 in the cerebral spinal fluid. So, because of the central chemoreceptors, respiration rate would be increased.

Renal compensation for metabolic alkalosis, less effective than respiratory compensation, consists of increased excretion of HCO_3^- (bicarbonate), as the filtered load of HCO_3^- exceeds the ability of the renal tubule to reabsorb it.

To calculate the expected pCO_2 in the setting of metabolic alkalosis, the following equations are used:

- $pCO_2 = 0.7 [HCO_3] + 20$ mmHg ± 5
- $pCO_2 = 0.7 [HCO_3] + 21$ mmHg

Treatment

To effectively treat metabolic alkalosis, the underlying cause(s) must be corrected. A trial of intravenous chloride-rich fluid is warranted if there is a high index of suspicion for chloride-responsive metabolic alkalosis caused by loss of gastrointestinal fluid (e.g., due to vomiting).

Terminology

- **Alkalosis** refers to a process by which the pH is increased.
- **Alkalemia** refers to a pH which is higher than normal, specifically in the blood.

RESPIRATORY ACIDOSIS

Respiratory acidosis is a state in which decreased ventilation (hypoventilation) increases the concentration of carbon dioxide in the blood and decreases the blood's pH (a condition generally called acidosis).

Carbon dioxide is produced continuously as the body's cells respire, and this CO_2 will accumulate rapidly if the lungs do not adequately expel it through alveolar ventilation. Alveolar hypoventilation thus leads to an increased $PaCO_2$ (a condition called hypercapnia). The increase in $PaCO_2$ in turn decreases the $HCO_3^-/PaCO_2$ ratio and decreases pH.

Types

Respiratory acidosis can be acute or chronic.

- In *acute respiratory acidosis*, the $PaCO_2$ is elevated above the upper limit of the reference range (over 6.3 kPa or 45 mm Hg) with an accompanying acidemia (pH <7.36).
- In *chronic respiratory acidosis*, the $PaCO_2$ is elevated above the upper limit of the reference range, with a normal blood pH (7.35 to 7.45) or near-normal pH secondary to renal compensation and an elevated serum bicarbonate (HCO_3^- >30 mEq/L).

Causes

Acute

Acute respiratory acidosis occurs when an abrupt failure of ventilation occurs. This failure in ventilation may be caused by depression of the central respiratory center by cerebral disease or drugs, inability to ventilate adequately due to neuromuscular disease (e.g., myasthenia gravis, amyotrophic lateral sclerosis, Guillain–Barré syndrome, muscular dystrophy), or airway obstruction related to asthma or chronic obstructive pulmonary disease (COPD) exacerbation.

Chronic

Chronic respiratory acidosis may be secondary to many disorders, including COPD. Hypoventilation in COPD involves multiple mechanisms, including decreased responsiveness to hypoxia and hypercapnia, increased ventilation-perfusion mismatch leading to increased dead space ventilation, and decreased diaphragm function secondary to fatigue and hyperinflation.

Chronic respiratory acidosis also may be secondary to obesity hypoventilation syndrome (i.e., Pickwickian syndrome), neuromuscular disorders such as amyotrophic lateral sclerosis, and severe restrictive ventilatory defects as observed in interstitial lung disease and thoracic deformities.

Lung diseases that primarily cause abnormality in alveolar gas exchange usually do not cause hypoventilation but tend to cause stimulation of ventilation and hypocapnia secondary to hypoxia. Hypercapnia only occurs if severe disease or respiratory muscle fatigue occurs.

Physiological response

Mechanism

Metabolism rapidly generates a large quantity of volatile acid (H_2CO_3) and nonvolatile acid. The metabolism of fats and carbohydrates leads to the formation of a large amount of CO_2. The CO_2 combines with H_2O to form carbonic acid (H_2CO_3). The lungs normally excrete the volatile fraction through ventilation, and acid accumulation does not occur. A significant alteration in ventilation that affects elimination of CO_2 can cause a respiratory acid-base disorder. The $PaCO_2$ is maintained within a range of 35–45 mm Hg in normal states.

Alveolar ventilation is under the control of the respiratory center, which is located in the pons and the medulla. Ventilation is influenced and regulated by chemoreceptors for $PaCO_2$, PaO_2, and pH located in the brainstem, and in the aortic and carotid bodies as well as by neural impulses from lung stretch receptors and impulses from the cerebral cortex. Failure of ventilation quickly increases the $PaCO_2$.

In acute respiratory acidosis, compensation occurs in 2 steps.

- The initial response is cellular buffering (plasma protein buffers) that occurs over minutes to hours. Cellular buffering elevates plasma bicarbonate (HCO_3^-) only slightly, approximately 1 mEq/L for each 10-mm Hg increase in $PaCO_2$.
- The second step is renal compensation that occurs over 3–5 days. With renal compensation, renal excretion of carbonic acid is increased and bicarbonate reabsorption is increased. For instance, PEPCK is upregulated in renal proximal tubule brush border cells, in order to secrete more NH_3 and thus to produce more HCO_3^-.

Estimated changes

In renal compensation, plasma bicarbonate rises 3.5 mEq/L for each increase of 10 mm Hg in $PaCO_2$. The expected change in serum bicarbonate concentration in respiratory acidosis can be estimated as follows:

- Acute respiratory acidosis: HCO_3^- increases 1 mEq/L for each 10 mm Hg rise in $PaCO_2$.
- Chronic respiratory acidosis: HCO_3^- rises 3.5 mEq/L for each 10 mm Hg rise in $PaCO_2$.

The expected change in pH with respiratory acidosis can be estimated with the following equations:

- Acute respiratory acidosis: Change in pH = $0.08 \times ((40 - PaCO_2)/10)$
- Chronic respiratory acidosis: Change in pH = $0.03 \times ((40 - PaCO_2)/10)$

Respiratory acidosis does not have a great effect on electrolyte levels. Some small effects occur on calcium and potassium levels. Acidosis decreases binding of calcium to albumin and tends to increase serum ionized calcium levels. In addition, acidemia causes an extracellular shift of potassium, but respiratory acidosis rarely causes clinically significant hyperkalemia.

Diagnosis

Diagnoses can be done by doing an ABG (Arterial Blood Gas) laboratory study, with a pH <7.35 and a PaCO2 >45 mmHg in an acute setting. Patients with COPD and other Chronic respiratory diseases will sometimes display higher numbers of PaCO2 with HCO3- >30 and normal pH.

Terminology

- Acidosis refers to disorders that lower cell/tissue pH to < 7.35.
- Acidemia refers to an arterial pH < 7.36.

RESPIRATORY ALKALOSIS

Respiratory alkalosis is a medical condition in which increased respiration elevates the blood pH beyond the normal range (7.35–7.45) with a concurrent reduction in arterial levels of carbon dioxide. This condition is one of the four primary disturbance of acid–base homeostasis.

Signs and symptoms

Signs and symptoms of respiratory alkalosis are as follows:

- Palpitation
- Tetany
- Convulsion
- Sweating

Causes

Respiratory alkalosis may be produced as a result of the following causes:

- Stress
- Pulmonary disorder
- Thermal insult
- High altitude areas
- Salicylate poisoning (aspirin overdose)
- Fever
- Hyperventilation (due to heart disorder or other, including improper mechanical ventilation)
- Vocal cord paralysis (compensation for loss of vocal volume results in over-breathing/breathlessness).
- Liver disease

Mechanism

Carbonic-acid

The mechanism of respiratory alkalosis generally occurs when some stimulus makes a person hyperventilate. The increased breathing produces increased alveolar respiration, expelling CO_2 from the circulation. This alters the dynamic chemical equilibrium of carbon dioxide in the circulatory system. Circulating hydrogen ions and bicarbonate are shifted through the carbonic acid (H_2CO_3) intermediate to make more CO_2 via the enzyme carbonic anhydrase according to the following reaction: HCO3−+H+→H2CO3→CO2+H2OThis causes decreased circulating hydrogen ion concentration, and increased pH (alkalosis).

Diagnosis

The diagnosis of respiratory alkalosis is done via test that measure the oxygen and carbon dioxide levels (in the blood), chest x-ray and a pulmonary function test of the individual.

Classification

There are two types of respiratory alkalosis: chronic and acute as a result of the 3–5 day delay in kidney compensation of the abnormality.

- *Acute respiratory alkalosis* occurs rapidly, have a high pH because the response of the kidneys is slow.
- *Chronic respiratory alkalosis* is a more long-standing condition, here one finds the kidneys have time to decrease the bicarbonate level.

pH

- *Alkalosis* refers to the process due to which there is elevation of blood pH.
- *Alkalemia* refers to an arterial blood pH of greater than 7.45.

Treatment

Respiratory alkalosis is very rarely life-threatening, though pH level should not be 7.5 or greater. The aim in treatment is to detect the underlying cause. When PaCO2 is adjusted rapidly in individuals with chronic respiratory alkalosis, metabolic acidosis may occur. If the individual is on a mechanical ventilator then preventing hyperventilation is done via monitoring ABG levels.

CHAPTER THIRTEEN

CLINICAL CASES

Case 1:

A 62year old man is 2 days post-colectomy. He is euvolaemic, and is allowed to drink 500ml. His urine output is 63 ml/hour:

1. How much IV fluid does he need today?

This man has a normal total body water content, and you aim is to maintain that.

A urine output of 63 ml / hr gives him a total daily urine loss of 1.5 litres.

His insensible losses are likely to be 500 ml. He therefore needs a total fluid intake of 2 litres to balance his losses. He is only allowed to drink 500 ml.

He therefore needs 1.5 litres of fluid IV today.

2. What type of IV fluid does he need?

As he is euvolaemic, this man does not need resuscita:on, so he should only receive crystalloid. His losses will include water and electrolytes. Giving him just 5% dextrose will cause osmolality to fall and hyponatraemia to follow. Giving him just 0.9% saline will cause gradual hypernatraemia and hypertonicity.

This man needs a mixture of crystalloids. He is ge.ng water orally which might help to offset the sodium load of saline. Even so, it is reasonable to use saline and dextrose in a 2:1 ratio; this proportion can be changed in response to changes in his clinical state and serum sodium.

Case 2:

3 days after her admission, a 43year old woman with diabe9c ketoacidosis has a blood pressure of 88/46 mmHg & pulse of 110 bpm. Her charts show that her urine output over the last 3 days was 26.5 litres, whilst her total intake was 18 litres:

1. How much IV fluid does he need to regain a normal BP?

The hyperglycaemia of diabetic ketoacidosis causes glycosuria which results in an osmotic diuresis.

This causes high losses of water and dehydration occurs if fluid balance is not attended to.

In this case, the lady has lost 26.5 litres of urine plus at least 1.5 litres insensible losses over the last 3 days; her input has been 18 litres. This equals a deficit of 10 litres, and it is not surprising that she appears to be hypovolemic with hypotension and tachycardia.

Assuming that she was euvolaemic to start with, she needs to gain 10 litres in order to regain a normal BP.

2. What type of IV fluid would you use?

As she has a low BP, we can assume that her blood volume is low, and that organ perfusion is at risk.

She therefore needs to be resuscitated. The initial fluids to use would be colloid in order to normalise BP and pulse. There is no need to use only colloid; indeed, this would cause intravascular overload and heart failure. Aver using perhaps 1 or 2 litres of colloid, her remaining fluids should be crystalloid. As she has lost mainly water, a large part of this should be dextrose, and serum [Na^+] should be monitored in order to assess the need for IV saline.

Case 3:

An 85 year old man receives IV fluids for 3 days following a stroke; he is not allowed to eat. He has ankle oedema and a JVP of +5 cms; his charts reveal a total input of 9 l and a urine output of 6 litres over these 3 days.

1. How much excess fluid does he carry?

This man has become hypervolaemic with inters::al oedema and intravascular excess, because he has received 3 litres more fluid than he has passed out in his urine. Remember however that he loses 500 ml/day insensible losses.

His total fluid excess is therefore around 1.5 litres.

2. What would you do with his IV fluids?

Although he is not drinking, he is overloaded and his IV fluids should be stopped. Aver a day without IV fluids, he should be euvolaemic, and IV fluids can be recommenced at 2.5 litres a day without overloading him.

Case 4:

5 days after a liver transplant, a 48year old man has a pyrexia of 40.8oC. His charts for the last 24 hours reveal:

urine output: 2.7 litres

drain output: 525 ml

nasogastric output: 1.475 litres

blood transfusion: 2 units (350 ml each)

IV crystalloid: 2.5 litres

oral fluids: 500 ml

On examination he is tachycardic; his supine BP is OK, but you can't sit him up to check his erect BP. His serum [Na^+] is 140 mmol/l.

1. How much IV fluid does he need?

As is oven the case with complex surgical patients, this man has multiple sources of luid loss. In each case, urine, drain or tube, the fluid lost will be a mixture of fluid and solutes.

Indeed, drain fluid will have an electrolyte content very similar to plasma.

His obvious losses (urine + drain + NG tube) total 4.7 litres.

His insensible losses are higher than normal because of his fever, and will be about 800 ml, giving a total loss of 5.5 litres.

His total intake was 3.7 litres, and he is therefore deficient by 1.8 litres.

Assuming that his total losses for this day are similar to those of the day before, he will need about 7.3 litres in order to become euvolaemic.

2. What fluid would you use?

He will almost undoubtedly need a mixture of fluids. He will need colloid or further blood in order to fill the intravascular compartment and maintain organ perfusion. He will need saline to replace water and solute losses, and will need some dextrose in order to prevent hypernatraemia.

In practice, a case of this complexity will require repeated re-evaluation, adjustment of his fluids throughout the day with serial blood tests in order to guide you.

CHAPTER FOURTEEN

ACIDOSIS DUE TO TOXINS

General Considerations

- Ingestion of alcohols, such as ethanol, methanol, and ethylene glycol, or administration of propylene glycol generates not only hyperosmolality but also metabolic acidosis with high AG. Whenever ingestion of these alcohols is suspected, it is important to measure and calculate serum osmolality to identify osmolal gap.
- *Osmolal gap* is defined as the difference between the measured and calculated serum osmolality. Generally, the measured osmolality is 10 mOsm higher than the calculated osmolality. Values >10 mOsm represent the presence of an osmolal gap.
- Note that in one study, the osmolal gap in healthy volunteers varied from −14 to 10 mOsm, suggesting that >10 is found to be abnormal.
- Elevated osmolal gap suggests the presence of osmotically active substances that are measured, but not included in the calculation of osmolality.
- Lactate and ketoacids also cause high osmolal gap.
- Traditionally, the presence of an osmolal gap and an elevated anion gap is considered to represent the ingestion of toxic alcohols such as methanol, ethylene glycol, and others (Table 28.4) This table shows the number of mOsm contributed by 100 mg/dL of each substance present in the serum.
- Metabolism: the first step in the metabolism of all toxic alcohols is catalyzed by the enzyme alcohol dehydrogenase (ADH), which is the most critical step in metabolism.
- Administration of an antidote to inhibit the enzyme ADH prevents the toxic metabolites of the parent alcohol. Table 28.5 shows metabolic end products that cause toxicity.

Let us discuss each one of these alcohols and others in detail.

Methanol

- Common names: methyl alcohol, wood alcohol, wood spirit, and carbinol.
- Sources: antifreeze, additive to gasoline and diesel oil, windshield wiper fluid (most common abuse in the USA), dyes, varnishes, and cheap alcohols.
- Lethal dose is 30 mL of absolute methanol.
- Easily absorbed from the gastrointestinal (GI) tract. Other less routes of exposure are inhalation and skin absorption.
- Methanol is not itself toxic, but its metabolites, formaldehyde, and formic acid are extremely toxic.
- Half-life of methanol in low dose is 14–24 h, and in higher doses, the half-life is prolonged to 24–30 h.

Clinical Manifestations Mostly due to formic acid (formate)

- Signs and symptoms of methanol intoxication are related to central nervous and GI systems:
  - Lethargy, headache, confusion, and vertigo are common.
  - Eye pain, blurred vision, photophobia, and blindness are common at presentation in 50% of patients.

– Dilated pupils, constriction of the visual fields, and papilledema are the ophthalmoscopic findings.
– Nausea, vomiting, pancreatitis, and abdominal pain are common GI complaints.

• Coingestion of ethanol delays the manifestations of methanol intoxication.

Diagnosis

• Serum electrolytes, BUN, creatinine, glucose, serum osmolality, serum Ca^{2+}, Mg^{2+}, ethanol, ethylene glycol, and ketone levels, urine microscopy, and ABG.

• Visual impairment, high osmolal gap, and high AG metabolic acidosis should alert the physician of methanol intoxication and warrants immediate treatment to prevent blindness. High AG is contributed by formic acid, lactic acid, and ketoacids.

Treatment The criteria for the initiation of therapy in patients with known or suspected methanol poisoning are:

Plasma methanol level of ≥ 20 mg/dL

or

Documented recent history of toxic amounts of methanol ingestion and an osmolal gap >10 mOsm/L

or

Suspected methanol ingestion and at least two of the following criteria:

Arterial pH <7.30

Serum [HCO_3^-] <20 mEq/L

Serum osmolal gap > 10 mOsm/L

• Immediate supportive care includes:

1. Hydration with normal saline, and glucose for hypoglycemia.
2. Intravenous $NaHCO_3$ to maintain blood pH >7.2.
3. Intravenous folinic acid (1 mg/kg) one dose and then folate supplementation to accelerate formate metabolism to CO_2 and water by tetrahydrofolate synthetase. This may benefit some alcoholics with folate deficiency
4. The American Academy of Clinical Toxicology recommendations are:

Fomepizole (4-methylpyrazole), the drug of choice in the USA.

Ethanol, if fomepizole not available.

Fomepizole is a competitive inhibitor of ADH, and the recommended dosages are as follows:

• *Without dialysis*
• Loading dose: 15 mg/kg
• Maintenance dose: 10 mg/kg Q12 h for four doses
• After 48 h or four doses, 15 mg/kg Q12 h until methanol levels are < 20 mg/dL
• *With dialysis*
• The same doses as above except that the drug is given 6 h after the first dose and then Q4 h thereafter

Ethanol is a substrate for ADH, and its administration decreases the metabolism of methanol. It has 10–20 times greater affinity for ADH than other alcohols. Ethanol at a serum concentration of 100 mg/dL inhibits completely the enzyme ADH. The recommended dosage is as follows:

Dose	Absolute alcohol	10% IV solution
Loading	600 mg/kg	7.6 mL/kg
Maintenance (nondrinker)	66 mg/kg/h	0.83 mL/kg/h
Maintenance (drinker)	154 mg/kg/h	1.96 mL/kg/h
Maintenance during dialysis (nondrinker)	169 mg/kg/h	2.13 mL/kg/h

Maintenance during dialysis (drinkers) 257 mg/kg/h 3.26 mL/kg/h

Hemodialysis: With the introduction of fomepizole, routine use of hemodialysis has diminished, and it has become an adjunctive therapy. However, hemodialysis is indicated in the following situations:

1. Ethanol-treated patient with methanol level >50 mg/dL
2. Renal dysfunction
3. Visual impairment
4. Severe acidemia

• It is important to understand the advantages and disadvantages of each of these treatment modalities for judicious use in the management of methanol poisoning

• Severe acidemia has a prognostic significance. Serum [HCO3−] <20 mEq/L carries 10% mortality, whereas [HCO3−] <10 mEq/L has the mortality of 50%.

Therefore, maintenance of arterial pH >7.2 is important.

Ethylene Glycol (EG)

• Colorless, odorless, and sweet-tasting alcohol.
• Sources: antifreeze, de-icers, and many industrial products.
• EG intoxication is more common than methanol intoxication.
• Oral ingestion of EG is the most common route of EG intoxication.
• EG is metabolized to glycolic and oxalic acids.
• Glycolic acid is the major cause of high AG acidosis.
• Oxalic acid is the major cause of AKI and myocardial, neurologic, and pulmonary dysfunction due to deposition of calcium oxalate in these organ systems.
• Lethal dose of EG is 1.4 mL/kg.

Clinical Manifestations (Classified into Three Stages)

Stage 1 (0.5–12 h after ingestion): Transient inebriation and euphoria with progression to cerebral edema and coma.

Stage 2 (12–24 h after ingestion): Tachycardia and hypertension, severe metabolic acidosis. ARDS may develop. Most deaths occur during this stage.

Stage 3 (24–72 h after ingestion): Oliguria, anuria, and severe renal dysfunction, requiring hemodialysis.

Note that neurologic, cardiopulmonary, and renal abnormalities can present at the time of admission in some patients.

Coingestion of ethanol delays the manifestations of methanol intoxication.

Diagnosis

• Serum electrolytes, BUN, creatinine, glucose, serum osmolality, serum Ca2+, Mg2+, ethanol, EG, ketones, lactate, urine microscopy, and ABG.
• Severe high AG metabolic acidosis, increased osmolal gap, and, at times, the presence of oxalate crystals in the urine are suggestive of EG intoxication.
• Note that osmolal gap is not always present because of small contribution of osmoles by EG compared to other alcohols and also the absence of glycolic acid due to rapid conversion to oxalic acid.
• Hypocalcemia may be present.
• High AG and high osmolal gap are associated with high mortality.

Treatment The criteria for the initiation of therapy in patients with known or suspected EG poisoning are:

Plasma EG level of ≥20 mg/dL

or

Documented recent history of toxic amounts of EG ingestion and an osmolal gap >10 mOsm/L or

Suspected EG ingestion and at least two of the following criteria:

Arterial pH <7.30

Serum [HCO3−] <20 mEq/L

Serum osmolal gap > 10 mOsm/L

Presence of oxalate crystals in urine

Propylene Glycol (PG)

- PG is used as a diluent in IV and oral drugs, including phenytoin, diazepam, lorazepam, phenobarbital, nitroglycerine, hydralazine, and trimethoprim–sulfamethoxazole.
- Most of the cases of PG intoxications are from IV administration of drugs.
- Toxicity of PG occurs at blood concentrations >100 mg/dL.
- Patients with liver and kidney dysfunction are at risk for PG toxicity.

Clinical Manifestations Include disorientation, depression, nystagmus, ataxia, hypotension, and cardiac arrhythmias.

Diagnosis

- Metabolic acidosis with high AG due to lactic acid (both l- and d-forms). Renal failure occurs in some patients.

Treatment Includes discontinuation of the offending agent. Hemodialysis helps in correcting renal failure and lowering PG levels.

Isopropyl Alcohol

- Usually called rubbing alcohol
- Sources: rubbing alcohol, cleaning agents, de-icer, and industrial solvents
- Route of exposure: skin and GI tract absorption as well as inhalation by lungs
- Metabolized to acetone by ADH

Clinical Manifestations Depend on serum levels of isopropanol: levels >150 mg/dL are associated with hypotension and coma, and levels >400 mg/dL carry poor prognosis.

Diagnosis

- High serum osmolality with large osmolal gap and normal acid–base disorder are common findings in subjects with isopropyl alcohol intoxication.

Treatment guidelines for EG ingestion

Treatment Indications

Supportive care Volume depletion and hypoglycemia: correct volume deficit with normal saline and D5W to improve glucose levels

NaHCO3, if pH <7.20

Pyridoxine and thiamine, particularly in alcoholics, to expedite glyoxylate metabolism

Follow serum EG levels, Ca2+, creatinine, lactate, and ABG

Ingestion of multiple substances with depressed level of consciousness

Fomepizole Altered mental status

Inadequate ICU staffing or laboratory support to monitor ethanol administration

Relative contraindication to ethanol (liver disease)

Critically ill patient with high AG metabolic acidosis of unknown etiology and potential exposure to EG

Ethanol Unavailability of fomepizole

Hemodialysis Severe metabolic acidosis refractory to fomepizole and ethanol or NaHCO3

Anuria

Renal failure

• Acetone breath and positive serum and urine nitroprusside reaction usually mislead to the diagnosis of diabetic ketoacidosis. Only serum glucose levels differentiate between these two conditions.

• If high AG metabolic acidosis is present, suspect lactic acidosis due to hypotension.

Treatment Supportive care, as the intoxication is self-limited. Hemodialysis is indicated in subjects with serum levels >200 mg/dL and hypotension.

Salicylate Intoxication

• Aspirin (acetylsalicylic acid or ASA) is the most commonly used salicylate.

• Exposure is topical and oral forms. ASA is readily absorbed in the GI tract, and salicylate is responsible for systemic toxic effects.

• Intake of ASA is usually accidental in children and suicidal or intentional in adults.

• Serum half-life of salicylate is 2–4 h at low doses, approximately 12 h with therapeutic doses, and can be prolonged to 15–30 h or more with toxic doses.

• Two to 30% of salicylate is excreted unchanged in the urine, with less renal excretion occurring in acidic urine or in patients with renal failure.

• Metabolic effects are:

1. Uncoupling of oxidative phosphorylation and decreased ATP production.
2. Inhibition of conversion of α-ketoglutarate to succinate and succinate to fumarate, resulting in lipolysis, ketone formation, and stimulation of glycolysis.
3. Acid–base disorder in adults: Initially respiratory alkalosis due to stimulation of medullary respiratory center by salicylate and hyperventilation. Subsequently, metabolic acidosis develops due to lactic acid and ketoacid production. Respiratory alkalosis seems to be the main reason for lactic acid production.
4. In children, metabolic acidosis predominates initially.
5. Urate excretion is low with low doses of salicylate and high with high doses of salicylate.

Clinical Manifestations Depend on acute or chronic ingestion of ASA.

Acute Manifestations Nausea, vomiting, abdominal pain, hematemesis, tachypnea, tinnitus, deafness, lethargy, confusion, coma, and seizures.

Chronic Manifestations Occur mostly in elderly patients with chronic use of ASA. Most of the manifestations are similar to those of acute intoxication except for GI symptoms. Patients appear ill, and neurologic symptoms are more prominent, including agitation, confusion, slurred speech, coma, and seizures.

Diagnosis

• History is extremely important, if it can be obtained. Type of salicylate, amount ingested, time of ingestion, long-term use, use of other medications, and history of renal, hepatic, cardiac, and psychiatric diseases should help therapeutic decision.

• Fever is common in children.

• Serum electrolytes, BUN, creatinine, glucose, $Ca2+$, lactate, and ketones should be obtained.

• ABG: Respiratory alkalosis with AG metabolic acidosis with hyperventilation and tinnitus should suggest the diagnosis of salicylate poisoning.

• Urine pH is important, as acid pH increases salicylate toxicity.

• Serial serum salicylate levels are extremely important for therapeutic consideration.
• Obtain chest X-ray for edema and EKG for arrhythmias.

Treatment Four goals for symptomatic acute or chronic toxicity, as there are no antidotes:

1. Supportive care
2. Reduce GI absorption of salicylate
3. Promote renal excretion of salicylate
4. Lowering plasma levels of salicylate by hemodialysis

• *Supportive care*: Should start in the emergency department for the following:
– Endotracheal intubation for protection of airways, hypoxia, and continuation of hyperventilation to prevent further drop in pH
– Correction of volume deficit and electrolyte abnormalities to maintain hemodynamic stability
• *Reduce GI absorption of salicylate*: Use oral activated charcoal at 1 g/kg to a maximum of 50 g in children and 100 g in adults. The minimum dose is 30 g. Repeat the dose of charcoal. The use of sorbitol with charcoal is advocated in adults by some physicians. The use of ipecac is controversial.
• *Promote renal excretion of salicylate*: Adequate fluid administration and alkalinization of urine promote the excretion of salicylic acid. Acidosis promotes tissue transfer of salicylate, particularly into the brain, and alkalinization prevents tissue penetration. One way to alkalinize the body fluids and urine is to give 1.5 L of 150 mEq/L of $NaHCO_3$ solution over 4 h. Blood pH should be followed with serum K^+ and Ca^{2+}. Continue urinary alkalinization until serum salicylate levels drop to therapeutic range (30 mg/dL).
• *Lowering plasma levels of salicylate by hemodialysis*: Hemodialysis is indicated for serum salicylate levels >120 mg/dL, refractory acidosis, fluid overload, renal failure, noncardiogenic pulmonary edema, coma, and seizures. Hemoperfusion is efficient in removing salicylate, but may not be that effective in correcting renal failure or fluid overload or severe acidosis. Peritoneal dialysis is not effective. Hemodialysis is also effective in symptomatic patient with chronic overdose and salicylate levels exceed 60–80 mg/dL.

5-Oxoproline (Pyroglutamic Acid)

• Pyroglutamic acid is a degradative product of reduced glutathione (GSH), and its accumulation in blood causes high AG metabolic acidosis (Fig. 28.1).
• The synthesis and degradation of glutathione occurs by reactions of the γ-glutamyl cycle.
• Glutathione is a tripeptide, consisting of glutamate, cysteine, and glycine (usually written as L-γ-glutamyl-l-cysteinylglycine). The synthesis and degradation of glutathione involves six enzymes: two enzymes for synthesis (γ-glutamylcysteine synthetase and glutathione synthetase) and four enzymes for degradation (γ-glutamyl transpeptidase, γ-glutamylcyclotransferase, 5- oxoprolinase, and dipeptidase).
• GSH is found in most cells in high (millimolar) concentrations. It has several functions, including amino acid transport and maintenance of thiol/disulfide balance.
• Under normal circumstances, glutathione inhibits γ-glutamylcysteine synthetase so that excess production of γ-glutamylcysteine is prevented. When glutathione

levels decrease, the feedback inhibition is relieved, resulting in accumulation of γ-glutamylcysteine and conversion to pyroglutamic acid by the enzyme γ-glutamylcyclotransferase.

• Elevated levels of pyroglutamic acid in blood cause high AG metabolic acidosis. Initially, pyroglutamic acidemia was described in infants with inherited deficiencies of glutathione synthetase and 5-oxoprolinase.

• These inherited enzyme deficiencies are rather rare, but acquired pyroglutamic acidemia and aciduria have been reported in adults in several clinical settings.

• Clinical conditions associated with pyroglutamic acidosis are sepsis, malnutrition, pregnancy, vegetarian, and modified diets.

• Drugs that cause pyroglutamic acidosis include acetaminophen (paracetamol), vigabatrin, an antiepileptic drug, monosodium glutamate, and antibiotics such as flucloxacillin or netilmicin.

• The common underlying mechanism for pyroglutamic acidemia and aciduria is depletion of tissue glutathione. However, vigabatrin and flucloxacillin seem to inhibit the enzyme 5-oxoprolinase.

Diagnosis

• History of drugs and antibiotics is very important. Chronic clinical conditions, such as rheumatoid arthritis, disc diseases, trauma, neuropathies, and surgeries, can give a clue of pain medication and antibiotic use.

• Unexplained AG metabolic acidosis, like d-lactic acidosis, may be a clue to the diagnosis of pyroglutamic acidosis. Osmolal gap is normal.

Treatment Includes discontinuation of the offending agent. Hemodialysis is needed to improve refractory acidosis and renal failure. N-acetylcysteine (NAC) can provide cysteine to replenish glutathione levels. It is, therefore, suggested that NAC may improve pyroglutamic acidemia.

Toluene

• Other names: methylbenzene or phenylmethane.

• Sources: acrylic paints, varnishes, paint thinners, glues, adhesives, shoe polish, gasoline, transmission fluid, and industrial solvents.

• Poisoning occurs by inhalation to induce euphoria.

• Children and adolescents are common users with male predominance.

• Levels of 200 PPM (parts per million) are dangerous.

• Metabolized to benzyl alcohol, then to benzoic acid, and finally to hippuric acid (hippurate).

• Hippurate is rapidly excreted by the kidneys, if renal function is normal.

• Because of this rapid excretion, hippurate levels are normal at the time of evaluation.

Clinical Manifestations

• Primarily CNS effects, such as euphoria, confusion, dizziness, stupor, and coma. Bronchospasm is common.

• Chronic abuse leads to neuropsychosis, ataxia, optic and peripheral neuropathies, blindness, and decreased cognitive ability.

Diagnosis

• High AG metabolic acidosis is common when serum hippurate levels are high; otherwise, hyperchloremic metabolic acidosis with severe hypokalemia is the common presentation, and serum hippurate levels are normal.

• Hyperchloremic metabolic acidosis and hypokalemia are thought to be due to distal renal tubular acidosis. Some patients also develop Fanconi syndrome.

• Acute kidney injury is also common, which is due to hypotension and/or rhabdomyolysis.

Treatment Includes supportive care and volume expansion with KCl supplementation. There is no antidote. Hemodialysis is recommended for severe renal failure.

Paraldehyde

• Used as a sedative and also for treatment of delirium tremens.

• It is replaced by many other drugs for delirium tremens, so cases of paraldehyde intoxication are rare.

• Metabolized to probably acetaldehyde and acetic acid, causing a high AG metabolic acidosis.

• No osmolal gap is seen.

Treatment Removal of the drug and supportive care.

CHAPTER FIFTEEN

CASE SCENARIOS

Case 1 A 54-year-old woman was admitted through the emergency department (ED) for shortness of breath, "unwell" feeling, and weakness of few days duration.

Her blood pressure was 114/51 mmHg with a pulse rate of 69 beats per minute. She was afebrile. Her medical history is significant for cervical and lumbosacral disc disease, hypertension, depression, anxiety, ataxia, and chronic pulmonary obstructive disease. She had carpal tunnel and cervical disc surgery, cholecystectomy, and hysterectomy. Her medications included combivent (ipratropium bromide 18 μg and albuterol 90 μg) one puff every 8 h, metoprolol 12.5 mg twice daily, klonopin (clonazepam) 0.5 mg every 8 h, as needed, and vicodin ES (hydrocodone bitartrate 7.5 mg and acetaminophen 750 mg) every 8 h, as needed. The patient was previously admitted with similar complaints and found to have a high AG metabolic acidosis and acute kidney injury, requiring short-term hemodialysis.

Hemoglobin was 13.4 g % and a platelet count of 430,000. Serum glucose was 80 mg/dL. ABG: pH of 7.20, pCO2 15 mmHg, pO2 91 mmHg, and calculated HCO3 – of 6 mEq/L. The AG was 16. Other pertinent laboratory results are normal. Serum osmolality was 293 mOsm/L. Serum ketones and lactate were negative, and urinalysis was normal.

Question 1Characterize the acid–base disorder in ED.

AnswerBased on pH and pCO2 and serum [HCO3−], the acid–base disorder is high AG metabolic acidosis and respiratory alkalosis.

Question 2Is calculation of osmolal gap important?

Answer Yes. In this patient, the osmolal gap is 6 mOsm/L. Therefore, methanol, ethylene glycol, ketoacidosis, and lactic acidosis (lactate levels are normal) can be excluded.

Question 3Is aspirin overdose possible in this patient?

AnswerYes. However, the initial acid–base disorder in aspirin overdose is respiratory alkalosis followed by the development of high AG metabolic acidosis. In this patient, serum salicylate levels were normal, excluding the diagnosis of aspirin overdose.

Question 4How does this acid–base disorder differ from that of toluene inhalation?

AnswerToluene inhalation causes a transient high AG metabolic acidosis and then hyperchloremic (non-AG) metabolic acidosis. In this patient, a slight increase in AG existed until the third day of admission, excluding the possibility of toluene inhalation. Also, the patient did not have any clinical manifestations of toluene inhalation or ingestion.

Question 5What other laboratory test you order at this time based on her medications?

AnswerShe is on high doses of acetaminophen (750 mg Q8 h); ordering urinary pyroglutamic acid is appropriate.

Question 6What is the diagnosis of her high AG metabolic acidosis with normal osmolal gap?

Answer Her urinary pyroglutamic acid level was >11,500 mmol/mol creatinine (reference range 0–100 mmol/mol creatinine). Also, acetaminophen and its metabolites were present. Therefore, the diagnosis was pyroglutamic acidosis due to daily high doses of acetaminophen (Tylenol) use. Tylenol depletes GSH, which promotes pyroglutamic acid production. She was started on fentanyl patch, and her serum[HCO_3^-] has been normal.

Case 2 A 40-year-old woman with history of short-bowel surgery is seen for slurred speech, confusion, weakness, impaired motor coordination, and irritability.

She likes ice cream and develops mild neurologic problems following large quantities of ice cream. She is not on any medications or special diets. ABG: pH 7.27, pCO_2 24 mmHg, and calculated HCO_3^- 16 mEq/L. Urine ketones are negative. Serum lactate levels are 1.5 mmol/L. Serum creatinine is normal. The anion gap is 20, but osmolal gap is normal.

Which one of the following is the MOST likely cause of acid–base disturbance in this patient?

(A) l-Lactic acid

(B) Pyroglutamic acid

(C) d-Lactic acid

(D) Methanol

(E) Topiramate

The answer is CExcept for topiramate, all other causes generate high AG metabolic acidosis. Topiramate causes non-AG metabolic acidosis due to inhibition of carbonic anhydrase. Serum lactate is normal; therefore, lactic acidosis is excluded.

Also, methanol intoxication is excluded based on normal osmolal gap. There is no history of medication (Tylenol or Tylenol-containing narcotics) or antibiotic use.

Therefore, pyroglutamic acidosis is ruled out. Based on the surgical history, high carbohydrate intake, and neurologic manifestations, the most likely diagnosis is d-lactic acidosis. Thus, option C is correct.

Case 3A 17-year-old female student is admitted for confusion and acute kidney injury. She is able to give some history that she had a fight with her boyfriend 2 days ago, and she drank some liquid that was in their garage. She has no other significant medical or illicit drug history. In the ED, her vital signs are stable. Other than altered mental status and confusion, her physical examination is normal. She weighs 60 kg.

Laboratory results are as follows:

Serum

Na^+ = 141 mEq/L Osmolality = 320 mOsm/kg H_2O

K^+ = 4.2 mEq/L pH = 5.2

Cl^- = 110 mEq/L Protein = trace

HCO_3^- = 7 mEq/L Blood = negative

BUN = 28 mg/dL Urine sediment = envelope-like crystals

Creatinine = 1.8 mg/dL

Glucose = 72 mg/dL

Serum osmolality = 312 mOsm/kg H_2O

ABG = pH 7.21, pCO_2 17 mmHg, pO_2 94 mmHg, calculated HCO_3^- 6 mEq/L

Question 1Characterize the acid–base disorder.

Answer High AG metabolic acidosis with respiratory alkalosis.

Question 2What is her osmolal gap?

Answer Osmolal gap is the difference between measured serum osmolality and calculated serum osmolality. Therefore, her osmolal gap is 16 (312–296 = 16 mOsm), which is high.

Question 3What is your diagnosis of this acid–base disorder?

Answer The presence of calcium oxalate crystals (envelope-like) in the urine sediment

is the clue for her acid–base disturbance, which is ethylene glycol ingestion.
One of the final products of ethylene glycol is oxalic acid, which is excreted as oxalate.

Question 4What is your initial management?

AnswerAntidote for ethylene glycol is fomepizole. The initial dose is 15 mg/kg followed by 10 mg/kg every 12 h for 4 doses. Continue fomepizole, if ethylene glycol levels are not below 20 mg/dL. At the same time, hydration with D5W and three ampules (150 mEq) of NaHCO3 to run at 120 mL/h to improve volume status should be started.

Question 5Is dialysis needed in this patient?

AnswerYes, if no improvement in renal function and metabolic acidosis following adequate hydration and administration of fomepizole and NaHCO3.

Case 4A 55-year-old man with chronic alcoholism presents to the ED with agitation, blurred vision, and eye pain. Blood pressure and pulse rate are normal. He is afebrile. He has a high AG metabolic acidosis with an osmolal gap of 26 mOsm/L.

Which one of the following toxic alcohol ingestions is the MOST likely cause of his symptoms?

(A) Ethanol
(B) Ethylene glycol
(C) Methanol
(D) Toluene
(E) Isopropyl alcohol

The answer is COnly formic acid formed from methanol is toxic to the optic nerve, causing visual impairment, blurred vision, eye pain, and blindness. Therefore, early institution of fomepizole is recommended to inhibit ADH and conversion of methanol to formaldehyde and formic acid.

Case 5 A 60-year-old man is admitted for a 2-week history of cyclic fever, weight loss of 10 lb, nausea, vomiting, and night sweats. He is not on any medications, and he has not seen a physician in years. Physical examination is normal except for a blood pressure of 100/40 mmHg and a pulse rate of 102 beats per minute. There is no lymphadenopathy. He weighs 74 kg. Pertinent laboratory results are as follows:

Serum
Na+ = 142 mEq/L pH = 7.20
K+ = 4.2 mEq/L pCO2 = 20 mmHg
Cl− = 104 mEq/L pO2 = 92 mmHg
HCO3− = 8 mEq/L
BUN = 32 mg/dL
Creatinine = 1.8 mg/dL
Glucose = 64 mg/dL
Measured serum osmolality = 312 mOsm/kg H2O
Alanine aminotransferase = 60 U/L (normal < 38 U/L)
Aspartate aminotransferase = 58 U/L (normal < 41 U/L)
Lactate dehydrogenase = 690 U/L (normal 115–221 U/L)
White cell count = 8.2 × 103/mm3

Question 1What is the acid–base disturbance?

AnswerBased on the pH, serum [HCO3−], and AG of 30, the primary acid–base disorder is a high AG metabolic acidosis with appropriate respiratory response.

Question 2Based on the osmolal gap of 14, do you suspect any alcohol intoxication?

AnswerNo. There are no clinical manifestations that are attributable to toxic alcohol ingestion with such a high AG. The osmolal gap of 14 can be attributable to causes other than alcohols.

Question 3What other pertinent laboratory tests you order at this time?

AnswerSerum lactate and ketones are the appropriate laboratory tests at this

time. Serum lactate levels were 14 mmol/L, and ketones were positive. Thus,

there are 20 (ΔAG 20; observed AG – normal AG: 30–10 = 20) excess anions in this patient. Of the 20 excess anions, lactate accounts for 14, and the remaining anions are possibly from ketoacids (due to starvation) and sulfate and phosphate from renal failure.

Question 4Based on clinical presentation and high lactate level, what other consult you request now?

AnswerHematology/oncology consult is extremely important. The hematologist

felt that a bone marrow biopsy is valuable in making the diagnosis in the presence of normal white cell count and lymph nodes. The biopsy revealed extranodal T-cell lymphoma, and the lactic acidosis was attributed to lymphoma.

The patient's condition deteriorates, and his pH drops from 7.20 to 7.00 and

HCO3– from 8 to 6 mEq/L. You intend to start the patient on NaHCO3 drip to raise his serum [HCO3–] from 6 to 10 mEq/L.

Question 6What is your next approach to improve lactate?

AnswerContinuous venovenous hemofiltration (CVVH) with NaHCO3 replacement

can be tried, as CVVH is also useful in metformin-induced lactic acidosis.

Case 6A 28-year-old woman was brought to the emergency department for agitation and respiratory distress, requiring intubation. She required fentanyl and lorazepam for sedation. Renal function was normal. Two days later she had a low serum [HCO3–] of 12 mEq/L, a drop of 10 mEq/L from baseline value. An ABG shows a high anion gap metabolic acidosis.

Which one of the following acids may have contributed to her anion gap metabolic

acidosis?

(A) Acetoacetate

(B) Methanol

(C) Ethylene glycol

(D) Lactic acid

(E) Hippuric acid

The answer is D The patient received lorazepam probably at high doses for sedation.

Propylene glycol (PG) is a diluent found in many intravenous and oral drugs,

including lorazepam. PG is metabolized by alcohol and aldehyde dehydrogenases to lactic acid. Each milliliter of lorazepam injection contains 828 mg of PG. Thus, high doses of lorazepam administration results in high circulating levels of lactic acid. PG is water soluble and is removed by hemodialysis and also continuous venovenous hemofiltration. Thus, choice D is correct.

CHAPTER SIXTEEN

CONCLUSION

Management of postoperative fluid therapy should be done considering both patients' unique status and intraoperative events. Thus, surgeons must be aware of pros and cons of current fluid management strategies and their effects on surgical outcome. Although there has been a significant progress on fluid status monitoring and fluid management strategies, most clinicians still prefer their traditional approaches for postoperative fluid management. This tendency towards empirical fluid management can be replaced by evidence based strategies, only if significant benefits of new strategies are proved with multicenter randomized controlled trials which use standardized criteria. GDS is the most rational approach to assess the patient and maintain optimum fluid balance. However, accessible and applicable monitoring tools for determining patient's actual fluid need should be further studied and universalized. The debate around colloids and crystalloids should also be considered with goal directed therapies. Advantages and disadvantages of each solution must be evaluated with the patient's specific condition.

KEY POINTS

1. **Proper management of fluid and electrolytes facilitates crucial homeostasis that allows cardiovascular perfusion, organ system function, and cellular mechanisms to respond to surgical illness.**
2. **Knowledge of the compartmentalization of body fluids forms the basis for understanding pathologic shifts in these fluid spaces in disease states. Although difficult to quantify, a deficiency in the functional extracellular fluid compartment often requires resuscitation with isotonic fluids in surgical and trauma patients.**
3. **Alterations in the concentration of serum sodium have profound effects on cellular function due to water shifts between the intracellular and extracellular spaces.**
4. **Different rates of compensation between respiratory and metabolic components of acid-base homeostasis require frequent laboratory reassessment during therapy.**
5. **Although active investigation continues, alternative resuscitation fluids have limited clinical utility, other than the correction of specific electrolyte abnormalities.**
6. **Most acute surgical illnesses are accompanied by some degree of volume loss or redistribution. Consequently, isotonic fluid administration is the most common initial intravenous fluid strategy, while attention is being given to alterations in concentration and composition.**
7. **Some surgical patients with neurologic illness, malnutrition, acute renal failure, or cancer require special attention to well-defined, disease-specific abnormalities in fluid and electrolyte status.**

CHAPTER SEVENTEEN

References

1. Linke GR, Mieth M, Hofer S, Trierweiler-Hauke B, Weitz J, Martin E, Buchler MW. Surgical intensive care unit - essential for good outcome in major abdominal surgery. *Langenbecks Arch Surg.* 2011;396:417–428.

2. Johnson JL, Moore EE, Aasen AO, Rogy MA, Wang JE, Alsanea O, Aikawa N, Neira JA, Tisminetzky GJ. The role of the surgeon as intensivist: an international perspective. *Curr Opin Crit Care.* 2006;12:357–369.

3. Bamboat ZM, Bordeianou L. Perioperative fluid management. *Clin Colon Rectal Surg.* 2009;22:28–33.

4. Shires T, Williams J, Brown F. Acute change in extracellular fluids associated with major surgical procedures. *Ann Surg.* 1961;154:803–810.

5. Starling EH. On the Absorption of Fluids from the Connective Tissue Spaces. *J Physiol.* 1896;19:312–326.

6. Adamson RH, Lenz JF, Zhang X, Adamson GN, Weinbaum S, Curry FE. Oncotic pressures opposing filtration across non-fenestrated rat microvessels. *J Physiol.* 2004;557:889–907.

7. Reitsma S, Slaaf DW, Vink H, van Zandvoort MA, oude Egbrink MG. The endothelial glycocalyx: composition, functions, and visualization. *Pflugers Arch.* 2007;454:345–359.

8. Strunden MS, Heckel K, Goetz AE, Reuter DA. Perioperative fluid and volume management: physiological basis, tools and strategies. *Ann Intensive Care.* 2011;1:2.

9. Rehm M, Zahler S, Lötsch M, Welsch U, Conzen P, Jacob M, Becker BF. Endothelial glycocalyx as an additional barrier determining extravasation of 6% hydroxyethyl starch or 5% albumin solutions in the coronary vascular bed. *Anesthesiology.* 2004;100:1211–1223.

10. Carrico CJ, Coln CD, Lightfoot SA, Allsman A, Shires GT. Extracellular fluid volume replacement in hemorrhagic shock. *Surg Forum.* 1963;14:10–12.

11. Shires T, Coln D, Carrico J, Lightfoot S. Fluid therapy in hemorrhagic shock. *Arch Surg.* 1964;88:688–693.

12. Fukuda Y, Fujita T, Shibuya J, Albert SN. The distribution between the intravascular and interstitial compartments of commonly utilized replacement fluids. *Anesth Analg.* 1977;48:831–838.

13. Jacob M, Chappell D, Rehm M. The 'third space'--fact or fiction. *Best Pract Res Clin Anaesthesiol.* 2009;23:145–157.

14. Gumpert JR, Zollinger RM, Riddell AG. Proceedings: the measurement of extracellular fluid volume with radiobromide simultaneous plasma and lymph disappearance in man. *Br J Surg.* 1973;60:903.

15. Breckenridge IM, Digerness SB, Kirklin JW. Validity of concept of increased extracellular fluid after open heart surgery. *Surg Forum.* 1969;20:169–171.

16. Nielsen OM, Engell HC. Extracellular fluid volume and distribution in relation to changes in plasma colloid osmotic pressure after major surgery. A randomized study. *Acta Chir Scand.* 1985;151:221–225.

17. Marik PE, Monnet X, Teboul JL. Hemodynamic parameters to guide fluid therapy. *Ann Intensive Care.* 2011;1:1.

18. Marik PE, Cavallazzi R, Vasu T, Hirani A. Dynamic changes in arterial waveform derived variables and fluid responsiveness in mechanically ventilated patients: a systematic review of the literature. *Crit Care Med.* 2009;37:2642–2647.

19. McIntyre LA, Hébert PC, Fergusson D, Cook DJ, Aziz A; Canadian Critical Care Trials Group. A survey of Canadian intensivists' resuscitation practices in early septic shock. *Crit Care.* 2007;11:R74.

20. Kastrup M, Markewitz A, Spies C, Carl M, Erb J, Grosse J, Schirmer U. Current practice of hemodynamic monitoring and vasopressor and inotropic therapy in post-operative cardiac surgery patients in Germany: results

from a postal survey. *Acta Anaesthesiol Scand.* 2007;51:347–358.

21. Marik PE, Cavallazzi R. Does the central venous pressure predict fluid responsiveness An updated meta-analysis and a plea for some common sense. *Crit Care Med.* 2013;41:1774–1781.

22. Solus-Biguenet H, Fleyfel M, Tavernier B, Kipnis E, Onimus J, Robin E, Lebuffe G, Decoene C, Pruvot FR, Vallet B. Non-invasive prediction of fluid responsiveness during major hepatic surgery. *Br J Anaesth.* 2006;97:808–816.

23. Michard F, Teboul JL. Using heart-lung interactions to assess fluid responsiveness during mechanical ventilation. *Crit Care.* 2000;4:282–289.

24. Theres H, Binkau J, Laule M, Heinze R, Hundertmark J, Blobner M, Erhardt W, Baumann G, Stangl K. Phase-related changes in right ventricular cardiac output under volume-controlled mechanical ventilation with positive end-expiratory pressure. *Crit Care Med.* 1999;27:953–958.

25. Monnet X, Teboul JL. Passive leg raising. *Intensive Care Med.* 2008;34:659–663.

26. Monnet X, Rienzo M, Osman D, Anguel N, Richard C, Pinsky MR, Teboul JL. Passive leg raising predicts fluid responsiveness in the critically ill. *Crit Care Med.* 2006;34:1402–1407.

27. Boulain T, Achard JM, Teboul JL, Richard C, Perrotin D, Ginies G. Changes in BP induced by passive leg raising predict response to fluid loading in critically ill patients. *Chest.* 2002;121:1245–1252.

28. Lafanechère A, Pène F, Goulenok C, Delahaye A, Mallet V, Choukroun G, Chiche JD, Mira JP, Cariou A. Changes in aortic blood flow induced by passive leg raising predict fluid responsiveness in critically ill patients. *Crit Care.* 2006;10:R132.

29. Lamia B, Ochagavia A, Monnet X, Chemla D, Richard C, Teboul JL. Echocardiographic prediction of volume responsiveness in critically ill patients with spontaneously breathing activity. *Intensive Care Med.* 2007;33:1125–1132.

30. Kinsella SM, Pirlet M, Mills MS, Tuckey JP, Thomas TA. Randomized study of intravenous fluid preload before epidural analgesia during labour. *Br J Anaesth.* 2000;85:311–313.

31. Stein L, Beraud JJ, Morissette M, Luz PD, Weil MH, Shubin H. Pulmonary edema during volume infusion. *Circulation.* 1975;52:483–489.

32. Waters JH, Gottlieb A, Schoenwald P, Popovich MJ, Sprung J, Nelson DR. Normal saline versus lactated Ringer's solution for intraoperative fluid management in patients undergoing abdominal aortic aneurysm repair: an outcome study. *Anesth Analg.* 2001;93:817–822.

33. Yim JM, Vermeulen LC, Erstad BL, Matuszewski KA, Burnett DA, Vlasses PH. Albumin and nonprotein colloid solution use in US academic health centers. *Arch Intern Med.* 1995;155:2450–2455.

34. Alderson P, Bunn F, Lefebvre C, Li WP, Li L, Roberts I, Schierhout G. Human albumin solution for resuscitation and volume expansion in critically ill patients. *Cochrane Database Syst Rev.* 2004;(4):CD001208.

35. Roberts I, Alderson P, Bunn F, Chinnock P, Ker K, Schierhout G. Colloids versus crystalloids for fluid resuscitation in critically ill patients. *Cochrane Database Syst Rev.* 2004;(4):CD000567.

36. Taylor DM. Inactivation of TSE agents: safety of blood and blood-derived products. *Transfus Clin Biol.* 2003;10:23–25.

37. Grobben AH, Steele PJ, Somerville RA, Taylor DM, Schreuder BE. Inactivation of the BSE agent by the heat and pressure process for manufacturing gelatine. *Vet Rec.* 2005;157:277–281.

38. Lamke LO, Liljedahl SO. Plasma volume changes after infusion of various plasma expanders. *Resuscitation.* 1976;5:93–102.

39. Mortelmans YJ, Vermaut G, Verbruggen AM, Arnout JM, Vermylen J, Van Aken H, Mortelmans LA. Effects of 6% hydroxyethyl starch and 3% modified fluid gelatin on intravascular volume and coagulation during intraoperative hemodilution. *Anesth Analg.* 1995;81:1235–1242.

40. Van der Linden PJ, De Hert SG, Deraedt D, Cromheecke S, De Decker K, De Paep R, Rodrigus I, Daper A, Trenchant A. Hydroxyethyl starch 130/0.4 versus modified fluid gelatin for volume expansion in cardiac surgery patients: the effects on perioperative bleeding and transfusion needs. *Anesth Analg.* 2005;101:629–634, table of contents.

41. Dubniks M, Persson J, Grände PO. Plasma volume expansion of 5% albumin, 4% gelatin, 6% HES 130/0.4, and normal saline under increased microvascular permeability in the rat. *Intensive Care Med.* 2007;33:293–299.

42. Persson J, Grände PO. Volume expansion of albumin, gelatin, hydroxyethyl starch, saline and erythrocytes after haemorrhage in the rat. *Intensive Care Med.* 2005;31:296–301.

43. Beyer R, Harmening U, Rittmeyer O, Zielmann S, Mielck F, Kazmaier S, Kettler D. Use of modified fluid gelatin and hydroxyethyl starch for colloidal volume replacement in major orthopaedic surgery. *Br J Anaesth.* 1997;78:44–50

44. Grocott MP, Mythen MG, Gan TJ. Perioperative fluid management and clinical outcomes in adults. *Anesth Analg.* 2005;100:1093–1106.

45. Freyburger G, Dubreuil M, Boisseau MR, Janvier G. Rheological properties of commonly used plasma substitutes during preoperative normovolaemic acute haemodilution. *Br J Anaesth.* 1996;76:519–525.

46. Korosue K, Heros RC, Ogilvy CS, Hyodo A, Tu YK, Graichen R. Comparison of crystalloids and colloids for hemodilution in a model of focal cerebral ischemia. *J Neurosurg.* 1990;73:576–584.

47. Neff TA, Fischler L, Mark M, Stocker R, Reinhart WH. The influence of two different hydroxyethyl starch solutions (6% HES 130/0.4 and 200/0.5) on blood viscosity. *Anesth Analg.* 2005;100:1773–1780.

48. de Jonge E, Levi M. Effects of different plasma substitutes on blood coagulation: a comparative review. *Crit Care Med.* 2001;29:1261–1267.

49. Aberg M, Hedner U, Bergentz SE. Effect of dextran on factor VIII (antihemophilic factor) and platelet function. *Ann Surg.* 1979;189:243–247.

50. Jones CI, Payne DA, Hayes PD, Naylor AR, Bell PR, Thompson MM, Goodall AH. The antithrombotic effect of dextran-40 in man is due to enhanced fibrinolysis in vivo. *J Vasc Surg.* 2008;48:715–722.

51. Salemark L, Wieslander JB, Dougan P, Arnljots B. Studies of the antithrombotic effects of dextran 40 following microarterial trauma. *Br J Plast Surg.* 1991;44:15–22.

52. Baum TD, Wang H, Rothschild HR, Gang DL, Fink MP. Mesenteric oxygen metabolism, ileal mucosal hydrogen ion concentration, and tissue edema after crystalloid or colloid resuscitation in porcine endotoxic shock: comparison of Ringer's lactate and 6% hetastarch. *Circ Shock.* 1990;30:385–397.

53. Marjanovic G, Villain C, Timme S, zur Hausen A, Hoeppner J, Makowiec F, Holzner P, Hopt UT, Obermaier R. Colloid vs. crystalloid infusions in gastrointestinal surgery and their different impact on the healing of intestinal anastomoses. *Int J Colorectal Dis.* 2010;25:491–498.

54. Annane D, Siami S, Jaber S, Martin C, Elatrous S, Declère AD, Preiser JC, Outin H, Troché G, Charpentier C, et al. Effects of fluid resuscitation with colloids vs crystalloids on mortality in critically ill patients presenting with hypovolemic shock: the CRISTAL randomized trial. *JAMA.* 2013;310:1809–1817.

55. Perel P, Roberts I. Colloids versus crystalloids for fluid resuscitation in critically ill patients. *Cochrane Database Syst Rev.* 2007;(4):CD000567.

56. Prien T, Backhaus N, Pelster F, Pircher W, Bünte H, Lawin P. Effect of intraoperative fluid administration and colloid osmotic pressure on the formation of intestinal edema during gastrointestinal surgery. *J Clin Anesth.* 1990;2:317–323.

57. Choi PT, Yip G, Quinonez LG, Cook DJ. Crystalloids vs. colloids in fluid resuscitation: a systematic review. *Crit Care Med.* 1999;27:200–210.

58. Schierhout G, Roberts I. Fluid resuscitation with colloid or crystalloid solutions in critically ill patients: a systematic review of randomised trials. *BMJ.* 1998;316:961–964.

59. Mailloux L, Swartz CD, Capizzi R, Kim KE, Onesti G, Ramirez O, Brest AN. Acute renal failure after administration of low-molecular weight dextran. *N Engl J Med.* 1967;277:1113–1118.

60. Diomi P, Ericsson JL, Matheson NA, Shearer JR. Studies on renal tubular morphology and toxicity after large doses of dextran 40 in the rabbit. *Lab Invest.* 1970;22:355–360.

61. Biesenbach G, Kaiser W, Zazgornik J. Incidence of acute oligoanuric renal failure in dextran 40 treated patients with acute ischemic stroke stage III or IV. *Ren Fail.* 1997;19:69–75.

62. Legendre C, Thervet E, Page B, Percheron A, Noël LH, Kreis H. Hydroxyethylstarch and osmotic-nephrosis-like lesions in kidney transplantation. *Lancet.* 1993;342:248–249.

63. Brunkhorst FM, Engel C, Bloos F, Meier-Hellmann A, Ragaller M, Weiler N, Moerer O, Gruendling M, Oppert M, Grond S, et al. Intensive insulin therapy and pentastarch resuscitation in severe sepsis. *N Engl J Med.* 2008;358:125–139.

64. Schortgen F, Girou E, Deye N, Brochard L. The risk associated with hyperoncotic colloids in patients with shock. *Intensive Care Med.* 2008;34:2157–2168.

65. Sakr Y, Payen D, Reinhart K, Sipmann FS, Zavala E, Bewley J, Marx G, Vincent JL. Effects of hydroxyethyl starch administration on renal function in critically ill patients. *Br J Anaesth.* 2007;98:216–224.

66. Boldt J, Priebe HJ. Intravascular volume replacement therapy with synthetic colloids: is there an influence on renal function. *Anesth Analg.* 2003;96:376–382, table of contents.

67. Finfer S, Bellomo R, Boyce N, French J, Myburgh J, Norton R. A comparison of albumin and saline for fluid resuscitation in the intensive care unit. *N Engl J Med.* 2004;350:2247–2256.

68. Roche AM, James MF. Colloids and crystalloids: does it matter to the kidney. *Curr Opin Crit Care.* 2009;15:520–524.

69. Velanovich V. Crystalloid versus colloid fluid resuscitation: a meta-analysis of mortality. *Surgery.* 1989;105:65–71.

70. Brandstrup B, Tønnesen H, Beier-Holgersen R, Hjortsø E, Ørding H, Lindorff-Larsen K, Rasmussen MS, Lanng C, Wallin L, Iversen LH, et al. Effects of intravenous fluid restriction on postoperative complications: comparison of two perioperative fluid regimens: a randomized assessor-blinded multicenter trial. *Ann Surg.* 2003;238:641–648.

71. MacKay G, Fearon K, McConnachie A, Serpell MG, Molloy RG, O'Dwyer PJ. Randomized clinical trial of the effect of postoperative intravenous fluid restriction on recovery after elective colorectal surgery. *Br J Surg.* 2006;93:1469–1474.

72. Lobo SM, Ronchi LS, Oliveira NE, Brandão PG, Froes A, Cunrath GS, Nishiyama KG, Netinho JG, Lobo FR. Restrictive strategy of intraoperative fluid maintenance during optimization of oxygen delivery decreases major complications after high-risk surgery. *Crit Care.* 2011;15:R226.

73. Nisanevich V, Felsenstein I, Almogy G, Weissman C, Einav S, Matot I. Effect of intraoperative fluid management on outcome after intraabdominal surgery. *Anesthesiology.* 2005;103:25–32.

74. Rahbari NN, Zimmermann JB, Schmidt T, Koch M, Weigand MA, Weitz J. Meta-analysis of standard, restrictive and supplemental fluid administration in colorectal surgery. *Br J Surg.* 2009;96:331–341.

75. Baker JW, Deitch EA, Li M, Berg RD, Specian RD. Hemorrhagic shock induces bacterial translocation from the gut. *J Trauma.* 1988;28:896–906.

76. Wilmore DW, Smith RJ, O'Dwyer ST, Jacobs DO, Ziegler TR, Wang XD. The gut: a central organ after surgical stress. *Surgery.* 1988;104:917–923.

77. Maharaj CH, Kallam SR, Malik A, Hassett P, Grady D, Laffey JG. Preoperative intravenous fluid therapy decreases postoperative nausea and pain in high risk patients. *Anesth Analg.* 2005;100:675–682, table of contents.

78. Moretti EW, Robertson KM, El-Moalem H, Gan TJ. Intraoperative colloid administration reduces postoperative nausea and vomiting and improves postoperative outcomes compared with crystalloid administration. *Anesth Analg.* 2003;96:611–617, table of contents.

79. Rivers EP, Nguyen HB, Huang DT, Donnino M. Early goal-directed therapy. *Crit Care Med.* 2004;32:314–315; author reply 315.

80. Abbas SM, Hill AG. Systematic review of the literature for the use of oesophageal Doppler monitor for fluid replacement in major abdominal surgery. *Anaesthesia.* 2008;63:44–51.

81. Wakeling HG, McFall MR, Jenkins CS, Woods WG, Miles WF, Barclay GR, Fleming SC. Intraoperative oesophageal Doppler guided fluid management shortens postoperative hospital stay after major bowel surgery. *Br J Anaesth.* 2005;95:634–642.

82. Noblett SE, Snowden CP, Shenton BK, Horgan AF. Randomized clinical trial assessing the effect of Doppler-optimized fluid management on outcome after elective colorectal resection. *Br J Surg.* 2006;93:1069–1076.

83. Hamilton MA. Perioperative fluid management: progress despite lingering controversies. *Cleve Clin J Med.* 2009;76 Suppl 4:S28–S31.

84. Poeze M, Greve JW, Ramsay G. Meta-analysis of hemodynamic optimization: relationship to methodological quality. *Crit Care.* 2005;9:R771–R779.

85. Giglio MT, Marucci M, Testini M, Brienza N. Goal-directed haemodynamic therapy and gastrointestinal complications in major surgery: a meta-analysis of randomized controlled trials. *Br J Anaesth.* 2009;103:637–646.

86. Gattinoni L, Brazzi L, Pelosi P, Latini R, Tognoni G, Pesenti A, Fumagalli R. A trial of goal-oriented hemodynamic therapy in critically ill patients. SvO2 Collaborative Group. *N Engl J Med.* 1995; 333: 1025–1032.

Printed by Libri Plureos GmbH in Hamburg,
Germany